CW00857923

STANDING FIRM IN THE FAITH

STANDING FIRM IN THE FAITH

✦

Finding God's Strength in Challenging Times

James L. Morrisson

iUniverse, Inc.
New York Lincoln Shanghai

STANDING FIRM IN THE FAITH
Finding God's Strength in Challenging Times

iUniverse books may be ordered through booksellers or by contacting:

iUniverse
2021 Pine Lake Road, Suite 100
Lincoln, NE 68512
www.iuniverse.com
1-800-Authors (1-800-288-4677)

You may quote from *Standing Firm in the Faith* as long as you do it fairly and accurately.

NOTE: Sometimes the author has added boldface type to Scripture quotations for emphasis.

ISBN-13: 978-0-595-33667-8 (pbk)
ISBN-13: 978-0-595-84194-3 (cloth)
ISBN-13: 978-0-595-78469-1 (ebk)
ISBN-10: 0-595-33667-1 (pbk)
ISBN-10: 0-595-84194-5 (cloth)
ISBN-10: 0-595-78469-0 (ebk)

Printed in the United States of America

To Frances, my beautiful bride of 63 years.
And to our children, whose prayers
helped bring us into the Kingdom of God.

Contents

Foreword

My theme is that these are increasingly challenging times for Christians. Not only is there an international conflict with radical Islamists, but there is a spiritual war for the soul of our nation. To survive, Christians need to stand firm for what we believe in, rather than allow everything we stand for to be progressively eroded. And to do this we need to be quite sure of what we believe, and quite sure that we really believe it and are willing to apply it in our own lives. In particular, I stress the importance of growing to Christian maturity.

I have tried to emphasize the things that unite us and that I hope most, if not all, committed Christians can believe. The book is in part a personal testimony, but it is primarily a discussion of Scriptures that have meant a lot to me. I make no claim to have said anything new. Rather, my purpose has been to stir people up by putting us in remembrance of what we should already know. (See 2 Peter 1:12-13.) Although written in a fairly low key style, I think there is quite a bit of passion in the book.

One reason for some of the passion is that, for the past two years, I have been dealing with advanced cancer. The medical prognosis is not very good. I've been on chemotherapy, and the cancer has not spread much, but it is still there. I know that God can heal me completely, and I am praying that he will heal me. This has put us in a situation where it has become vividly clear that our trust, in all things, has to be in God. There are words I have said in the past, but they have acquired a new reality for me. And it has been good. There's been a considerable change in priorities, and quite a few things that used to be head knowledge have become heart knowledge. Perhaps all this has happened to test and strengthen our faith. (See 1 Peter 1:7.)

My wife, Frances, and I feel that this has been one of the best years of our lives. We have found a deeper love for each other, and a new peace and joy that are quite wonderful. We lead a quiet life, but we have a good deal of fun together, and at times we get downright silly and laugh a lot.

Whatever God does will be for the best. (See Romans 8:28.) If I die soon, I'll go to be with God, and that's a good place to be. If I live for some time longer, I'll have more time to write other things and to serve him, and that's a good place to be. At any rate, my faith in him and commitment to him depend on who he is and not on what he does for me.

James L. Morrisson
December 29, 2004

James Morrisson died in April 2005.
This Foreword is taken from a letter
that he wrote to his nephew.

Author's Preface

The purpose of *Standing Firm in the Faith* is very practical—to let Scripture stir people into action. The Bible says that Scripture is living and active. It can profoundly impact our lives if we allow it to. It has impacted my life greatly. I hope that *Standing Firm in the Faith* will encourage all of us to allow Scripture to affect the way we live our lives.

What I have written is a discussion of basic Christian principles that I think need to be more clearly understood and more fully applied. It is also an account of how these principles have impacted my life. I hope that this will suggest how they may impact the lives of others.

I have sought to keep my presentation simple and non-technical. My brother, an engineer, used to say that if he could not express his ideas in ordinary lay language, he probably didn't understand them himself. I have tried to follow that example. I also believe that, for most laymen, the important thing is to have a solid grasp of the basic essentials of Christian belief. Supreme Court Justice Oliver Wendell Holmes, Jr. once said (to the best of my recollection), "The vindication of the obvious is often more important than the elucidation of the obscure."

I came to Jesus Christ late in life, in my 60s. Hence I did not grow up within the confines of any one denominational or theological outlook. The one principle that underlies everything in this book is that all Scripture is true and authoritative. I try to form my understanding as much as possible from the words of Scripture itself, believing that the Scriptures were meant to be understood by ordinary people. I hope that this may sometimes enable me to bring a freshness of approach that has some value.

It is essential to have sound, Scripturally based doctrine on basic issues. Our doctrinal beliefs will affect our actions, for good or for evil. There are some doctrines that all who would call themselves Christians must adhere to. Understanding the basic essentials of these doctrines is, for most laymen, far more important than pursuing all their refinements.

Most of what I have written applies to myself as much as to anyone else. Often, I am dealing with goals which Scripture has set for us and which few, if any, people on earth have fully achieved. We are all in the process of learning and growing. But it is good to be clear as to our goals even though they are seldom fully achievable on this earth.

I have quoted and referred to a considerable amount of Scripture. I have several purposes in doing so. (1) As a lawyer, I like to document what I say. (2) I want to encourage my readers to read Scripture, and to read it in context. (3) I want to encourage my readers to check Scripture for themselves to see whether these things are so. (See Acts 17:11.) (4) I like to let Scripture speak for itself. The language of Scripture is far more powerful, and more capable of reaching people's hearts, than any words I could write. (5) One of the things I enjoy about Scripture is the repeated discovery that different human authors, writing at very different times, have said essentially the same thing under the inspiration of the Holy Spirit. I delight in the way different parts of Scripture fit together.

I have referred to some Greek and Hebrew words. I have studied a little Greek and Hebrew, but do not read either language. I believe that, with today's resources (which I discuss briefly at the end of Chapter 4), the average layman can get a sense of what some of the original words of Scripture mean, and even of some of their nuances. At times, in this book, I shall show how I have found this to be so in my own reading of Scripture.

I have tried to let each chapter be complete in itself, so that those who wish may browse through this book rather than reading it from start to finish. This may have resulted in some repetition of material and thought. I have tried to minimize any repetition. But I also think there can be value in hearing the same thought repeated in different contexts. We get exposed hourly to so much that is false and ungodly, that we need to make a conscious effort to put God's principles into our mind. Repetition is one way to do this.

I sometimes refer to personal events in my life. I do this, not out of any desire to call attention to myself, but in the hope that this may help bring Scriptural principles to life, and may demonstrate that God's principles work. Our God is a very practical God.

I use the term "man" in its generic sense of mankind, the human race, what biologists call *homo sapiens*. This is the sense in which it is often used in Scripture. For example, Genesis 1:27 says, "So God created man in his own image, in the image of God created he him; male and female created he them." In following this traditional use of the word, I do not imply any suggestion of superiority or inferiority of either sex.

What qualifications do I have for writing such a book? A brief biographical note is in order. My primary professional training and experience is as a lawyer. I had the privilege of being law clerk to Chief Justice Harlan F. Stone of the U.S.

Supreme Court from 1942 to 1944. I served in various capacities as a lawyer in the U.S. Government. I have argued a number of cases in the U.S. Supreme Court and participated in the briefing of many others, including some of major Constitutional significance.

As a lawyer, I attained some skill in interpreting a written text. Our understanding of Scripture must always be based on the guidance of the Holy Spirit. Someone who does not have the Holy Spirit cannot understand spiritual things (1 Corinthians 2:14). But I believe my legal training can help me organize and present what the Holy Spirit has shown me is in the Scriptures. As a student and performer of classical music, I had a different kind of experience in interpreting a written text in accordance with the intent of its author.

During much of my life I was a humanist, believing in the power of man to improve himself by his own efforts. I eventually found that this was false. In seeking for a more spiritual dimension to my life, I joined a New Age organization. After a number of years I left it, because I concluded that its teachings were inconsistent with Scripture, and I decided to believe Scripture. I later earned a Master's Degree in Biblical Studies.

When I left the New Age organization, I adopted, as a description of my situation, the words of Psalm 40:2 (NIV), "He lifted me out of the slimy pit, out of the mud and mire; he set my feet on a rock and gave me a firm place to stand." Ever since, I have taken my stand on the rock of Scripture. I find it a great comfort that, in a world in which so much seems like quicksand, there is a solid rock on which to stand.

I do not claim any special value for my own thoughts. However, I do claim that everything I have written is based on Scripture. Some may disagree with my interpretation of Scripture, or may feel that I have emphasized one aspect of it and given inadequate attention to other aspects. This is fine; I encourage my readers to check everything out for themselves. But I do claim that everything I say has Scriptural support, and for that reason deserves your serious consideration.

The basic message of this book is both simple and Scriptural. I ask that you not allow differences of opinion over some details to detract from that basic message.

I thank my family and friends and many others for their love, encouragement, and prayers as I worked on this book while at the same time fighting cancer. I thank my wife and daughter for their many contributions, including their poems, and for bearing with patience the time-consuming process of putting the book together. I thank others who have contributed in various ways to this book. I thank my son Bob for taking care of my website and keeping my computer going. I thank all three of my children for their prayers, which eventually brought my wife and me to salvation. I thank all who, in various ways, have shown me God's extraordinary love and the blessings he bestows on those who serve him.

May God bless us all as we seek to know and understand him better!

James L. Morrisson
October 26, 2004

◆ ◆ ◆

Notice

I believe that, because of the challenging times in which we live, many Christians need to be able to read *Standing Firm in the Faith*. Therefore, I have made the entire book available online at the following website. Please let people know about it. If you have a website, please feel free to link to it.

www.StandingFirmInTheFaith.com

Although written for Christians (both new believers and old timers), *Standing Firm in the Faith* is also helpful for people who are considering the claims of Christianity.

You can order the book by phone from the publisher (1-800-288-4677). You can also buy it online from Amazon.com and iUniverse.com. (The best way to find the book is to search for the title because my last name has an unusual spelling.) Bookstores, including Internet stores, can get discounts if they order from the publisher by phone.

PART I
THE CHALLENGE

1

The Challenge

o o o o o o o o o o o o o o o o o o o o o o o o o o o o o o o

"Be on your guard; stand firm in the faith; be men of courage; be strong."

—*(1 Corinthians 16:13 NIV)*

We live in challenging times.

Ours is a fast-paced, stressful society where many people lack strong, long-term personal relationships. We are bombarded with so much secularism that Christian beliefs and values can become eroded. As a result, it is more difficult to deal with health problems, personal crises, and other hardships. Now, more than ever, Christians need to be solidly grounded in their faith so that they can stand firm in the face of difficulties.

Our nation is at war against terrorism. In the Middle East, changes are occurring whose implications and lasting effects are difficult to predict. We can expect the war against terrorism to continue for some time. Our enemy is very determined. This war has a profound spiritual dimension. The terrorists come from a branch of Islam that seeks to impose its religious views on the rest of the world by force, and that regards both Christians and Jews as infidels to be exterminated. They expect to succeed because they accept no limits on the tactics they use, and because they will persevere and they think that we will not.

In addition, the soul of our country is in danger. Will we be a godly nation? Or will we be a worldly nation that denies and excludes God? Will we return to the basis on which we were founded, which placed a strong reliance on the Christian faith which most of our founders shared? Or will we become a totally secular society in which Biblical principles are considered both irrelevant and inimical? We see the choice made in many areas today. I believe it is a very serious choice.

Our American culture has changed so much, and so rapidly, that things that were unthinkable 40 years ago are now commonplace. There are deadly new diseases, such as AIDS and SARS. We face the possibility of chemical and biological warfare, and nuclear bombs so small that they can be carried in a suitcase. Divorce rates are soaring, crime rates are soaring, and many children come from broken homes. Everything seems to be moving faster and more frantically. It feels as if things are falling apart.

George Washington considered that the victory of a ragged, ill-equipped American militia over the most powerful army in the world could be explained only by the intervention of Almighty God.[1] George Washington also warned, "We ought to be no less persuaded that the propitious smiles of heaven can never be expected on a nation that disregards the eternal rules of order which heaven itself has ordained."[2] John Adams, our second President, stated, "Our Constitution was made only for a religious and moral people. It is wholly inadequate for the government of any other."[3] Most of the other founders of our nation expressed similar principles. Yet, today, many seek to eliminate all mention of God from our public life and our schools, and they have to a large extent succeeded. Many seek the total rejection of godly moral principles, and they, too, have succeeded to an alarming degree. It seems that, as a nation, we are deliberately throwing away the source of our greatness.

These principles were well understood until fairly recently. In 1950, President Harry Truman wrote, "The fundamental basis of this nation's laws was given to Moses on the Mount. The fundamental basis of our Bill of Rights comes from the teachings we get from Exodus and St. Matthew, from Isaiah and St. Paul. I don't think we emphasize that enough these days. If we don't have a proper fundamental moral background, we will finally end up with a totalitarian government which does not believe in rights for anybody except the State."[4] In 1952 the U.S. Supreme Court declared, "We are a religious people and our institutions presuppose a Supreme Being."[5]

In the guise of protecting us from the "establishment" of the Christian religion, our courts have made possible, and have done nothing to stop, the effective establishment of the religion of secular humanism as the religion of our public school systems. Secular humanism, which the Supreme Court has said is a religion, asserts that there is no God, there is no absolute truth, there are no moral absolutes, the greatest virtue is tolerance (including tolerance of evil), and man is the measure of all things. We have established, as the religion of our public schools, a religion which is anti-Christian to its very core, while suppressing any reference to Christianity.

Thus far, our nation has succeeded and prospered to a remarkable degree. I believe this is largely because we have had God's favor and protection. If that favor and protection should be withdrawn, we cannot expect to continue to succeed, and we could find our nation disappearing, as so many powerful civilizations in the past have disappeared. I believe this is the greatest danger we face today. I consider it very real.

Some Christians have fought valiantly against this strong movement to eliminate God, and godly principles, from our public life. I am very grateful to them. But I think it fair to say that the majority of those who call themselves Christians have sat by passively and allowed it to happen. There are a number of reasons for this, some theological, some psychological. I am afraid that, as a whole, the body of Christ has demonstrated the truth of the principle that the only thing necessary for evil to prevail is for good men to do nothing.

God said many years ago, "Who will rise up for me against the evildoers? Who will stand up for me against the workers of iniquity?" (Psalm 94:16). God repeatedly warned his people not to be enticed into following the ways of pagans. (See, for example, Deuteronomy 4:15-19.) He has told us not to conform to this world (Romans 12:2). He is calling on Christians to be different, and to stand firmly for God's truth.

These themes have been developed by others in much greater detail.[6] It is not my purpose to discuss them further in this book. They form the background for what I do want to discuss. What I am dealing with is some changes that I believe need to occur in the minds and hearts of many who call themselves Christians, if we as individuals are to survive in this challenging world, and if we, and the church as a whole, are to play an effective part in stemming the tide of secularism in our nation.

THE CHRISTIAN CHURCH

Christianity is not just private faith and personal salvation. It affects our entire life. It is a framework, a world view, for understanding all of reality. I'm afraid there are some Christians whose religious faith is rather like a hood ornament on a car. It looks attractive, it may be interesting, but it has nothing to do with the functioning of the car. That is not Biblical Christianity. It is in God that we live and move and have our being (Acts 17:28). Everything we say or do is rooted in our belief in God and in Jesus Christ.

I think that God is calling on those who believe in him to move out of our comfortable church buildings and bring our faith to the world around us. This was what Jesus did. Most of his ministry was out on the streets, where the people were. We are called upon to be salt and light to the world, and we can do this only when we go out to where the people are.

When we move out of our comfort zone, however, two things happen:

- We encounter beliefs which contradict and oppose ours. Hence we need to be quite clear as to what we believe, we need to be able to express it in terms that ordinary people can understand, and we need to be able to stand firm against beliefs which conflict with God's word.
- We should expect opposition, dislike and even hatred. Jesus told his disciples to expect hatred. Just as the world had hated Jesus, it would hate his disciples. As the world persecuted Jesus, it would persecute his disciples. If we are to stand firm against opposition and hatred, we need to be very solidly grounded in what we believe.

One of the themes of this book is that true Christianity is not easy. It calls for effort and struggle. It is often difficult and challenging. We should not expect that it would be easy. In this life, few things that are worthwhile are attained without a good deal of effort. Jesus told his followers to count the cost of following him. For those early followers, and for the many Christians who today undergo severe persecution for their religion in various parts of the world, the cost was very great, but they were and are willing to pay it. We in America today are blessed by not having to face the cost of persecution and possible martyrdom, but there are other costs that we may face.[7]

Christianity expects that those who accept it will grow and change. It calls for radical change in our character and conduct. Growth and change are seldom easy. They can be quite painful.

In an effort to make Christianity appealing, some tend to make it seem easy and effortless. We should not do this. We should not water down the demands of Christ's gospel in order to gain a nominal acceptance of it from as many people as possible. Such a nominal acceptance often has shallow roots and does not last, and it may inoculate people so as to make it harder for them to receive the real thing.

God does not want Christians whose love grows cold (Matthew 24:12), or who have abandoned their first love (Revelation 2:4). He does not want lukewarm Christians. He spits them out of his mouth (Revelation 3:15). A lukewarm Christian cannot stand up to a deeply committed atheist or humanist.

God does not want Christians "who honor Me with their lips, but their heart is far from Me" (Matthew 15:8, quoting Isaiah 29:13). He does not want those who profess to believe him but do not do his will (Matthew 7:21). He does not want those who have a form of godliness but deny its power (2 Timothy 3:5). He does not want those who "…claim to know God, but by their actions they deny him" (Titus 1:16 NIV).

Some years ago, a Russian Communist said, "If you Westerners were half as committed to your beliefs as we Communists are to ours, we wouldn't stand a chance against you." The Communist revolution in Russia was a victory of a small, deeply committed minority (the Bolsheviks) over the majority. The radical Islamist movement today hopes to prevail because they are deeply committed and they perceive us as not committed. The early Christians, a tiny minority, turned the world around because they were committed. In the U.S. today, I think we can see that deeply committed minorities have had a disproportionate influence on public opinion and on politics. If we Christians want to affect the course of events in this nation, we need to be deeply committed.

If we are to stand firm in the faith, we need to be hot and not lukewarm.

In this book I tend to emphasize the demands of Christianity because I feel that, in our affluent society, there is great danger that our faith will be flabby and apathetic. But I must also say two other things, which I hope you will keep in mind.

First, Christianity is tremendously rewarding. To those who truly believe in Jesus Christ, it promises eternal life in heaven with God. It promises forgiveness of our sins, and freedom from many things that have held us down. It promises an abundant life on earth, in which we can overcome every adversity. It promises peace, joy and true fulfillment. These are not empty promises. I have seen them realized, in greater or lesser degree, in my own life and the lives of others around me. Whatever Christianity may cost, the rewards are much greater.

Second, God expects us to change, but he also accepts us and loves us as we are. His love is not conditioned on our changing. We don't have to earn his love and acceptance. They are just there for us. Wherever we are in our Christian life, God is there for us.

WHAT CAN WE DO ABOUT IT?

Scripture speaks of the "end times," the times just before Christ returns to earth in glory and power. Some think we are already in these end times. Others say that we are approaching them. Whichever view you take, the words of Jesus Christ, in his great end-time prophecy, are certainly relevant. I shall discuss this prophecy (Matthew, chapter 24) in more detail later. (See Chapter 22.) For now,

I want to emphasize one sentence of it. Jesus described very difficult times that would come, and said that many would turn away from the faith, and the love of many would grow cold. Then he said, "but he who stands firm to the end will be saved" (Matthew 24:13 NIV).

Other Scriptures repeat this admonition to stand firm. Paul told the Corinthians to "...stand firm in the faith..." (1 Corinthians 16:13 NIV). "...it is by faith you stand firm" (2 Corinthians 1:24 NIV). (Also see Galatians 5:1; Philippians 1:27, 4:1; 1 Thessalonians 3:8; 2 Thessalonians 2:15; James 5:8.) Peter told believers to resist the devil, "...standing firm in the faith..." (1 Peter 5:9 NIV). Paul also told believers to "...stand firm..." against the devil's schemes (Ephesians 6:13 NIV). (See Ephesians 6:11-18.) Jude told us to "contend earnestly for the faith" (Jude 3). The Old Testament says the same. "When the storm has swept by, the wicked are gone, but the righteous stand firm forever" (Proverbs 10:25 NIV). "...If you do not stand firm in your faith, you will not stand at all" (Isaiah 7:9 NIV).

How do we stand firm in the faith? We must be uncompromising about what we believe. God hates evil, and Scripture calls on us to hate evil. We must not water down the faith that Scripture declares for us. There are times when we need to take a stand publicly against that which Scripture says is evil. This may mean speaking out publicly for what is right, and taking political action to obtain election of godly men and women, and adoption of godly legislation.

In order to do any of these effectively, we need to be strong. Paul told Timothy to "be strong in the grace that is in Christ Jesus" (2 Timothy 2:1). He told the Corinthians to "be strong" (1 Corinthians 16:13). He prayed that the Colossians would be "strengthened with all might, according to His [God's] glorious power, for all patience and long-suffering with joy" (Colossians 1:11). He said, "God has not given us a spirit of fear, but of power and love and a sound mind" (2 Timothy 1:7). God wants Christians to be strong.

This includes being strong in our faith. We need to be quite clear about what we believe. We also need to believe it completely, with our whole being, and not just with our intellect. We need to believe and not doubt. Those whose faith is not deeply rooted will fall away; those whose faith is solid and who persevere will bear much fruit. (See Luke 8:13-15.)

We can stand firm on the words of the Bible. The Bible is true and reliable, and it can and should be the guide for everything we do. In Part II of this book, I give my reasons for believing this. That belief underlies everything else I say. If we accept Scripture on its own terms, as an authoritative revelation from God, then we have a solid rock to stand on. If we do not accept it as authoritative, then it becomes merely one among many expressions of fallible human opinion. It is largely because many Christians, today, do not accept Scripture as authoritative that we find such wide divergences of opinion among those who call themselves Christians.

The Bible tells us very clearly certain things about God, about Jesus Christ, and about our relationship with God. These basics of our Christian faith are things we need to stand firm on and not compromise. I shall touch very briefly on some of these in Part III.

Then we need to be able to apply what we believe to what is happening in our lives. If we can't apply it to the life situations we face, it is probable that we either don't understand it, or don't really believe it, or both. It is in our actions that our faith becomes real. Faith that does not result in action, that does not make a major difference in the way we view and respond to everything around us, is not real faith. In Part IV, I shall address this issue of application. I shall identify some practical issues that arise in the lives of many of us, and shall show, I hope, how the teachings of Scripture can give us guidance, confidence and strength in dealing with those issues.

It may seem, as you read this part of the book, that the magnitude of the task is overwhelming, but remember two things. First, we don't have to deal with all these issues at the same time. We deal with whatever God is showing us needs attention at the moment. And as we improve in one area, that will strengthen us in others. Second, we deal with all of them in God's power and not our own. Whatever he calls us to do, he will enable us to do.

I want to say something about that word "believe." We Americans often use "believe" to mean intellectual assent. In Scripture it means much more than that. The Biblical words for "believe" and "faith" mean to put our entire trust in, and obey. They imply a total commitment. In the Biblical sense, belief is something we do, not just with our mind, but with all of us. Jesus commanded us to "Love the Lord your God with all your heart, with all your soul, with all your mind, and with all your strength" (Mark 12:30). I think it fair to say that the whole Bible also tells us to **believe** "with all your heart and with all your soul and with all your mind and with all your strength." The belief that Scripture talks about is a belief that shows itself in action. It shows itself in your whole life.

One other thing about belief should be kept in mind. It is important for us to be clear, and Scripturally sound, about **what** we believe. It is even more important to know **whom** we believe. Paul wrote, "I know whom I have believed" (2 Timothy 1:12). Our Christian faith is not primarily a belief in doctrines. It is a belief in a person. It is a relationship with a person.

It is because we know who God is that we can put our trust in him. It is because we know who God is that we can say, with the Psalmist, "God is our refuge and strength, a very present help in trouble. Therefore we will not fear" (Psalm 46:1-2). No matter what happens, we will not fear. We are not victims of the circumstances. They are temporary and God is eternal. God is greater than the circumstances, he is faithful to his promises, and he wants what is best for us. He has promised us that, in him, we can be overcomers (1 John 5:4-5). (See Chapter 11.) No matter what happens, we can depend on God.

Everything I have written in this book is written for myself as much as it is for those who may read it. I need increasingly deeper faith. All of us are working to find a deeper and solider faith. All of us need to pray, "I do believe; help me overcome my unbelief!" (Mark 9:24 NIV). Hopefully we can help and encourage each other in this process. As times get more difficult, we must succeed in strengthening our faith and learning to stand firm in it.

The stakes are high—for ourselves as individuals, for our children, for the body of Christ, for our nation, and for the world. I think we are at a point where God is saying to us, as he said to the Israelites in the time of Moses,

> "I call heaven and earth as witnesses today against you, that I have set before you life and death, blessing and cursing; therefore choose life, that both you and your descendants may live; that you may love the LORD your God, that you may obey His voice, and that you may cling to Him, for He is your life and the length of your days" (Deuteronomy 30:19-20).

We have important choices to make and we need to make the right choices. But we also need to be confident that if we do make the right choices, we will prevail. Our situation in the United States today is very serious. We need to recognize its seriousness, and not shut our eyes to it. But God is greater than our situation. Our God is a great God. He is Almighty. His power will prevail. His plans and purposes will stand, and nothing can thwart or defeat them. If we put our trust in him, and act in his mighty power and not just our own, we need not fear. Those who trust in God will not be disappointed. (See Psalm 22:5.)

My wife's poem says it better than I can.

THESE TIMES

These days are days to search,
to think, to see, to know—
reaching out to You to find

This Hour clarified:
all History being available
to new Perspective, greater range.

This Time is the time
to know and do;
a time of Portent:
unknown future
stirring into suddenness
of drastic change.

These Times are times for strength,
strength to receive the faithfulness
coming forth from You:
the Hour, indeed,
to Hear and Do.

Part II
SCRIPTURE

2

The Authority of Scripture

o o o o o o o o o o o o o o o o o o o o o o o o o o o o o o

"All Scripture is given by inspiration of God, and is profitable for doctrine, for reproof, for correction, for instruction in righteousness, that the man of God may be complete, thoroughly equipped for every good work."

—*(2 Timothy 3:16-17)*

I grew up in a household where the Bible was not read. I can't recall that my father ever referred to it. My mother admired the literary qualities of the King James version, and sometimes quoted a phrase from it as one would quote from Shakespeare or Emerson, but that was about all. My own love of, and respect for, Scripture has come to me late in life.

My father was a man of great personal integrity and honesty. He considered himself an atheist. By that I think he meant that he tried to deal only with what he regarded as facts—things that could be measured or demonstrated scientifically, or dollars and cents business and economic data. For him, anything else either did not exist; or he couldn't handle it, and so he generally tried to ignore it. In Paul's terminology, my father considered only what is seen, and tried to deny or ignore the existence of the unseen things. (See 2 Corinthians 4:18.)

In the early 1940s, I came to Washington, D.C. as a New Deal lawyer. I believed in man's capacity to solve any problem by the correct application of enough intellect, energy and money. I have since learned better. We became active in the Unitarian Church, which, as I experienced it, believed in man's ability to perfect himself by his own efforts. Later my wife and I became members of a New Age organization.

At age 66 I decided that the New Age teachings and the Bible were inconsistent with each other, and I decided to trust the Bible and to take it at face value.

Since then, under various pastors and professors, I have read and studied the Bible quite a bit. The more I read it, the more amazed I am at how it all fits together. I am also amazed at how I can keep coming back to the same passages and find new material and new insight in them.

As I have accepted the Bible as true, and tried to apply its principles in my life, I keep being impressed with the fact that it works. The Bible is a very practical book. Its principles work. If you let it change you, it will, and the change is for good. If you live by it, you will find more peace and joy and confidence in your life. In the years since I first decided to accept Scripture as true and as a sure guide for my life, I have never regretted that decision, and I keep being confirmed in its rightness.

When, in 1983, I decided to put my faith in the Bible, and in the God it reveals, I felt that these words of Psalm 40 had a special meaning for me:

> "He lifted me out of the slimy pit, out of the mud and mire; he set my feet on a rock and gave me a firm place to stand. He put a new song in my mouth, a hymn of praise to our God…" (Psalm 40:2-3 NIV).

Scripture is the rock, the solid foundation, the firm place on which I can stand. When everything around me seems like quicksand, Scripture stands solid and secure. For me, Scripture has become the touchstone of truth, by which I evaluate everything else.

Scripture can only become such a rock, such a touchstone, if we accept its authority as the word of God. If we accept the Bible as authoritative, then our faith rests on revelation from God. If we do not accept the Bible as authoritative, then our faith rests only on what we choose to believe, and has no greater claim to authority than does any other human philosophy or belief system. In this chapter, I want to indicate why I have come to believe that we should accept the Bible as authoritative.

Much has been written about Scripture and its authority. I have drawn on some of this literature. But perhaps what I can best contribute is some personal sense of what the Bible has come to mean to me.

Before I go further, I need to say something about Bible translations. The Bible was originally written in Hebrew and Aramaic (Old Testament) and in Greek (New Testament). There are a number of good English translations available, which differ somewhat in flavor, but almost never, so far as I have found, in basic meaning. Among the good ones are the King James Version (KJV), the New King James Version (NKJV), the Revised Standard Version (RSV), the New Revised Standard Version (NRSV), the New American Standard Version

(NASB) and the New International Version (NIV). The Living Bible is easy to read, and I think is basically sound. However, it is not a translation, but a paraphrase; it seeks to give what its editors believe is the basic meaning of the Bible without necessarily adhering to the text. I am reliably informed that the New Living Translation (NLT) is a true translation. Some people use the Amplified Bible, which gives a number of alternative translations of significant words and phrases.

In *Standing Firm in the Faith* I have quoted from the NKJV, the NIV and the KJV, partly for reasons of copyright permission, and partly because their flavor is appropriate to the point I am making. Unless otherwise indicated, Scripture quotations are from the New King James Version.

There are also books, claiming to be translations or paraphrases, which depart seriously from the original text. Some of them, I think, can fairly be called "counterfeit Bibles." They can do great harm because they teach falsity. One, that I have seen, deletes parts of what Scripture says and substitutes New Age or other non-Christian concepts and phraseology. Recently a so-called translation appeared in England, which was much praised by some. Examination of part of the text shows that it simply omits, or totally rewrites, significant parts of Scripture. It is wise to be cautious, and consult other mature Christians, in choosing a Bible translation. The fact that a translation or version is widely used does not guarantee its reliability. If we are thoroughly grounded in the true texts of Scripture, we should be able to reject the false. We need to be alert to the warning signals our spirit will give us when we encounter something false. With so many dependable translations available, why take a chance on something questionable?

The good translations came to us at a cost. Five or six centuries ago, quite a few people, such as William Tyndale, were burned at the stake for translating the Bible into English or other contemporary languages. Others were burned for possessing such translations.

Many English-speaking Protestants have grown up with the King James Version, which has a beauty and an inspiration all its own. But the King James Version uses an English which is not spoken today, and which is hard for many today to understand. I prefer to use a modern translation, because it makes it easier for me to apply the words of Scripture to my own life. I hope that those who believe in using only the King James Version will be able to accept the Biblical truth in *Standing Firm in the Faith*.

THE IMPORTANCE OF SCRIPTURE

I start this book with three chapters about Scripture, because I believe that our acceptance of Scripture on its own terms—as the revealed, authoritative word of God—is basic to our Christian life and basic to everything else I have to say.

"Do not merely listen to the word, and so deceive yourselves. Do what it says" (James 1:22 NIV). James is telling us that, if we do not live by the words of Scripture, we deceive ourselves. We are not being internally honest. We say one thing and do something different. We pretend to be one thing and are something else. We are double-minded, and hence ineffectual.

We also deceive ourselves if we accept some of Scripture as true and reject other parts of it. When we do that, it is not Scripture that we put our faith in; it is our own, fallible human judgment.

If we are to live by the words of Scripture, we need to believe that they are true. Not just true as a matter of human opinion. Not just true for some times and situations. But true. True for all times and for all situations.

As I shall show in a moment, Scripture declares itself to be the revealed word of God. It declares itself to be authoritative. It declares itself to be true for all time. If we are to use Scripture at all, should we not accept it on its own terms? If we accept it on its own terms, it will change our lives. If we accept it on its own terms, it will give us a sure guide for most situations that we encounter in our lives. But we have to accept it on its own terms.

Jesus Christ said, "Man shall not live by bread alone, but by every word that proceeds from the mouth of God" (Matthew 4:4, quoting Deuteronomy 8:3). God's words, as revealed in Scripture, are our spiritual food. They are just as necessary to us as the physical food we eat. Living in a world in which we are assaulted daily by so much that is ungodly, we urgently need the words of Scripture if we would remain committed to God.

We need to read and study Scripture, to understand it correctly, to believe it with our hearts and not just our minds, and then to live by it.

THE BIBLE IS THE REVEALED WORD OF GOD

Physically, the Bible is a collection of 66 books, written by some 42 different human authors over a period of about 1500 years. But actually it has a single author. The entire Bible is the word of God. It declares this many times over.

This is an amazing assertion, but I believe it is true. We cannot get much benefit from the Bible unless we are willing to accept it as the word of God.

The Christian Bible has two basic divisions, which we call the Old Testament and the New Testament. I believe they are a seamless web. The Old Testament points to the New; the New Testament fulfills the Old. Both are inspired by the same author, who does not change. Everything I say in this chapter applies to both.

The Bible is a unique book. There is no other book like it. There is no other book that has so impacted so many lives. There is no other book that has had such an impact on the world's history.[8]

All Scripture Is Inspired by God

"All scripture is given **by inspiration of God**" (2 Timothy 3:16). The Greek word, *theopneustos* (from *theos*, "God" and *pneuma*, "breath" or "spirit") literally means "God-breathed" or "God-spirited." Everything in Scripture is breathed, or inspired, by God. Everything. Romans 3:2 says that the Jews, to whom the Old Testament Scriptures were given, had been entrusted with "the oracles [words] of God."

"God, who at various times and in various ways **spoke** in time past to the fathers by the prophets, has in these last days **spoken** to us by His Son, whom He has appointed heir of all things, through whom also He made the worlds" (Hebrews 1:1-2). What an amazing statement! God has spoken to men and women. The Bible is a record of words that God has spoken.

Paul commended the people of Thessalonica because, "when you received the word of God which you heard from us, you welcomed it not as the word of men, but as it is in truth, the **word of God**" (1 Thessalonians 2:13). (Also see Galatians 1:11-12.)

We find many specific examples that confirm these general statements.

Much of what we find in the Old Testament prophetic books is the direct words of God, spoken in the first person. For example, God said to Jeremiah, "Behold, I have put my words in your mouth" (Jeremiah 1:9). "Speak to them all that I command you" (Jeremiah 1:17). Isaiah declares, "Thus saith the Lord GOD" (Isaiah 28:16 KJV). (Also see Isaiah 42:5.) Amos says much the same (Amos 1:3, 6, 11,13, 2:1, 4, 6). The prophetic books are full of such statements. Much of Exodus and Deuteronomy consists of the direct words of God which were spoken to Moses and which Moses delivered to the people. (See, for example, Exodus 20:1; Deuteronomy 6:1.) I could give many further examples. The prophets also say that their predecessors spoke directly from God. Zechariah spoke of "the words which the LORD of hosts had sent by His Spirit through the former prophets" (Zechariah 7:12). Over and over, God rebukes the Israelites for not listening to the words he sent by his prophets. (See, for example, 2 Kings 17:13; Nehemiah 9:30.) Summarizing all this, Peter wrote, "...prophecy never had its origin in the will of man, but men **spoke from God** as they were **carried along by the Holy Spirit**" (2 Peter 1:21 NIV).

God also told his prophets to write down the words he spoke to them. He told Jeremiah to write on a scroll all the words God had spoken to him (Jeremiah 36:2). When the King burned that scroll, God told Jeremiah to write another scroll (Jeremiah 36:28). Moses wrote "the words of this law in a book" (Deuteronomy 31:24). "This law" refers, I believe, to all the words God spoke to Moses. God told Joshua to meditate day and night on "this Book of the Law" (Joshua 1:8).

David, who wrote many of the Psalms, said that he wrote by inspiration of the Holy Spirit. "The Spirit of the LORD spoke by me, and His word was on my tongue" (2 Samuel 23:2). Jesus said that David spoke by the Holy Spirit (Matthew 22:43). Peter said, "You [God] spoke by the Holy Spirit through the mouth of your servant, our father David..." (Acts 4:25 NIV). (Also see Acts 1:16.)

Joshua 1:2-9, 3:7-8; 7:10-15, and 24:2-13 record the very words of God. "For the LORD revealed Himself to Samuel" through his word (1 Samuel 3:21). (Also see 1 Samuel 8:7-9, 22.) Job, chapters 38-41, record the words of God spoken to Job. 2 Chronicles 7:12-22 record the words which God spoke to Solomon one night, words of promise and warning to the nation of Israel. 2 Chronicles 20:15-17 (KJV) gives a prophecy, "Thus saith the Lord unto you," by the prophet Jahaziel, giving hope, encouragement and a battle strategy to the kingdom of Judah. Genesis records many direct words of God, spoken to Adam, Noah, Abraham, Isaac, and Jacob. There are many other such examples.

Jesus said that the words he spoke (which are recorded in Scripture) were the very words of God. "I speak to the world those things which I heard from Him [God]" (John 8:26). "I have not spoken on My own authority; but the Father who sent Me gave Me a command, what I should say and what I should speak...just as the Father has told Me, so I speak" (John 12:49-50). "I have given to them the words which you [God] have given Me" (John 17:8).

Should we then say that these particular examples, and the many similar examples that could be given, are the words of God, while the rest of Scripture is not? No. The basic principle is that **all** scripture is inspired by God. **All** of it is what God wanted.

This is very important. It means that those who take the Bible as literature, or as human teachings or human historical accounts, are not taking it according to its own terms. It means that the whole Bible is inspired by God, breathed out by God, and we need to accept it on that basis.

The difference is vitally important. If the Bible is just a human book, then we are free to take what we like out of it and reject the rest. But if it is the word of God, then we must accept it all. If it is a human work, we can judge it. If it is the word of God, it judges us.

I point out in the next chapter that the Bible has great power in our lives. It can have this power only if we submit to it and treat it as authoritative. We should take the Bible on its own terms.

Did God Actually Speak to People?

Some may ask, "Did God really speak to the people who wrote the Bible? Did he give them his exact words, as many of the passages cited above say? How can this be?"

The question arises because such things are outside of our personal experience. In addition, we may have been exposed to some "flaky" people who claimed to hear from God, but obviously didn't. But Scripture records many cases in which God has spoken directly to certain individuals, and even carried on fairly extended conversations with them. Following are a few examples of such conversations. Adam (Genesis 3:8-19); Noah (Genesis 6:13-7:4; 9:1-17); Abraham (Genesis 15:1-9; chapter 18); Moses (Exodus 3:1-4:17); Isaiah (chapter 6); Paul and Ananias (Acts 9:4-16); Peter (Acts 10:13-20).

The record of Scripture is very clear that God does talk to people. God "spoke," he has "spoken" (Hebrews 1:1-2), and men have recorded his words. He has done so many times. To those who would still say, "But he can't do this," I simply reply that Scripture tells us that nothing is impossible with God (Luke 1:37). That is the very nature of God. He is the one for whom nothing is impossible. (See Chapter 5.)

On its own internal evidence, I think we must conclude that **all** Scripture is inspired by God. **All** of it is God's book, given in the words God wanted, to achieve God's purposes.

If we are to use the Bible, we need to take it on its own terms. It will not be of much benefit to us unless we take it on its own terms.

JESUS AND THE APOSTLES TREATED SCRIPTURE AS AUTHORITATIVE

The Old Testament Scriptures are quoted or referred to over 1,000 times in the New Testament. Always they are treated as authoritative.

Jesus spoke of his life on earth as the fulfillment of Scripture. He said that he had come "to fulfill" the Law and the Prophets—that is, the Old Testament Scriptures (Matthew 5:17). At the beginning of his ministry he said, "The time is fulfilled" (Mark 1:15). He read in the synagogue from Isaiah 61:1-2 and then said, "Today this scripture is fulfilled in your hearing" (Luke 4:21). He several times spoke of events in his life as the fulfillment of Scripture. (See Mark 14:49; John 13:18, 17:12.) He said of his parables, "In them the prophecy of Isaiah is fulfilled" (Matthew 13:14). He said that the Scriptures "testify of me" (John 5:39).

When Jesus was arrested shortly before his Crucifixion, Peter drew his sword and struck the High Priest's servant. Jesus said, "Do you think that I cannot now pray to My Father, and He will provide Me with more than twelve legions of angels? How then could the Scriptures be fulfilled, that it must happen thus?" (Matthew 26:53-54). (Also see Luke 24:46.) Jesus was so convinced that the Scriptures must be fulfilled that he deliberately went to an agonizing death. After his Resurrection, while walking with two disciples on the road to Emmaus, Jesus "...explained to them what was said in all the Scriptures concerning himself" (Luke 24:27 NIV). Later he said to the disciples, "These are the words which I spoke to you while I was still with you, that all things must be fulfilled which were written in the Law of Moses and the Prophets and the Psalms concerning Me" (Luke 24:44).

Jesus resisted the devil's temptation by quoting Scripture, saying, "it is written" (Matthew 4:4, 7, 10). He told some Sadducees, "You are mistaken, not knowing the Scriptures nor the power of God" (Matthew 22:29). He often referred to Scripture in his discussions and teachings. (See, for example, Matthew 26:31; Mark 12:10; Matthew 19:4, 18, 21:16, 42.) And always it is with the assumption that Scripture is true and authoritative. He said that God's "word is truth" (John 17:17)

The apostles similarly treated Scripture as authoritative. Peter quoted Psalms to show that it was necessary to choose one to take Judas' place among the twelve disciples (Acts 1:20-22). On the Day of Pentecost he said, "This is what was spoken by the prophet Joel" (Acts 2:16). Repeatedly he quoted from Scripture. (See, for example, Acts 2:25-28, 34-35; 4:11, 25-26.) The gospel writers repeatedly point out how events in Jesus' life are the fulfillment of prophecies in Scripture. The epistles repeatedly quote Scripture as authoritative. In 1 Corinthians 15:3-4, Paul summarizes the gospel he has taught, "For I delivered to you first of all that which I also received: that Christ died for our sins **according to the Scriptures**, and that He was buried, and that He rose again the third day **according to the Scriptures**."

If Jesus and the apostles treated Scripture as authoritative, should not we?

SCRIPTURE IS TRUTH THAT ENDURES FOREVER

Scripture declares that God's word is true. God's word is truth (John 17:17). It is "the word of truth" (Ephesians 1:13). (Also see Psalm 119:43; 2 Corinthians 6:7; Colossians 1:5; 2 Timothy 2:15; James 1:18.) "The entirety of your word is truth" (Psalm 119:160).

Scripture says that its truth endures forever. "Forever, O Lord, your word is settled in heaven" (Psalm 119:89). "The word of our God stands forever" (Isaiah 40:8). Jesus said, "Heaven and earth will pass away, but My words will by no means pass away" (Matthew 24:35). The word of God, as recorded in Scripture, is true eternally. It is not, as some today assert, just for a particular time and a particular group of people. It declares that it is true for all time, for all people, and for all situations. It is more lasting then the physical universe. God does not change (Malachi 3:6; James 1:17) and his truth does not change.

Should we not accept the Bible at face value on this, also?

My wife has said it well.

YEARNING

Your Word is Truth.
Lord, lead me where
only truth is living there.

SCRIPTURE WORKS

My experience has been that when I accept Scripture as authoritative, and seek to do what is says, it works. It works in my life. It works in the lives of those around me. It leads to a better, richer, more satisfying life. To me this is one of the most compelling reasons for accepting its authority.

I am absolutely convinced of this in my own life. Scripture says that, after we accept Jesus Christ as our Savior and Lord, we should be transformed. (See Chapter 14.) Scripture is the principal agent for that transformation. I have seen this transformation happening in my own life, and in the lives of other Christians around me. It is real. It is one of the best things that has happened in my life. Through Scripture I have found hope, joy, peace and fulfillment that I could not have found in any other way. I simply don't see how people can get along without it!

In a sense, the rest of this book can be seen as a demonstration of the fact that Scripture works. I have taken Scriptural principles that apply to many of the situations we find ourselves in as humans, and I believe I have shown that they make practical sense. That, at least, has been my purpose.

I do want to deal with one misconception that some people have. Many tend to see Scripture as a bunch of rules—of "dos" and "don'ts"—which limit their freedom. My experience has been the opposite. I have found that living by Scriptural principles has freed me up from a great many mindsets, preconceptions, and attitudes that were limiting me and keeping me from functioning as God intended me to. Jesus promised this. He said, "If you abide in My word [Scripture], you are My disciples indeed. And you shall know the truth, and the truth shall make you free" (John 8:31-32). I have found this promise fulfilled often in my life.

THREE AREAS IN WHICH SOME FIND PROBLEMS

Before I go any further, I want to deal with three areas which may make it difficult for some to accept the Bible as true.

Predictive Prophecy

Seventeen books of the Old Testament are referred to as prophetic books. Prophecy is simply God speaking through a human. "Thus saith the LORD" (Amos 1:3 KJV). Often these words of God are saying how God sees what is going on in the world. Sometimes they include predictions of future events.

Prophecy in the Old Testament is not limited to these 17 books. Moses is said to have been the greatest prophet (Deuteronomy 34:10) and the book of Deuteronomy begins with these words, "Moses spoke to the children of Israel according to all that the LORD had given him as commandments to them" (Deuteronomy 1:3). There are many other prophecies in the Old Testament outside the 17 prophetic books. (See, for example, 2 Samuel 2:4-16, 12:7-12; 1 Kings 13:1-6, 22:17-28; 2 Chronicles 20:15-17.)

There are a number of predictive prophecies in the New Testament. Jesus, who referred to himself as a "prophet" (Matthew 13:57), gave a tremendous end-time prophecy (a prophecy of what would occur at his Second Coming) recorded in Matthew, chapter 24. Jesus gave a number of other predictive prophecies. He frequently prophesied his own crucifixion and resurrection (for example, see Matthew 16:21), and his second coming (Matthew 25:31, 26:64; Luke 17:24-25). He said that he would judge all men. (See Matthew 25:31-46; John 5:28-30; Matthew 13:41.) He said that he would be seated at the right hand of God (Matthew 26:64). He said that he would send the Holy Spirit to dwell in us (John 14:15-18). (Also see Acts 1:8.) He said that heaven and earth would pass away (Matthew 24:35). He said that the kingdom of God would be taken away from the Jewish religious leaders and given to a people that will bring forth its fruits (Matthew 21:43). (Also see Matthew 8:11-12.) He prophesied that his disciples would all fall away and that Peter would deny him three times (Matthew 26:31). He said that the disciples would be arrested and flogged (whipped or beaten) and brought before governors and kings (Acts 5:40-41). He prophesied about the woman who washed his feet with her tears and dried them with her hair (Mark 14:9).

Both Paul and Peter gave predictive prophecies. (See 1 Corinthians 15:51-57; 1 Thessalonians 4:13-5:11; 2 Thessalonians 1:5-2:12; 1 Timothy 4:1-5; 2 Timothy 3:1-9; 2 Peter 3:10-13.) The Book of Revelation is a "prophecy" (Revelation 1:3, 22:18), a vision of "things which must take place after this" (Revelation 4:1).

As I have already noted, both Jesus and the gospel writers repeatedly spoke of aspects of Jesus' life as the fulfillment of prophecy.

Some have trouble with these passages of Scripture because they do not believe future events can be predicted. My answer is, very simply, if all things are possible with God, why cannot God give his chosen prophets advance knowledge of things that are going to happen? This is exactly what he says he does. God declares "the end from the beginning, and from ancient times things that are not yet done" (Isaiah 46:10). "I have declared the former things from the beginning; They went forth from My mouth, and I caused them to hear it. Suddenly I did them, and they came to pass" (Isaiah 48:3). Jesus warned his disciples of what would happen in the end times, and said, "See, I have told you beforehand"

(Matthew 24:25). God says, "Surely the Lord GOD does nothing, unless He reveals His secret to his servants the prophets" (Amos 3:7). Should we not believe him?

Scripture records a great many predictive prophecies that have been fulfilled. I shall mention only three.

- **THE BABYLONIAN CAPTIVITY**—Soon after a group of people were taken from Jerusalem to Babylon, the prophet Jeremiah prophesied that the captivity in Babylon would last 70 years (Jeremiah 29:10). When the 70 years were up, Daniel, who was one of the captives, prayed earnestly for his people (Daniel 9:1-19). The result was that "...in order to fulfill the word of the LORD spoken by Jeremiah, the LORD moved the heart of Cyrus king of Persia..." to allow the Israelites to return to Jerusalem and rebuild the Temple (Ezra 1:1 NIV). (By this time Persia had conquered Babylon.)
- **THE CRUCIFIXION OF JESUS**—Psalm 22 (written about 1000 B.C.) and Isaiah, chapter 53 (written about 700 B.C.) give remarkably vivid descriptions of the Crucifixion of Jesus, which occurred about 30 A.D. It's almost as if the prophets were actually seeing it happen.
- **THE DESTRUCTION OF THE TEMPLE**—Jesus, just before his Crucifixion, predicted that the great Temple in Jerusalem would be destroyed and "not one stone shall be left here upon another" (Matthew 24:2). About 40 years later, in 70 A.D., the Temple was utterly destroyed by the Romans; not one stone was left standing.

Some critics who cannot accept the idea of predictive prophecy have assumed that these writings must have been written after the date of the event prophesied. For example, they ascribe quite late dates for the second half of Isaiah and for Daniel. There are three major problems with this.

- It is contrary to the fact that the words are given as prophecies of **future** events. In effect, these critics are saying that Scripture, in this respect, is false. They are saying that the authors of these books are liars and deceivers, who claim to be predicting as future events things that have already occurred.
- Isaiah gave many prophecies of the coming of Jesus. We know that they were given before the event occurred, because one of the Dead Sea scrolls, dated a century or more B.C., is a manuscript of the book of Isaiah.

- It fails to deal with other predictions by the same prophets of events which have not yet occurred. Both Isaiah and Daniel prophesied events which have not yet occurred. The logic of these critics' position would seem to require us to conclude that the books of Isaiah and Daniel have not yet been written! In this area, as in all others, the wisest course is to take the Bible on its own terms.

Miracles and the Supernatural

The Bible is full of miracles and supernatural events. There are miraculous healings by Jesus, by his disciples, and by Elijah and Elisha. People are raised from the dead. There is multiplication of food, calming of a storm, walking on water, and much else. There are crossings, dry shod, of the Red Sea and the Jordan River. Three young men were thrown into a very hot furnace and not burned. Daniel was thrown into a den of lions and not harmed. At Elijah's command, there was no rain or dew in Israel for 3½ years. At Moses' command, many plagues came upon Egypt. At Joshua's command, the sun stood still for a day.

There are miraculous victories in battle: the walls of Jericho falling, Gideon's army of 300 defeating many thousands, Jehoshaphat defeating a much larger army without even having to fight, an angel striking 185,000 Assyrians dead and saving Jerusalem from attack.

There are appearances of angels, and casting out of demons.

There are even more amazing things than these. At God's command, the physical universe was created. God caused a flood that destroyed the whole world. Jesus was fully God and fully man. Jesus was resurrected from the dead. Jesus, Elijah and Enoch were taken up bodily into heaven.

How can anyone believe that such things actually occurred? And if they did not occur, why should anyone believe the Bible? How can it be said to have been inspired of God if it tells of things that are simply not credible?

To our western, scientific/materialist minds, the question may seem unanswerable. But I have no problem with it. I have no problem with accepting all of these supernatural things as having actually happened.

If God is God, then he is all-powerful. That's what it means to be God. It's part of his nature. He is God Almighty, as Scripture repeatedly says.

If he is all-powerful, then he can do anything. This is exactly what Scripture tells us. God "can do everything" (Job 42:2). "With God nothing will be impossible" (Luke 1:37). "With God all things are possible" (Matthew 19:26). "Is anything too hard for the LORD?" (Genesis 18:14). God's power is "...incomparably great..." (Ephesians 1:19 NIV). "'To whom will you compare me? Or who is my equal?' says the Holy One" (Isaiah 40:25 NIV).

Scripture says that God is above everything. God said, "I am God, and there is no other; I am God, and there is none like Me" (Isaiah 46:8). Jesus Christ (who is God, see Chapter 6) is "far above all rule and authority, power and dominion, and every title that can be given, not only in the present age but also in the one to come" (Ephesians 1:21 NIV). God is not limited by the "laws of nature" or anything else. His power and authority have no limits.

This may be hard for our modern Western minds to accept. But it is what God's word tells us over and over. If we can once really accept it, then there should be no difficulty accepting the Bible at face value when it tells of supernatural events.

Some will say, "Does this mean that God can violate the laws of nature?" I think the question has a faulty premise. What we call "the laws of nature" are not laws at all. They are the best efforts of scientists to describe what God has created and to predict how it will function. Scientists have done a good job of this, and their descriptions and predictions usually work. But their descriptions and predictions are necessarily incomplete because they have no tools with which to describe God or to predict how he will act. God is not limited by the descriptions men have formulated. He is not limited by man-made "laws." Much as we may admire science, the human scientists have no power or authority to tell God what he can or cannot do.

Consider the fact that "the laws of nature" change from time to time. It used to be said that matter cannot be destroyed. Now it is said that matter can be converted into energy and vice versa. It used to be said that one chemical element could not change into another. With the discovery of radioactivity, we know they can. It used to be said that everything operated by a principle of continuity. Now many scientists believe there was a discontinuous creative event, a "big bang," that got everything started. Etc. Does this mean that the "laws of nature" have changed? Does "nature" operate differently than it used to? Of course not. It merely means that scientific descriptions have become more nearly accurate.

Someone once commented to a scientist that "the Bible is not a science textbook." To which he responded, "I know. I have written several science textbooks and they all have to be revised every few years."

When God does a miracle, he is not acting outside of, or contrary to, the "laws" of the universe. He is merely acting outside the comprehension, and sphere of activity, of some scientists.

As a lawyer, I understand that any laws or rules have validity only to the extent that those issuing them had authority to issue them. An Act of Congress is binding and enforceable because Congress has, by the U.S. Constitution, been granted authority to legislate. If an Act of Congress deals with something outside the authority delegated to Congress, the courts will (or should) declare it unenforceable. So, I ask, who has given scientists, individually or collectively, the authority to declare what God can or cannot do? Certainly not God, for his Scripture declares, "…who are you, O man, to talk back to God?…" (Romans 9:20 NIV). (Also see Isaiah 29:4, 45:9.) When looked at in this light, I suggest that for scientists, individually or collectively, to think that they can tell God what he can or cannot do, is an astonishing act of presumption.

There have been some who, in an effort to make the Bible more acceptable to our Western scientific mindset, have sought to remove the miracles, the supernatural events, from the Bible. Sometimes they try to explain them in naturalistic terms—which are often harder to accept than the Biblical, supernatural, explanations. Sometimes they assert that these passages are not authentic, because they say something that the critic is not willing to accept. The effort is bound to fail. God, by definition, is supernatural. To take the supernatural out of the Bible is to take God out of the Bible. Then it is no longer the Bible—it is no longer the record of God's words and actions; and it has no greater claim to authority or truth than any other human writing.

Does Science Contradict the Bible?

Much has been written about this. I can only suggest a little perspective.

When we consider this question, we need to consider the character and function of both the Bible and scientific knowledge.

The Bible does not purport to be a scientific textbook. For example, when Psalm 19 speaks of the sun as rising at one end of the heavens and making his circuit to the other, this is a poem, describing in poetic imagery how it appears to men. Actually, it is expressing much the same metaphor as we use today, in our newspapers and almanacs, when we speak of "sunrise" and "sunset." Quite a bit of the Bible is in the form of poetry, and no one should expect poetry to be scientifically precise. That is not its function.

On the other hand, scientists cannot really tell us about first causes. They can describe what they see now. They may be able to make some inferences as to how such phenomena **might** have occurred. But they cannot tell with certainty what **actually** occurred.

Today, the great conflict is over the issue of creation vs. evolution. There the Bible is very clear. It says that God created **all** the physical universe. The fact that he created it is basic to many other things that the Bible says. If we are to take the Bible at face value, we must accept its statements that God is the Creator of all things.

Does science contradict those statements? I don't think so. The theory of evolution denies that there was an intelligent Creator, but that is a theory and not an established fact. Scientists have taken a large body of observed facts, and tried to come up with an explanation for them. This is part of the job of scientists, but we need to distinguish sharply between what is proven fact and what is unproven theory. Some scientific theories have been proven. Repeated experiments or engineering applications have been conducted which consistently confirm these theories, so that they can be regarded as established fact, at least until a new theory is developed. But evolution is not like that. No one has ever seen it happen. No one can devise an experiment or application to cause it to happen. There is no way to verify it experimentally or practically. It is simply a set of logical inferences from the observed facts. And there are respected scientists who, on the basis of strict scientific analysis, with no reference to the Bible or any religious belief, find major flaws with the theory.

The real conflict, I believe, is between two religious viewpoints. On the one hand, we have Christianity (and Judaism), which assert that God created the physical universe, and that man, God's creation, is accountable to God for his actions and decisions. On the other hand, we have secular humanism (which the U.S. Supreme Court has declared to be a religion). Secular humanism denies that there is any Creator or God. It asserts that man is the measure of all things, that the physical universe came about by accident, and that there is no higher power to whom man is accountable. I suggest that the main body of evolutionists today have started with the premise that God either does not exist or is irrelevant. Having made this assumption, they then tried to develop a theory consistent with that premise to fit the known facts. This is legitimate; it is the way science works. But should we not also try starting with the premise that God created the universe and see whether the known facts fit that premise? Some well-qualified scientists have done this, with considerable success.

My own sense is that purely scientific reasoning and analysis will never "prove" or "disprove" either creation or evolution. The issue is basically not a scientific one but a religious one.

THE AUTHENTICITY OF THE BIBLE

Much has been written about the authenticity of the Bible.[9] There has been an enormous literature of so-called "higher criticism," which often questions the authorship of various books of the Bible, the validity of various portions of the text, etc. Indeed, there is a myth, that is fairly widely current in the news media and elsewhere, that all "scholars" question or discredit the Bible, while only ignorant or superstitious people accept it as true. Actually, there are many well-qualified Bible scholars whose study has convinced them that the Bible is true and authentic, and who document that conclusion impressively, not only with evidence from the Bible, but with evidence from history, archeology and other branches of knowledge.

In the interest of brevity, I shall just give a few highlights on this issue of authenticity.

The Reliability of the Texts

For the New Testament, we have a great many more manuscripts, dating far closer to the time of the original composition, than for any other ancient writing. I can only give a few highlights. There are in existence today over 5,600 Greek manuscript texts of part or all of the New Testament, as well as almost 20,000 manuscripts of early translations into Latin and other languages. One of the fragments dates back to within 50 years of the date of composition of the writing. There are a number of others, including complete texts of some of the gospels, dating back to 200 A.D. or earlier. There are also a very large number of quotations from the New Testament in early Christian writings, quite a few of which date back to the First and Second centuries A.D. We have almost complete texts of the New Testament dating back to 350 and 400 A.D.

By way of contrast, we have only 7 copies of Plato's writings; the earliest available one was written some 1,300 years after Plato died. For Caesar's *Gallic Wars*, the oldest available manuscript is dated 900 years after Caesar wrote it. For some other recognized ancient texts, we have one or two available manuscripts. Compared with other widely accepted ancient writings, whose authenticity is rarely questioned, the number of copies of the New Testament, and their closeness in time to the original writing and the events recorded, is very impressive. We can have much greater confidence in the authenticity of the Greek texts on which our modern translations are based than in any other ancient writing.[10]

For the Old Testament, we have a substantial number of manuscripts. Among these are the Dead Sea Scrolls, dated 300 to 100 B.C., containing the entire book of Isaiah and fragments from almost every other book in the Old Testament. We also know that the Hebrew copyists exercised extreme care to produce accurate copies. A Greek translation of the Old Testament, known as the Septuagint, was made starting about 200 B.C., and the New Testament contains about 1,000 references to and quotations from that translation.[11]

There is impressive archeological evidence to support the truth of what is stated in both Old and New Testaments.[12]

There are some minor variations among the available texts, as is almost always the case when dealing with hand-written copies of the same text, but in general they are in remarkable agreement.

There are a number of English translations available today. Translation is an art, and not a science. Often there is no one English word or phrase that can accurately convey the full meaning of the Hebrew or Greek original. Hence different translators render the same passage somewhat differently. It is unusual to find any significant difference in meaning among the good translations. Moreover, especially with the computer programs available, it is not difficult for the layman who does not know Hebrew or Greek to compare different translations, to consult dictionaries for the meaning of the original words, to do word studies, and to have access to commentaries, so as to get a pretty accurate picture of the meaning of a passage.

Authorship and Date

Much has been written about the human authorship and the date of composition of various books of the Bible. I shall only touch on two questions that have been raised which are of major importance, and shall deal even with them very summarily.

THE FIRST FIVE BOOKS (THE PENTATEUCH)—The traditional view is that these were all written by Moses. This would place their dates somewhere in the range of 1450-1300 B.C., depending on which date you use for the Exodus. The view that Moses is their author is well supported by the words of Scripture, which say that Moses "wrote all the words of the LORD" (Exodus 24:4), that he then "took the Book of the Covenant and read in the hearing of the people" (Exodus 24:7), that he "wrote this law" and commanded that it be read to the people every seven years (Deuteronomy 31:9-11), and that he "completed writing the words of this law in a book" and directed that "this Book of the Law" be placed beside the ark of the covenant (Deuteronomy 31:24, 26). (Also see Exodus 17:14; Deuteronomy 17:18.) (The ark of the covenant was placed in the innermost part of the tabernacle, and later the Temple.) Through Moses, God directed the people of Israel to "obey the voice of the LORD your God, to keep His commandments and His statutes which are written in this Book of the Law" (Deuteronomy 30:10). Before the Israelites entered into Canaan, God told Joshua, "This Book of the Law shall not depart from your mouth, but you shall meditate in it day and night, that you may observe to do according to all that is written in it" (Joshua 1:8). Evidently by the time of Moses' death there was a "Book of the Law" in written form which Moses had written.

Then, beginning early in the nineteenth century A.D. and reaching its complete form by the 1870s, a view developed which said that none of these books were written by Moses, but that they were written by at least four different authors, or groups of authors, at various times between about 850 and 450 B.C. In other words, the writing of these five books is said to have begun a little more than a century before the Assyrians destroyed the Northern Kingdom, and to have continued until after parts of the Southern Kingdom returned from captivity in Babylon and Persia. This "documentary theory," as it came to be called, became very popular and is still widely taught.

There are a lot of problems with this theory.

- It results in extreme artificiality. Proponents of the theory say that, in many cases, a single verse of the Bible was written by two, three or even four different authors over a period of several hundred years.
- It portrays God as destroying the Northern Kingdom for violating rules that were not officially or definitively formulated until shortly before he took that action, rules that were not finally formulated until many centuries later. This is contrary to God's character.
- As originally proposed, it rested on an assumption that there was no writing in Moses' time. This assumption has since been proven false. We now know that there was writing in the Near East long before the time of Moses. Since Moses had been trained to become a leader in the court of Egypt, the greatest nation of that time, it is reasonable to suppose that he knew how to write.
- Much emphasis was placed on the use of two different words for God—*Elohim* and *Jehovah*—which was thought to imply two different authors. However, it is not unusual for a single author to use more than

one name for God, particularly where, as in this case, the text sometimes focusses on God in his universal aspect and sometimes on his special relationship with Israel. *Jehovah* and *Elohim* are not synonyms. They have different shades of meaning. It is also interesting that the combined term *Jehovah Elohim* appears over 250 times in the Old Testament. Are we to assume that each time it appears, *Jehovah* was written by one author and *Elohim* by another author, perhaps a hundred years earlier?

- It was also assumed that the religion of the Jewish people evolved and did not become truly monotheistic until the time of Amos, about 750 B.C. This assumption treats the Bible as a purely human product and denies that it is a revelation from God. There have been archeological finds that show that some Israelites had idols of pagan gods. These finds merely confirm the truth of Scripture, which tells over and over of the Israelites turning away from the true God and worshiping Canaanite or other pagan gods, a practice recorded as early as Judges, chapter 2, and for which God repeatedly rebuked them through his prophets. (See, for example, Jeremiah 2:11-13.) These archeological finds confirm, rather than refute, the Scriptural account.

Modern scholarship has developed persuasive evidence for Moses' authorship of these five books.[13] If this is so, then four of them—Exodus, Leviticus, Numbers and Deuteronomy—are essentially eyewitness accounts by Moses of the events and words of God which they record and in which he participated. (Deuteronomy 34:5-12 would have been added by someone else.) Moreover they are eyewitness accounts by a well-educated man who had been trained for a leadership position in the court of Egypt. As such they are reliable evidence of the truth of what they record.

Moses was, of course, not an eyewitness of the events recorded in Genesis. However, I believe a persuasive argument has been made that Genesis is a compilation, by Moses, of earlier written accounts, most of which could have been made by one of the participants. Some have seen, in the word *toledoth* (usually translated "these are the generations of" or "this is the account of"), which appears at various places in the Genesis narrative, an indication of the ending of one such document and the beginning of another.

THE GOSPELS—Many questions have been raised about the authorship and date of the four gospels. Based on what I have read, I believe that the first three gospels and the book of Acts were probably written in the period 55-75

A.D. (and probably the earlier part of that period), and the gospel of John was written about 90-95 A.D. I believe that their authors are:

- Matthew, one of Jesus' twelve original disciples (Matthew 9:9).
- John Mark, who was so close to the disciple Peter that Peter called him his son (1 Peter 5:13). Several of the early church writers say that Mark's gospel reflects Peter's teachings. Mark was also a traveling companion of Paul on his first missionary journey, and appears to have been with him during part of his imprisonment in Rome (Colossians 4:10; Philemon 24). It was at the house of Mark's mother in Jerusalem that the disciples met for prayer when Peter was imprisoned by Herod (Acts 12:12); possibly they met there on other occasions. Mark may well have been the young man present at Jesus' arrest, referred to in Mark 14:51.
- Luke, a Gentile physician, who accompanied Paul on some of Paul's journeys and was evidently with him when he was in prison in Rome. Luke also wrote the Book of Acts (Acts 1:1).
- John, one of Jesus' original twelve disciples (John 21:24).

If I am right, Matthew and John were written by members of the original 12 disciples, and Mark, Luke and Acts were written by men who had ready access to the first disciples and to others who had been with Jesus during his earthly ministry. All but the gospel of John were written at a time when many would still have been alive who were alive during Jesus' ministry on earth, including people who were hostile to the gospel and had strong reasons for wanting to discredit these writings. (Much the same can be said of the rest of the New Testament.) This gives the gospels and Acts strong historical credibility.

The New Testament emphasizes that it is based on eyewitness evidence. John wrote, "The Word [Jesus] became flesh and dwelt among us, and **we beheld His glory**" (John 1:14). "That which was from the beginning, **which we have heard, which we have seen with our eyes, which we have looked upon** and **our hands have handled**, concerning the Word of life—the life was manifested, and **we have seen and bear witness**, and declare to you that eternal life which was with the Father and was manifested to us—**that which we have seen and heard we declare to you**" (1 John 1:1-3). At the end of his gospel John refers to the disciple "...who had leaned back against Jesus at the supper..." (John 21:20 NIV) and then says, "This is the disciple who **testifies of these things, and wrote these things**; and we know that his testimony is true" (John 21:24).

Peter wrote that he was "a witness of the sufferings of Christ" (1 Peter 5:1). He wrote, "We did not follow cleverly invented stories when we told you about the power and coming of our Lord Jesus Christ, but we were **eyewitnesses** of his majesty. For he received honor and glory from God the Father when the voice came to him from the Majestic Glory, saying, 'This is my Son, whom I love; with him I am well pleased.' **We ourselves heard this voice** that came from heaven when we were with him on the sacred mountain" (2 Peter 1:16-18 NIV). (Also see Matthew 17:1-8.)

All of the apostles, and those who followed Jesus, were witnesses of his ministry and testified to what they saw. "We are His **witnesses** of these things" (Acts 5:32). Those who traveled with him are "His **witnesses** to the people" (Acts 13:31). (Also see Acts 1:8, 22; 2:32; 10:41.) When the Jewish leaders tried to silence Peter and John, they replied, "...we cannot help speaking about **what we have seen and heard**" (Acts 4:20 NIV).

These writers are proclaiming what they personally observed as eyewitnesses.

Luke begins his gospel, "Many have undertaken to draw up an account of the things that have been fulfilled among us, just as they were handed down to us by those who from the first were **eyewitnesses** and servants of the word. Therefore, since I myself have **carefully investigated** everything from the beginning, it seemed good also to me to write an orderly account for you, most excellent Theophilus, so that you may know the **certainty** of the things you have been taught" (Luke 11:4 NIV). Luke says that he carefully investigated these eyewitness accounts, and then wrote it all down in an orderly way.

Part of Luke's account in Acts is an eyewitness account, as is shown by his use of the pronouns "we" and "us." This evidences that he was with Paul during parts of Paul's second and third missionary journeys (Acts 16:10-17; 20:6-21:19) and during his trip to Rome (Acts, chapters 27-28). He was also with him during his imprisonment in Rome. (See Colossians 4:14; Philemon 24.) Whether he was with him at other times we do not know, but he was evidently very close to Paul, who referred to him as a dear friend.

Thus the historical books of the New Testament were written by men who had either been among the original twelve disciples, or were in very close contact with those disciples. They are based on eyewitness testimony. All but one were written within 25 to 45 years after Jesus' death, at a time when many who had been alive during his earthly ministry were still living, including many who did not accept the gospel and had every motive to try to discredit it. This gives these books a high level of credibility as historical records.

The style of these records is remarkable. They tell of the most extraordinary events in a very brief, matter-of-fact way. For instance, Matthew's account of the transfiguration (Matthew 17:1-8), when Jesus shone with a brilliant white light, Elijah and Moses appeared, and the voice of God was heard, takes eight verses. There is no "hype," no exaggerated rhetoric, no overblown language; just a simple recitation of fact. Also remarkable is the way in which they record the shortcomings of the disciples. They record several occasions in which Jesus told his disciples that they lacked faith (Matthew 14:31, 17:19-20) or understanding (Matthew 16:9-11; John 14:9). They record many shortcomings by Peter, who became one of the apparent leaders of the disciples after Jesus' death. He was confused and frightened on the mount of transfiguration (Mark 9:6). Earlier Jesus had said to him, "Get behind me Satan! You are an offense to Me" (Matthew 16:23). He denied Jesus three times (Matthew 26:69-75). They record other times when the disciples were confused or seeking personal glory.

In assessing these records, we should also consider that most of the disciples died martyrs' deaths, often very painfully, for their Lord Jesus. (No sane person would willingly die for a known lie, let alone endure crucifixion or other acutely painful forms of death.) Jesus had taught them that he is the truth (John 14:6) and that the truth would set them free (John 8:32), while the devil "is a liar and the father of it" (John 8:44). He warned against deceivers (Matthew 24:4-5, 24). Scripture records that Ananias and Sapphira fell down dead because they lied (Acts 5:1-11). It says that all liars will be excluded from the New Jerusalem (Revelation 21:8). It teaches "do not lie to one another" (Colossians 3:9), speak "the truth in love" (Ephesians 4:15), gird "your waist with truth" (Ephesians 6:14). It also warns against any form of deception (for example, 1 Corinthians 3:18; Colossians 2:4, 8; 1 Timothy 4:1; James 1:22; 2 Peter 2:1). I think we must assume that the writers of the New Testament made every effort to tell the truth and avoid any element of deception.

So-Called Discrepancies

Some have referred to seeming "discrepancies" in the Biblical accounts as evidence that the Bible cannot be inspired by God. Without going into excessive detail, I would like to indicate the approach I take to such arguments. (There are books that discuss such "discrepancies" far more fully.)

EYEWITNESS ACCOUNTS—Eyewitness accounts often differ in unessential details without thereby losing their credibility. Witnesses to the same events may see what happened quite differently; and they may remember, or choose to emphasize, different aspects. This is well-understood in modern jurisprudence. (In fact, if several witnesses' accounts are identical, we are inclined to suspect collusion.) We should not be surprised to find minor differences in accounts in the Bible. A case in point is the account, in three of the gospels, of the healing of a blind man or men near Jericho (Matthew 20:29-34; Mark 10:46-52; Luke 18:35-43). Matthew says there were two men healed. Mark and Luke mention only one man, and Mark gives his name, Bartimaeus. Evidently Bartimaeus was someone known to them; it is not surprising that Mark and Luke focus on this one individual. (There probably were many blind beggars by the roadside.) Matthew and Mark say this happened as they were leaving Jericho. Many translations of Luke say it happened as they were coming to or approaching Jericho, but the Greek word Luke uses is derived from a word meaning "nigh" or "near," so it could just mean that it was near Jericho. Also, I understand that there are several parts to the city of Jericho, so he could have been leaving one part while approaching another. All three accounts agree that there was a healing of blindness, that it happened near Jericho while Jesus and the disciples were on their way to Jerusalem just before Palm Sunday, that the blind man (men) persisted strongly, and that Jesus commended his (their) faith. There is no real inconsistency.

APPARENT INCONSISTENCIES—Sometimes an apparent inconsistency turns out, on closer examination, to be no inconsistency. A case in point is the death of Judas Iscariot. Matthew says he hanged himself (Matthew 27:5). Acts says he fell headlong in a field and his body burst open (Acts 1:18). The two accounts seem quite inconsistent. But consider for a moment. Suppose Judas did hang himself, and his body remained hanging for several days. (This would have been quite possible in a land where criminals hung on the cross for days. Moreover, this was during Passover, and no one would have wanted to make himself ceremonially impure by touching a dead body.) People would have been concerned with other things. Many extraordinary things had happened on the day of the Crucifixion, including an earthquake. During this time Judas' body would have started to decompose. (After four days in the tomb, Lazarus' body "stinketh," John 11:39 KJV.) After some days of rotting, Judas' body was taken down or fell down, rolled downhill to a field (Jerusalem is hilly), struck a rock or a tree, and burst. One account tells how it began; the other tells how it ended. They are not inconsistent.

DIFFERENCES IN TEACHINGS—At times there are accounts of teachings by Jesus, recorded in different gospels, that have some similarities but also differ in some respects. This is true of some of his parables. It is often assumed that these parables or other teachings are different accounts of the same words spoken by Jesus, which necessarily implies either that one or more accounts have been inaccurately reported or, as is sometimes suggested, that all have been inaccurately reported and the true account is something else which the scholar has created by speculation. But consider a minute. In real life, teachers typically teach the same material on many different occasions, and teach it differently each time. If they use stories to illustrate a point, they may use the same basic story materials a number of times, but vary the details and the emphasis to suit each particular occasion and audience. Why should we assume that Jesus was any different? If this common sense, real life, approach is adopted, then there is no discrepancy. The differing accounts simply reflect that Jesus used the same teaching or story material on two or more different occasions, in somewhat different ways.

Thus Matthew records a Sermon on the Mount (Matthew, chapters 5-7) and Luke records a Sermon on the Plain (Luke 6:17-49). They contain quite a bit of common material, but differ in some respects, and are said to have been given at different locations and different points in Jesus' ministry. The reasonable assumption is that these were two different teachings which cover some of the same material. Again, Jesus told two parables about a banquet, the Wedding Banquet of Matthew 22:1-14 and the Great Banquet of Luke 14:15-24. They differ in the place they were spoken, the audience they were spoken to, and some aspects of the story told. It is reasonable to assume that these were two different stories which Jesus told, to different audiences and for different purposes, using some of the same material in both.

I want to add a comment here. Some Bible critics seem to assume that Biblical characters behave differently from ordinary people. They assume that Jesus never told the same story more than once, or taught the same material more than once. They assume that two eyewitness accounts of an event must agree exactly in every detail. They assume that a Biblical writer, such as Paul, unlike any other writer the world has ever known, always used the same vocabulary, rather than tailoring his vocabulary to his audience and his subject matter, and developing it as his thinking progressed. On this basis, they reject as not authentic any writing that uses more than a certain number of words that do not appear in his other writings. What grounds have we for assuming that Biblical characters and writers are unlike ordinary people in these respects?

LIMITED HUMAN UNDERSTANDING—If none of these approaches work, I still do not reject Scripture. Rather I say, "There must be a good explanation but no one has yet been smart enough to figure it out." The fact that I can't explain something does not mean that there is no explanation. It may just mean that my understanding is limited—an assumption which I am quite willing to accept.

APPARENT CONFLICTS IN TEACHING—At times there are teachings in Scripture that may seem to conflict. For instance, there are passages that emphasize God's foreknowledge, that speak of predestination, and that say that everything works out according to God's plan. There are other passages that emphasize man's free will and the necessity for choice. Men have struggled for centuries trying to fit these two threads together into a consistent, systematic structure. With every such problem, my basic approach, after I have done what I can with it, is to say that since both threads are in Scripture, I must accept both and allow each one to keep me from carrying the other too far. Or, as with predestination and free will, I may say something like, "I need to act as if I have free will and God will hold me accountable for my choices. If he knows ahead of time how I will choose, that's his business and not mine." If I can't work out all the ramifications of how the teachings fit together, I can still understand enough to know how I must live and what I must do, and I can keep chewing at it until I come closer to understanding it fully.

MYSTERIES—There are also things in Scripture that I just don't understand. For example, I don't understand the Trinity. I don't understand how Jesus could have been fully God and fully man at the same time. I don't understand how the one who participated in the creation of the universe, and who holds all things together by his powerful word (Colossians 1:16-17; Hebrews 1:2-3), could also be a helpless baby in his mother's womb or her arms. I don't understand how the Holy Spirit of God can dwell in us. But God's ways and his thoughts are higher than ours (Isaiah 55:8-9) and so I don't have to understand it; I can just accept it and rejoice in it.

CONCLUSION

This chapter has only scratched the surface of many issues. I encourage you to read and study further on these issues.

Primarily, however, I encourage you to let the words of Scripture speak to you. Read them, reflect and meditate on them, memorize them if you can, and allow them to become a very part of you. You will find that they change your life. I also believe that as you work with Scripture and allow it to change your life, you will, as I have, become convinced that it is true and is authoritative.

At one point Jesus asked his disciples if they would leave him because of a "hard" teaching he had given. Peter replied, "Lord, to whom shall we go? You have the words of eternal life" (John 6:68). The words of the Bible are the words of eternal life, and all who truly immerse themselves in them, believing them, will be richly blessed.

3

The Power of God's Word

o o o o o o o o o o o o o o o o o o o o o o o o o o o o o o o o o o o

"The word of God is living and powerful."

—*(Hebrews 4:12)*

The Bible is like no other book. It is alive. It is life. It gives us light. It strengthens us, encourages us and guides us. It transforms us. It shows us what we need to change in our life and gives us the power to change. It works in us, deeply and powerfully. It gives us peace, joy and assurance. And much more. It has done all this for me and for many others, and it can do it for all who will accept it on its own terms. It can do this because it is the revealed word of God. In order for it to do this, we must accept it as the word of God, submit ourselves to it, and treat it as authoritative.

SOME BASIC PRINCIPLES

Here are some of the things Scripture says about the power it has and the ways in which it can affect our lives. I have seen them confirmed over and over in my own life and that of many others. Hopefully they will suggest how much the Bible has meant to many and how much it can mean to anyone who approaches it with the right attitude.

God's Word Is Alive and Powerful

"For the word of God is living and powerful, and sharper than any two-edged sword, piercing even to the division of soul and spirit, and of joints and marrow, and is a discerner of the thoughts and intents of the heart" (Hebrews 4:12). Much could be said about this remarkable passage, but for the present I wish to emphasize simply that it says that God's word, in Scripture, is alive and powerful; it cuts sharply; and it discloses and discerns our inner thoughts and intentions. I think everyone who has read and thought about Scripture, and applied it to their lives, will confirm this by his or her own experience. As we read and reflect on Scripture, there are passages that have a way of jumping out at us. They may bring a new revelation of who God is and what his ways are, or a new understanding of one's self. They may say to us forcefully, "This is something you need to deal with, **now**." The process is not always enjoyable, but the end result is always good. Perhaps one reason some do not like to read Scripture is that they do not wish to have the thoughts and intents of their heart discerned!

The prophet Jeremiah, about 600 years earlier, wrote something quite similar. "'Is not My word like a fire?' says the LORD, 'And like a hammer that breaks the rock in pieces?'" (Jeremiah 23:29). God's word is a hammer that can break down many of our emotional strongholds and preconceptions, if we will let it.

God's word created the physical universe. "And God said" (Genesis 1:3, 6, 9, 14, 20, 24, 26 KJV). "For he spoke, and it came to be; he commanded, and it stood firm" (Psalm 33:9 NIV). "...he commanded and they were created" (Psalm 148:5 NIV). "By faith we understand that the universe was formed at God's command..." (Hebrews 11:3 NIV). (Also see Romans 4:17.) If God's word had the power to create the physical universe out of nothing, it should not surprise us that his word has power to change our lives.

It Gives Us Life

"Your word has given me life" (Psalm 119:50). "I will never forget your precepts, for by them you have given me life" (Psalm 119:93). (Also see verses 25, 40, 88, 107, 149, 154, 156, and 159.) God's word "quickens" us (KJV). It revives us. It gives us life.

It Transforms Us

Paul has told us, "Be transformed by the renewing of your mind" (Romans 12:2). The transformation he is calling for is a radical one. We are to become like God in character. (See Chapter 14.) It is Scripture, more than anything else, that is the agent for this transformation. It is through reading Scripture, studying Scripture, reflecting on Scripture, living Scripture, making Scripture a part of us, that we come to know God's ways, his heart and his character, and can begin to bring ourselves into conformity with them. If Scripture does not transform us, it has done us little good.

God is at work in those who believe in him and his son Jesus Christ. "He who has begun a good work in you will complete it until the day of Jesus Christ" (Philippians 1:6). "It is God who works in you both to will and to do for his good pleasure" (Philippians 2:13). "...in all things God works for the good of those who love him, who have been called according to his purpose" (Romans 8:28 NIV). God is "able to do exceedingly abundantly above all that we ask or think, according to the power that works in us" (Ephesians 3:20). Paul said, "...I labor, struggling with all his energy, which so powerfully works in me" (Colossians 1:29 NIV). One of the principal ways God works in us is through his Scripture. Paul wrote that the gospel he preached is "the word of God, which also works effectively in you who believe" (1 Thessalonians 2:13).

The Christian life should be a life of spiritual growth. (See Chapter 10.) We are to grow "in the knowledge of God" (Colossians 1:10). We are to "...become mature, attaining to the whole measure of the fullness of Christ" and "...grow up into him who is the Head, that is, Christ" (Ephesians 4:13, 15 NIV). We are to add various qualities to our faith (2 Peter 1:5). Much of this growth is achieved through reading, study and application of the Bible. It is by Scripture that "the man of God may be complete, thoroughly equipped for every good work" (2 Timothy 3:17).

This process of transformation does not come quickly. It continues throughout our life. Near the end of his life, Paul had not yet attained it. But, he wrote, "I press on, that I may take hold of that for which Christ Jesus has also laid hold of me" (Philippians 3:12). Nor does the transformation come easily. The old self does not give up without a struggle. When Paul said we must go through "many tribulations" to enter the kingdom of God (Acts 14:22), he was speaking of physical things, but I think the statement applies also to the inner conflicts we often have to work through. Thanks be to God, we can prevail. "We are more than conquerors through Him who loved us" (Romans 8:37). Jesus never said it would be easy, but he said it would be worth the effort.

It is often hard to be aware of this process of transformation while it is going on. I have been told by others that I have changed significantly in recent years. I think I can begin to see it and believe it. And I know that the changes have been for the good. God's word does change us, if we will allow it to. The big problem is that we are often stubborn—"stiff-necked," as Scripture would say—and resist the change.

It Cleanses Us

Part of this transformation is a cleansing. Scripture tells us to "...throw off everything that hinders and the sin that so easily entangles..." (Hebrews 12:1 NIV). Living by Scripture enables us to do this. The Psalmist wrote, "Your word have I hidden in my heart, that I might not sin against You" (Psalm 119:11). (Also see verse 9.) Jesus prayed, "Sanctify them by Your truth. Your word is truth" (John 17:17). Peter said, "It is written: 'Be holy, for I am holy'" (1 Peter 1:16).

When Jesus was tempted in the desert, he resisted the temptation by standing on Scripture. Three times he said, "it is written," and then the devil left him (Matthew 4:1-11).

It Is Able to Save Us

"Receive with meekness the implanted word, which is able to save your souls" (James 1:21). We need to have the word of God planted in us, firmly established in us, so that it is a very part of us. Paul speaks of "the Holy Scriptures, which are able to make you wise for salvation through faith which is in Christ Jesus" (2 Timothy 3:15).

It Is Our Source of Truth

God's word is truth (John 17:17; Ephesians 1:13; Psalm 119:160). Jesus told his disciples, "If you abide [dwell] in my Word...you shall know the truth" (John 8:31-32). Jesus told the Sadducees, "You are mistaken, not knowing the Scriptures nor the power of God" (Matthew 22:29). Scripture commends the Bereans because, after Paul had taught them, they "...examined the Scriptures every day to see if what Paul said was true" (Acts 17:11 NIV).

It is against Scripture that we measure our own thoughts and what we hear from others. Scripture is the touchstone by which we know what is true. "Your word is a lamp to my feet and a light to my path" (Psalm 119:105). "Direct my steps by Your word" (Psalm 119:133). "The entrance of Your words gives light; it gives understanding unto the simple" (Psalm 119:130). "Give me understanding according to Your word" (Psalm 119:169).

Scripture tells us to bring "every thought into captivity to the obedience of Christ" (2 Corinthians 10:5). One of the best ways to do this is to compare our thoughts with Scripture. We identify every thought that is not Scriptural and replace it with the truth of Scripture.

It Is Our Spiritual Food

Jesus, quoting Deuteronomy 8:3, said, "It is written, 'Man shall not live by bread alone, but by every word that proceeds from the mouth of God'" (Matthew 4:4). In Deuteronomy 8:3, God's word is compared to the manna, which was given daily as physical food. The implication is that we need the spiritual food of God's word daily. (The same comparison is suggested in John 6:47-51.) I believe that when Jesus prayed, "give us this day our daily bread," he was speaking, not only of physical nourishment, but also of spiritual nourishment from the word of God. Hebrews 5:12 says, "you need someone to teach you again the first principles of the oracles of God; and you have come to need milk and not solid food." (Also see 1 Corinthians 3:2.) Again we see the comparison between God's word and physical food. God's word is our spiritual food that we need daily.

It Teaches, Encourages and Strengthens Us

All Scripture is "...useful for teaching, rebuking, correcting and training in righteousness, so that the man of God may be thoroughly equipped for every good work" (2 Timothy 3:16-17 NIV). "For everything that was written in the past was written to teach us, so that through endurance and the encouragement of the Scriptures we might have hope" (Romans 15:4 NIV).

In order for it to do this, we must be willing to accept it. We must be willing to learn. We must be willing to accept rebuke and correction. We must be willing to be trained. We must be willing to be encouraged. We must, as James says, receive the word of God with meekness and humility, and then allow it to do in us whatever it needs to do.

It Sets Us Free

Jesus said, "If you abide in My Word, you are my disciples indeed. And you shall know the truth, and the truth shall make you free" (John 8:31-32). Free from what? I would suggest that reading Scripture, living by Scripture, continuing in Scripture, can free us from addictions, mindsets, emotional and spiritual strongholds, bitterness, unforgiveness, and much else. It can enable us to "...throw off everything that hinders..." (Hebrews 12:1 NIV).

The Christian life is not a life of constraints and limitations—of "don'ts"—as many seem to believe. It is a life of freedom. We are free because we can function as we were designed to function.

It Enables Us to Succeed

God told Joshua, just before he began the conquest of Canaan, "Do not let this Book of the Law depart from your mouth; meditate on it day and night, so that you may be careful to do everything written in it. Then you will be prosperous and successful" (Joshua 1:8 NIV). The Psalmist wrote of the man whose "delight is in the law of the LORD, and in His law he meditates day and night"; he said, that man "shall be like a tree planted by the rivers of water, that brings forth its fruit in its season; whose leaf also shall not wither; and whatever he does shall prosper" (Psalm 1:2-3). Jesus taught, "Therefore everyone who hears these words of mine and puts them into practice is like a wise man who built his house on the rock. The rain came down, the streams rose, and the winds blew and beat against that house; yet it did not fall, because it had its foundation on the rock. But everyone who hears these words of mine and does not put them into practice is like a foolish man who built his house on sand. The rain came down, the streams rose, and the winds blew and beat against that house, and it fell with a great crash" (Matthew 7:24-27 NIV).

In his explanation of the parable of the sower, Jesus said that when "the word of God" is sown, it can fall on different kinds of soil. It can be stolen, or wither away, or be choked out. "But the seed on good soil stands for those with a noble and good heart, who hear the word, retain it, and by persevering produce a crop" (Luke 8:15 NIV). It is those who receive the word of God, retain it and persevere who bear good fruit.

Peter wrote, "His divine power has given us everything we need for life and godliness through our knowledge of him who called us by his own glory and goodness. Through these he has given us his very great and precious promises, so that through them you may participate in the divine nature and escape the corruption in the world caused by evil desires" (2 Peter 1:3-4 NIV). It is primarily through Scripture that we gain our knowledge of God, and it is in Scripture that God's promises are recorded.

I sometimes like to compare Scripture to an owner's manual, in which the manufacturer of a product tells us how his product is intended to operate and how it needs to be cared for and maintained. If we don't follow the owner's manual for our car—if we don't change the oil and replace it with the right kind of oil, or keep the tires properly inflated, etc.—the car will not function as it should and may break down. In the Bible, God, who created us, tells us how we are expected to function. If we understand and follow his instructions, we will be successful. If we do not follow them, we can expect to have a lot of trouble.

To avoid misunderstanding, I need to point out that God's idea of succeeding and prospering is usually different from ours. We tend to use material wealth as the measure of success. These passages of Scripture are talking about succeeding and prospering in the sense of doing what you set out to do, accomplishing the task that God has given you. I am not saying that reading the Bible will make you wealthy or give you a position of prestige or power. I am saying that if you allow the Bible to work in your life and change you, you are much more apt to lead a life that is truly satisfying and fulfilling.

A PERSONAL EXPERIENCE

Let me illustrate some of what I have been saying by a personal experience that I have been going through as I work on this book.

In October, 2002 I found that I had a cancerous tumor in my colon. It was removed, and we thought we had gotten all of it. I went through a course of chemotherapy to make sure. In July, 2003 we learned that the cancer had spread to my liver and lungs. The prognosis in such cases is not good. My doctor, when I pressed him, said that I might have one to three years to live. He added that sometimes patients survive who were not expected to, and the doctors don't understand why. (Almighty God is not bound by medical statistics.) We went on a new course of chemotherapy, but the cancer grew. We changed the chemotherapy, and the cancer remained about the same. Just recently (October 2004), we found that it has begun to grow again. We are changing to a new regime of chemotherapy.

My family and I are praying that I will be totally healed. We have been praying a lot, and have been receiving a lot of prayer from my church, my family and friends, and many others. I have been doing far better than my doctor expected, and I believe this is primarily the result of prayer.

We have also been spending a lot of time in Scripture. Since we learned that the cancer had spread, my wife, my daughter and I have read aloud, and discussed, most of the New Testament, and quite a bit in Psalms, Isaiah, Deuteronomy and other parts of the Old Testament.

How has this helped? Let me give some of the ways. Please read this entire section before coming to any conclusions. The first part of it is balanced by other

Scriptural principles that I discuss later. I try to follow the whole counsel of Scripture in everything I write.

We read about the healings which God did through Elijah, Elisha, Jesus and the disciples, and about the fact that nothing is too difficult for God, and this strengthens our faith that God is much bigger than this illness and he can heal it totally. He "heals all your diseases" (Psalm 103:3). We will not be afraid of "the pestilence that walketh in darkness, nor of the destruction that lays waste at noonday" (Psalm 91:6). He "shall give his angels charge over you to keep you in all your ways" (Psalm 91:11). "By his stripes [the wounds from the whipping that Jesus endured] we are healed" (Isaiah 53:5). We can say, as the prophet did to King Jehoshaphat of Judah, "...Do not be afraid or discouraged because of this vast army. For the battle is not yours, but God's" (2 Chronicles 20:15 NIV). We can say, as Jesus did to Jairus after he was told that his daughter had died, "Do not be afraid; only believe" (Mark 5:36). All of this strengthens our faith that God can heal me totally.

We read about the father who prayed, "Lord, I believe; help my unbelief" (Mark 9:23) just before Jesus healed his son. We have prayed that prayer often. I have spent a good deal of time asking God to show me what it is that causes me sometimes to doubt. As I became aware of something, I would try to deal with it. This is part of the process of taking your thoughts captive to obey Jesus Christ. (See 2 Corinthians 10:5.) It can involve identifying a thought we have been having that is not in conformity with Scripture, and consciously replacing it with one that is Scriptural. For example, some of us tend to think, "I am not worthy to receive healing, or blessing, or whatever." The answer, based on what God tells us in his word, is, "Of course. No one is worthy. It doesn't depend on your worthiness. Jesus suffered and died for those who were unworthy. It depends on God's compassion and his plan for your life." Once we start this process, it is surprising how many kinds of thoughts will come up that we now realize we need to take captive to obey Jesus Christ. Once we have identified and rejected them, these thoughts will come to our mind again, and we need to keep telling them, "Get out. You don't belong here. I repudiate you." And then we replace them with the truth of God's word.

We read in Scripture about the need for perseverance. (See, for example, Luke 18:1; James 1:4.) And so we keep on praying even when we see no visible results.

We get a medical test result that seems somewhat discouraging, and then we remind ourselves that "we walk by faith, not by sight" (2 Corinthians 5:7) and that we "do not look at the things which are seen, but at the things which are not seen. For the things which are seen are temporary, but the things which are not seen are eternal" (2 Corinthians 4:18).

I have had times when I say, "Lord, am I doing something to hold this healing back? Do I hold bitterness or unforgiveness against anyone? Do I give in to self-pity, which I know is very destructive? Are there other kinds of thoughts I allow myself that I need to get rid of?" This kind of process is not enjoyable, but when your life is at stake you become willing to go through it.

Scripture says, "…we know that in all things God works for the good of those who love him, who have been called according to his purpose" (Romans 8:28 NIV). It tells us to rejoice in testing and trials because we learn and grow from them (James 1:2). So I have asked, "Lord, are you teaching me something by this?" Then I came upon 1 Peter 1:7 (NIV), which speaks of trials that "…have come so that your faith—of greater worth than gold, which perishes even though refined by fire—may be proved genuine and may result in praise, glory and honor when Jesus Christ is revealed." Is God using all of this to build in me, and my family, a much stronger faith than we have had before? I think so.

We have begun to see that God is using this illness to strengthen my faith and that of my family, to cleanse me of thought patterns that have hindered me from growing, to strengthen my prayer life and my commitment to him, and to do other needful things. As a result, we have even come to the point of saying, "Lord, it is a good thing that this has happened. You really do work all things for good for those who love you and are called according to your purposes." We can identify with the Psalmist who said, "It is good for me that I have been afflicted, that I may learn your statutes" (Psalm 119:71). (Also see verse 67.)

You don't have to go through this process alone. I have shared much of the process with my family, and also, as seemed appropriate, with other mature Christians who are well grounded in Scripture. We need this kind of support (and sometimes correction) from each other.

I want to make one thing clear. In our prayers, and in what I have written above, I have emphasized the affirmative promises of Scripture, because they were what I needed at that point. I am quite aware that God does not always answer our prayers in the way we expect him to or want him to. I am quite aware that, in today's imperfect world, not everyone is healed. God is sovereign. He will do, or allow, what he sees best, and he doesn't owe us any explanations or apologies. At Gethsemane, Jesus prayed three times not to have to go through the Crucifixion, and God denied that prayer. We need to put our trust in God, and commit ourselves to God, no matter how he answers our prayers.

I call this principle the "but even if not" principle. When King Nebuchadnezzar of Babylon threatened to throw the three young Hebrew men into a fiery furnace, they replied, "If we are thrown into the blazing furnace, the God we serve is able to save us from it, and he will rescue us from your hand, O king. **But even if he does not**, we want you to know, O king, that we will not serve your gods or worship the image of gold you have set up" (Daniel 3:17-18 NIV). Their faith was in God as a person, and they kept that faith regardless of whether God did what they hoped and expected him to do. That is where my family and I are. We expect God to heal me fully. But even if he does not, we will still worship him and serve him. And it will be OK.

Indeed, I see my situation as a "win, win" situation. If I should die soon, I will go to be with God in heaven. That's a very good place to be! And I am sure that God will watch over and provide for my family. If I live quite a bit longer, perhaps I can do more to serve God, and also I can learn more and grow more. That's also a good place to be. Either alternative is good.

I could go on, but I hope I have said enough to suggest how very helpful Scripture can be in the face of a pretty severe test. It is remarkable how much there is in Scripture, if you will look for it, that applies directly and specifically to almost any situation we may encounter. I can't imagine what it would be like to have to deal with something like this without the resources of Scripture.

Psalm 119:92 says, "If your law had not been my delight, I would have perished in my affliction." I think I can say, in all truth, that if I had not had the word of Scripture to encourage and strengthen me time and again—to lean on, to rely on, and to delight in—I would have perished in my present affliction.

Let me sum this up with a poem by my wife.

TRUST

Suddenly the Everyday
is wrenched away.

Lord, please guard and grow
the fulness of my love and trust in You.

When all I know
is set afloat today,

pilot my boat and nudge me to
the harbor of the Narrow Way.

There let me find a clearer, newer view
where all that's upside down
resolves; makes sense;
steady in the light of love and Trust in You.

CONCLUSION

I have tried to give you some of what Scripture says, and what my own experience confirms, about the power of God's word to change our lives. Much of the rest of this book is a demonstration of the power of God's word in various situations we may encounter in our lives.

I encourage you to try it. If you are willing to submit yourselves to God's word, to accept it as true and authoritative, and to live by it, I believe you will find that it will transform your life. The process is neither quick nor easy. Few things are that are worth doing. But it does work. Why don't you give it a try?

4

Reading and Understanding Scripture

o o o o o o o o o o o o o o o o o o o o o o o o o o o o o o

"Open my eyes, that I may see wondrous things from Your law."

—*(Psalm 119:18)*

Much has been written on this.[14] I want simply to give a few ideas that I have found helpful. If what I say seems simplistic to some, it is because I am trying to make my meaning very easily understood.

Working with Scripture involves three steps: Observation, Interpretation and Application.

Observation means noticing everything in the text and its context. This can include the meaning of the words used; the grammatical, logical and literary structure; the persons to whom the text was addressed; the characters involved and their relationship; the social and historical setting; the kind of writing involved; and much more. The more carefully we observe all these things, the better we will be able to proceed to the next two steps.

Interpretation asks, "What does it mean?" "What is the author saying to us?"

Application asks, "What do I need to do about it in my own life?" This is the point to which the first two steps lead. We do not really understand anything until we have applied it to our own life and experience. I find that it is as I try to live by Scripture, try to follow its guidance, and try to do what it calls on me to do in my life, that my faith in God grows, my understanding of Scripture deepens, and my confidence in the reliability of Scripture increases.

In this chapter, I shall touch on some aspects of observation and interpretation. Most of the rest of this book deals with issues of application.

HOW TO READ SCRIPTURE

There are many ways to read Scripture. The most important thing is to read it. Find a dependable translation you can understand and are comfortable with. (See Chapter 2.) Some grew up with the King James Version and like to use it; I prefer a modern translation because I find it easier, with contemporary language, to see how the Bible applies to my life.

Sometimes I like to read large chunks of Scripture at a time, to get a sense of the overview, the continuity. Sometimes I will spend a lot of time on one or a few verses. Martin Luther said that in Scripture every daisy becomes a meadow, and I have often found that to be so. Sometimes the Holy Spirit will call a passage to mind and I will keep reading it or thinking about it day after day. Some people like to sing or listen to songs based on Scripture and let the words sink in. Some like to listen to tapes in which Scripture is read aloud.

I like to read Scripture out loud with my family. We discuss it, look up cross-relationships with other passages of Scripture and read those other passages, etc. Sometimes we pray a passage through, putting it into the first person and applying it to our lives. We especially like to do this with such passages as the marvelous prayers in Ephesians (chapters 1 and 3) and Colossians (chapter 1).

There are times when it is good to read Scripture in a disciplined way, to set yourself a program for reading through the whole Bible in a certain period of time, for example. There are also times when it is good to feel free to go wherever you feel led to go. There are no set formulas. I would strongly caution you, however, not to confine your reading to a few favorite or familiar passages. We need to become familiar with the whole counsel of Scripture. Work through some of the difficult or unfamiliar passages. Don't just stay with the familiar and comfortable.

Some like to use a commentary or guide in reading Scripture. I will use various secondary sources when needed, but I generally prefer to let the words of Scripture speak for themselves. It's a matter of choice.

I enjoy seeing how different passages of Scripture fit together. For example, compare the following: Deuteronomy 4:29 (about 1350 B.C.); Psalm 9:10 (about 1000 B.C.); Jeremiah 29:13 (about 600 B.C.); Matthew 7:7-8 (spoken about 30 A.D.); and James 4:8 (about 45 A.D.). I delight to see how, over a period of almost 1,400 years, five different human writers, all led by the Holy Spirit, are saying essentially the same thing. The margins of my Bible are full of this kind of cross-reference.

I enjoy doing word studies—seeing how the same word is used in different passages in Scripture. Anyone can do these with a good Concordance; with today's computer programs they are easy to do. I find they can give you a much more detailed sense of the meaning of particular words in Scripture.

The important thing, however, is that with Scripture you don't just want to read it. You want to immerse yourself in it, let it sink in to your very being, let it change your attitudes and the way you think, let it transform you, let it challenge you and convict you. Sometimes you want to let it really bother you.

It is a good idea, whenever you take up the Scriptures, to ask the Holy Spirit to show you what he wants to show you. When you do this, you may find that certain words seem to jump off the page at you!

Sometimes, in reading Scripture, I come across something I just don't understand. I may want to dig into it then, look up definitions of words, consult a commentary or other source, talk to a mature Christian about it, etc. Quite often, however, I find that if I just put the question aside and go on trying to apply what I do understand, then when I come back to the passage a few months or years later, after having worked with other portions of Scripture, the difficulty seems to have disappeared. My sense is that there will always be passages in Scripture that I don't understand, and I don't want to let them distract me from working with what I do understand. I like the comment (I think it was by Mark Twain), "It isn't the parts of Scripture I don't understand that bother me; it's the ones I do understand." Being able to change our lives by what is clear in Scripture is more important, and usually more difficult, than unraveling every obscurity.

We also need to remember that we don't just understand Scripture with our mind, but with our heart. It is the Holy Spirit who gives us real understanding. (See 1 Corinthians 2:14-15.) It is good to approach Scripture with a prayer, "Lord, give me understanding" (Psalm 119:73).

The most important thing is the attitude with which we come to Scripture. Scripture can do much for us, as I have pointed out in the previous chapter. But it can do these things only if we come to it in a spirit of humility and of seeking. Jesus said, "Ask, and it will be given to you; seek, and you will find; knock, and it will be opened to you" (Matthew 7:7). I understand that the tense of the Greek verbs means "keep on asking," "keep on seeking," "keep on knocking." Jesus expects us to persevere. "Men always ought to pray and not lose heart" (Luke 18:1). James says, "You do not have because you do not ask" (James 4:2).

If we approach Scripture in a spirit of humility and seeking, it will be a "discerner of the thoughts and intents of the heart" (Hebrews 4:12), it will change us, it will do all the things I have talked about in the previous chapter. I try to come to Scripture asking God to "Search me, O God, and know my heart: try me, and know my thoughts" (Psalm 139:23 KJV). I ask, "Open my eyes, that I may see wondrous things from Your law" (Psalm 119:18). Our spirit in coming to the Scriptures should be that which Paul expressed in Ephesians 1:17-18 (NIV): "I keep asking that the God of our Lord Jesus Christ, the glorious Father, may give you the spirit of wisdom and revelation, so that you may know him better. I pray also that the eyes of your heart may be enlightened..." If we approach Scripture in that spirit, there is no limit to what we can get from it. God "...is able to do immeasurably more than all we ask or imagine, according to his power that is at work within us" (Ephesians 3:20 NIV). "Eye has not seen, nor ear heard, nor have entered into the heart of man, the things which God has prepared for those who love Him" (1 Corinthians 2:9).

Psalm 119 is a wonderful Psalm about God's word. Its author wrote, "O how I love Your law!" (verse 97). (Also see verse 163.) "I will delight myself in Your commandments, which I love" (verse 47). God's words "are the rejoicing of my heart" (verse 111). "Great peace have those who love Your law" (verse 165). "I love Your commandments more than gold, yes, than fine gold" (verse 127). (Also see Psalm 19:10.) My experience, and that of others I know, tells me that if we come to Scripture with the right attitude of humility and searching, we shall find all these and more in it.

SOME THOUGHTS ABOUT INTERPRETING SCRIPTURE

It is sometimes said that there is only one interpretation of Scripture, but many applications. If this is so, why do so many committed Christians, who know their Bible well, differ so often in their interpretations? My experience is that, in interpreting a verse or passage, there often are some arguments pointing one way and other arguments pointing another way, and I have to weigh them and see which seem to me the weightier and more reasonable. Words are often capable of more that one meaning. You may have observations that pull in more than one direction. Different principles of interpretation may pull in different directions.

Let me give one example by way of illustration.

In Romans 7:14-25, Paul talks of warfare inside him between God's law and his sinful desires. Is he speaking of a time before he was saved, or after? It makes quite a difference in how you understand and apply the passage. Because it is written in the present tense, and appears between chapters 6 and 8 of Romans, I believe it is talking of a time after he was saved. I see it as an illustration of the inner conflict (also referred to in Galatians 5:17) that occurs between the Holy Spirit and our fleshly desires after we have been saved and have received the Holy Spirit. (See Chapter 15.) But I can understand how some people, whom I respect, could think that Paul is speaking of a time before he was saved. I am convinced by my interpretation, but I don't think the issue is proved beyond a doubt. We must, as in many issues of life, go with what, on balance, seems most likely.

A great deal has been written about how to interpret Scripture. It has a scholarly term—hermeneutics—and courses are given in it. Let me suggest, in very simple terms, a few basic principles that I have found helpful.

The Basic Message of Scripture Is Simple

My starting point is that God intended, by his scripture, to communicate a message that would be understood by ordinary people. He is not communicating in some code that only a few could decipher. He is not just talking to experts and theologians. He is talking to all of us. John R.W. Stott, British teacher and preacher, puts it this way:

> "We may be quite sure, therefore, that He [God] has spoken in order to be understood, and that he has intended Scripture (the record of the divine speech) to be plain to its readers. For the whole purpose of revelation is clarity not confusion, a readily intelligible message, not a set of dark and mysterious riddles...God's whole purpose in speaking and in causing His speech to be preserved is that He wanted to communicate to ordinary people and save them."[15]

I think we should always keep this in mind in our reading and understanding of Scripture. Scripture has some complexities. Translating from the realm of the Spirit to the realm of the material is never easy. But the basic message of the Bible is simple, and we do well to focus on that basic message and not let ourselves be caught up in difficulties of detail.

Take Scripture at Face Value

As with any writing, we start by trying to see what the author intended. Usually this means taking it literally. But there are exceptions to this. For example:

METAPHORS—When Scripture uses metaphors, they should be read as metaphors. Thus Jesus is variously referred to as the lamb of God, the lion of Judah, the light of the world, a stone of stumbling, a cornerstone. Obviously these statements do not mean that Jesus was literally a four-legged beast with wool or a mane, or that he is a lamp burning oil, or that he is made of granite or limestone. They mean that he has some of the qualities of these things to which he is compared.

PARABLES—Jesus often taught in parables. These are not things that actually happened; they are stories he invented to make a point, and are best interpreted by looking at the context to see what point he was making. He showed us how to do this by giving the interpretation of some of his parables.

VIVID LANGUAGE—Sometimes Jesus used very vivid language to make a point. When he said we should cut off a hand or foot or pluck out an eye that causes us to sin (Mark 9:42-48), he was not really telling people to mutilate themselves; he was simply expressing very graphically how essential it is to get rid of sin. There is no example in the Bible where anyone actually mutilated himself in response to this teaching.

KINDS OF WRITING—We need always to look at what kind of writing we are dealing with. Parts of the Bible are poetry. Not everything in poetry is meant to be taken literally. Parts of the Bible are prophecy. Predictive prophecy should not be read as one would read an expository statement.

What we must not do is to read our own preconceptions, or desires, into Scripture. Scripture was written by people living in the Near East during the period of about 1350 B.C. to 95 A.D. Its human authors believed that God does supernatural things. If it says that a miraculous or supernatural event occurred, what right have we to impose our 19th to 21st century Western mindsets on it and either seek to find a naturalistic explanation, or interpret the words contrary to their evident intent, or find some plausible or implausible ground for rejecting them as not authentic because they do not fit our mindsets?

Jesus made many extraordinary statements about himself. If we believe Scripture, then we must accept such statements at face value. We cannot ignore them, or interpret them to mean something other than what they say, or reject them as not authentic, and say that we are being true to Scripture. Scripture itself warns against those who distort or twist Scripture "to their own destruction" (2 Peter 3:16).

Draw the Meaning Out of the Text

Two Greek words that I find helpful are *exegesis,* drawing the meaning **out of** the text, and *eisegesis,* putting a meaning **into** the text. In *exegesis* we look at the text, the meaning of the words used, the grammatical structure, the textual and historical context, parallel passages, and other aspects of the document to find the meaning. In *eisegesis* we impose on the text a meaning derived from our own preconceptions and mindsets. It's a matter of mental attitude. Are we coming to Scripture to learn, to see what God wants to say to us, to see how we need to change? Or are we seeking to use (and sometimes misuse) anything we can find in Scripture to justify where we are now?

It is sometimes said, "You can find support in Scripture for anything you want." The statement implies a totally wrong attitude. If you are looking for support for a preconceived position, you can often find in Scripture a verse which, if distorted or taken out of context, could be thought to support whatever you want it to support. But if you are genuinely looking for the truth of Scripture, and seeking to draw the meaning out of what is written, you will often find that it convicts you that your preconceived position or attitude is wrong and needs to be changed.

It is easy to see instances in the past where people used Scripture to justify a wrong position. For example, before the Civil War many southern pastors sought to justify the slavery of blacks by Scripture. We now can see how false their reasoning was, but at the time they were persuaded by it. Today there are "white supremacists" who seek to find support for their position in Scripture, despite the clear statement of Galatians 3:28 that "There is neither Jew nor Greek, there is neither slave nor free, there is neither male nor female; for you are all one in Christ Jesus." We need to be careful that we do not fall into similar errors.

One of the most serious forms of *eisegesis* today is the attempt of some to make Scripture conform to our contemporary Western scientific/materialistic mindsets. To do this is to distort the intention of its authors and to destroy its power and value. Paul wrote, "Do not conform any longer to the pattern of this world…" (Romans 12:2 NIV). We make a serious mistake if we try to conform Scripture to any pattern of this world, or to any viewpoint other than that which it itself expresses. We need to conform to Scripture, rather than distort it to conform to our way of thinking.

Interpret Scripture by Scripture

I believe Scripture is basically consistent with itself. The more I work with it, the more convinced of this I become. One of the principles of interpreting any writing is that, where possible, we avoid putting a meaning on one passage which makes it conflict with another.

When Jesus was tempted by the devil in the wilderness, the devil quoted Scripture at him, saying, "it is written" (Matthew 4:6). Jesus replied with another passage, saying "…it is also written…" (Matthew 4:7 NIV). We need to look for the "it is also writtens" of Scripture. I think one major cause of false teaching is a tendency to rely heavily on certain passages in Scripture and ignore others that tend to qualify or limit their scope.

At times there are passages in Scripture which, to our limited human logic, may appear inconsistent with themselves or each other. My experience is that often, as I mature in my understanding, I come to realize that they are not inconsistent at all. For example, Philippians 2:12-13 says, "…work out your own salvation with fear and trembling; for it is God who works in you both to will and to do for His good pleasure." I used to say, "Wait a minute. Do we do it? Or does God do it? Isn't this contradicting itself?" Now I realize that this passage is a beautiful example of a basic principle called co-laboring. In most of our Christian life, we and God are working together. We do it, and God does it, and together we get it done. "We are God's fellow workers" (1 Corinthians 3:9). Jesus gave the image of being yoked with him, as two oxen would be yoked together (Matthew 11:29). We can't do it without him, and he (usually) chooses not to do it without our participation. So a passage that I once thought self-contradictory turns out to be an excellent illustration of a very basic principle of how God works.

Other seeming inconsistencies often disappear on closer examination. For example, Jesus said that those who follow him must "hate" their own family (Luke 14:26 KJV). How can this be, when we are told to love our neighbors and our enemies? When we look at the Greek word translated "hate" (*miseo*), we find that it has several meanings. According to Strong's *Dictionary of the Greek Bible,* it can mean to "love less." According to Vine's *Expository Dictionary of Biblical Words,* it can refer to "relative preference for one thing over another." In a parallel passage in Matthew 10:37 (KJV), Jesus made this explicit, "He that loveth father or mother more than me." Jesus was not telling us to reject our families; he was telling us to put nothing ahead of him.

Where I still find an inconsistency, or have difficulty in reconciling two principles, I simply say, "God, I don't see how these two principles fit together, but you do. I hope some day you will show me. But even if you do not, I will work with both principles as best I can. I cannot reject anything that is in your Scripture just because it does not fit my limited logical understanding."

God did not give us a tightly organized, logical system of theology. He gave us living principles to work with and live by. I think he did this deliberately. He did not want us to be controlled by rules, but by an active love for him. He wanted us to be dependent on him rather than our own intellects. Our primary faith needs to be in a person—Jesus Christ—and not a set of doctrines. Even when we are not sure about doctrine, we can put our faith in the person of Jesus.

Theology is important. We need to have as clear an understanding of God as we can. But our theology is only man's inadequate attempt to describe who God is and what he does. Sometimes God has acted to shake up men's theology. Acts, chapter 10, is a beautiful example. God told Peter to go to a Gentile's house. Then he told him to eat food that was unclean under the law of Moses. Both statements must have shocked Peter to the core; they violated all his training and everything he had lived by. And then the people of Cornelius' household received the Holy Spirit before they had been baptized or had made any profession of salvation! (This one has puzzled many scholars ever since.)

God has often said, "Behold, I will do a new thing" (Isaiah 43:19). That's his privilege, as God. He is not bound by our theology. If he does something that seems contrary to our theology, he is not breaking the rules; he is merely showing us that our understanding of him was incomplete. We need to distinguish clearly between the words of Scripture, which are true, and the intellectual systems which men have erected on those words, which are useful but fallible.

Stay With What Is Written

God said, "You shall not add to the word which I command you, nor take from it" (Deuteronomy 4:2). (Also see Deuteronomy 12:32; Revelation 22:18-19.) "Every word of God is pure...Do not add to his words, lest He rebuke you, and you be found a liar" (Proverbs 30:5-6). Paul wrote, "Do not go beyond what is written" (1 Corinthians 4:6 NIV). Jesus rebuked those who "...nullify the word of God for the sake of your tradition" (Matthew 15:6 NIV). I think sometimes today we come very close to doing this.

This is a very basic principle. We must not ignore or disregard anything that is in Scripture, just because we do not like it, or it does not fit into our logical schemes. If we believe what we like in Scripture, and reject what we don't like, then our confidence is in ourselves—not in Scripture. We are leaning on our own understanding instead of trusting the Lord. (See Proverbs 3:5-7.)

We also need to take what is written at face value. Too often, we try to water down or explain away what Scripture clearly says. Or we read it and then ignore it. This can be a form of taking things away from the text of Scripture. In subsequent chapters, I shall give examples of passages in Scripture that I feel many Christians have not taken seriously enough.

We must also not add to what is written in Scripture. Sometimes, without meaning to, we seem to give to a human interpretation of Scripture an authority equal to the very words of Scripture themselves. If we learned it in seminary, or if our pastor or denomination has taught it, we tend to think of it as "gospel truth." It is good to be like the Bereans, who "searched the Scriptures daily to find out whether these things were so" (Acts 17:11).

Paul addressed this issue in two of his letters. Galatians was written because some were trying to add, to the Christian gospel, a requirement that Gentile Christians must adhere to every detail of the Jewish law, including many rules imposed by the Jewish rabbis. Paul wrote, "I am astonished that you are so quickly deserting the one who called you by the grace of Christ and are turning to a different gospel—which is really no gospel at all..." (Galatians 1:6-7 NIV). The Colossians were adding to the Christian gospel a number of rules and practices about celebrating particular days, worshiping angels, not handling or tasting certain things, etc. Paul warned, "See to it that no one takes you captive through hollow and deceptive philosophy, which depends on human tradition and the basic principles of this world, rather than on Christ" (Colossians 2:8 NIV). He emphasized that Christ is all we need.

We have similar problems today. There are those who seek to add other things to Christianity. Some of these additions include principles and practices from the New Age Movement (much of which is derived from ancient paganism, Far Eastern religions, native religions, and other non-Christian sources), or from Wicca (a modern pagan religion), or from Hinduism or Buddhism, or from various schools of psychology, or from other non-Christian sources.

But the principle of staying with what is written has a broader importance. Let me give a few further examples:

THE SUPERNATURAL—There has been a movement among some Bible scholars to "demythologize" the Bible. They say that modern man will not accept the supernatural things in the Bible. Therefore, to make it acceptable to modern man, they would delete, as not authentic, every passage that deals with the miraculous or other supernatural events. Basically, it seems to me, they are saying that the Holy Spirit made a mistake when he caused the Bible to be written as it was written, and they must correct the Holy Spirit's mistake. In doing so, they depart seriously from the purpose and intent of the original text.

PICKING AND CHOOSING—There have been some who would reject, as not authentic or irrelevant, any passages which do not conform with their idea of God's character and his ways. It is from Scripture that we learn of God's character and ways, and we therefore have to deal with everything that Scripture says about them. We cannot pick and choose only those passages that fit our preconceptions. For example, we may not like to have to deal with the ideas of judgment and of God's wrath, but the Bible (including the New Testament) speaks of them quite often, and so we must deal with them.

TRADITION—Jesus warned us that human traditions can "...nullify the word of God..." (Mark 7:13 NIV). (See verses 5-13.) We sometimes have doctrinal formulations, teachings, or practices which have become so entrenched that almost no one would consider re-examining them to see whether or not they are solidly based on Scripture. The test of any teaching should be, not "Does it conform to this or that doctrinal formulation or theological teaching?" but "Does it conform to Scripture?"

LOGICAL DEDUCTIONS—There are some teachings which rest on logical deductions from what Scripture says. The Bible tells us to distrust human logic. Scripture tells us that the human heart—which includes the mind—"is deceitful above all things, and desperately wicked" (Jeremiah 17:9). Proverbs tells us, "Trust in the LORD with all your heart, and lean not on your own understanding" (Proverbs 3:5). We should be reluctant to base our doctrine on human reasoning rather than on revelation from God. It is better not to add to what the Holy Spirit has written, or to attribute to him conclusions that may seem logical by human reasoning, but which he did not state.

Recognize That We Do Not Have All the Answers

Paul wrote that now "we see in a mirror, dimly" and we "know in part" (1 Corinthians 13:12). We shall not see clearly or know fully until we are with God in heaven. I believe these statements apply as much to our understanding of

Scripture as they do to anything else in this world. We should seek all the understanding we can get, but we need to recognize that it is still incomplete.

Scripture says, "Trust in the LORD with all your heart, and lean not on your own understanding" (Proverbs 3:5). If we think we understand everything in Scripture, we may run into the danger of leaning on our own understanding rather than trusting in God.

Paul wrote much of the New Testament and was probably the best educated and intellectually most acute of its human authors. Yet he keeps talking about the mysteries of God's ways. He writes, "Oh, the depth of the riches both of the wisdom and knowledge of God! How unsearchable are His judgments and His ways beyond finding out" (Romans 11:33). He speaks of the love of Christ "which passes knowledge" (Ephesians 3:19), and the peace of God "which surpasses all understanding" (Philippians 4:7). The Psalmist wrote that "…no one can fathom…" the greatness of God (Psalm 145:3 NIV). He wrote of knowledge of God's ways that is "too wonderful for me; it is high, I cannot attain it" (Psalm 139:6). God's ways and his thoughts are vastly higher than ours (Isaiah 55:8-9). No matter how profound our knowledge of Scripture may be, there will always be this element of mystery, of things that are beyond human understanding.

God has given us "…everything we need for life and godliness through our knowledge of him who called us by his own glory and goodness" (2 Peter 1:3 NIV). He has not answered all the questions our fertile minds can come up with. The Book of Job is instructive. Job asked all sorts of questions of God, deep questions that came out of his intense suffering. God answered none of them. He simply said, in effect, "Job, look at who I am." (See Job, chapters 38-41.) Job replied, "I have uttered what I did not understand, things too wonderful for me, which I did not know" (Job 42:3). Then God put an end to his suffering and blessed him richly.

This helps explain something which often troubles many. They say, "How can we believe Scripture when Christians so often disagree as to what it means?" I have said that Scripture is true. But our human interpretations of Scripture are fallible. Hence we humans can differ in our understanding of Scripture. (Actually most of the disagreements, while they attract a lot of attention, do not deal with the basics.) We also need to recognize that any human interpretation or teaching is probably incomplete and may be seriously wrong. This is not because the Bible is confusing or unclear. It is because anything humans do is subject to error.

Ask the Holy Spirit for Guidance

When we accept Jesus Christ as our Lord and Savior, the Holy Spirit comes to dwell in us (John 14:16-17). One of his functions is to "guide you into all truth" (John 16:13). Paul tells us that without the Holy Spirit we cannot understand spiritual things (1 Corinthians 2:14). On any question of interpretation, we should ask the Holy Spirit for guidance.

This leads me to a basic principle that I try to follow in everything involving Scripture. Our reading and study of Scripture involves the intellect. I find it as challenging intellectually as anything I have ever done. But the intellect must be guided by the Holy Spirit. The two work together.

Paul has told us that the letter kills but the Spirit gives life (2 Corinthians 3:6). I find that, after I have done what I can with the intellectual techniques previously discussed, there will sometimes come an insight, which I believe is from the Holy Spirit, that makes certain words in the text jump out at me, or that sheds a new light on the meaning of the text and its relationship to other texts, or that directs my attention to some "it is also writtens" that I need to consider. There are also insights that lead me to consider, or do a study on, particular issues. I believe that the Holy Spirit sometimes leads me through gentle nudges and suggestions, and I try to keep myself open to these.

There is another reason not to limit yourself to an intellectual understanding of Scripture. I find that, if left to itself, my intellect can often lead me to error. I think that God was warning us about this when he told Jeremiah that the heart is deceitful (Jeremiah 17:9). ("Heart" in the Old Testament is often used to mean the non-physical part of man; what we today would call the "soul." Thus it includes the intellect.) Proverbs 3:5 is even more explicit, "Trust in the LORD with all your heart, and lean not on your own understanding." When we rely solely on our own intellect in our reading and study of Scripture, are we not leaning on our own understanding?

Scripture is not of much value to us unless it results in a radically changed life. A purely intellectual understanding is not apt to produce this kind of change. Our understanding needs to move from "head knowledge" to "heart knowledge." We believe and we absorb Scripture, not only with all our mind, but also with all our heart and all our strength. To do this, we need the guidance and the power of the Holy Spirit.

I have experienced this recently. I am faced with advanced cancer. An intellectual understanding of God's love and faithfulness, while useful, will not accomplish much to give me the strength, encouragement, peace, and joy that I need to have in spite of the circumstances. I have needed to bring my faith, and my understanding, to a heartfelt level that involves my whole being. It has taken something fairly dramatic to bring me to that point. All of us need to make that transition from head knowledge to heart knowledge.

But we also need to be quite careful about our reliance on spiritual insights. The Holy Spirit does guide us, and we need to follow his guidance, but there are also counterfeit spirits that try to deceive us. (See Chapter 12.) So whenever we think we have gotten guidance from the Holy Spirit, we need to make sure (1) that it really is from the Holy Spirit, and (2) that we have understood it correctly. Part of this process involves checking it against our understanding of the language and context of Scripture. The Holy Spirit will not contradict his Scripture. It may be that our understanding of Scripture needs to change. But it also may be that what we thought was a prompting of the Holy Spirit needs to be re-examined carefully. This process involves considerable use of our intellect.

What I am saying is that in this, as in so many areas of our spiritual life, there needs to be a balance. Our intellect, and the guidance of the Holy Spirit, need to work in partnership. Our intellectual understanding needs to be deepened and enlivened by the Holy Spirit. But what we think of as spiritual guidance needs to be checked against our intellectual understanding.

Be Humble

Perhaps I can sum up much of what I have said by the words, "be humble." "God resists the proud, but gives grace to the humble" (James 4:6). (Also see 1 Peter 5:5.) James wrote, "Receive with meekness the engrafted word" (James 1:21 KJV).

If we approach Scripture seeking to use it for our purposes, to find support in it for our agendas, to confirm and approve the way we are already living, it will do us little good and may do us much harm. Peter speaks of those who distort Scripture "to their own destruction" (2 Peter 3:16). (Also see Psalm 119:21.)

If, on the other hand, we approach Scripture humbly, with meekness, seeking to know what it says, expecting to find wonderful things in it, willing to yield to what it says, eager to allow it to work in our hearts and change us, then we will find it to be an inexhaustible treasure house of riches that will transform our lives. This has been my experience, and that of many whom I know.

CONCLUSION

This chapter has only scratched the surface of many issues. There are many good books which deal with these areas in greater depth. You may wish to consult some of them. In addition, this book has an Appendix that describes some good resources for studying Scripture.

I encourage you to let the words of Scripture speak to you. Read them, reflect and meditate on them, memorize them if you can, and allow them to become a very part of you. You will find that they change your life. At one point Jesus asked his disciples if they would leave him because of a "hard" teaching he had given. Peter replied, "Lord, to whom shall we go? You have the words of eternal life" (John 6:68). The words of the Bible are the words of eternal life, and all who truly immerse themselves in them will be richly blessed.

PART III
SOME BASIC BELIEFS

5

God

o o o o o o o o o o o o o o o o o o o o o o o o o o o o o o o

"I am God, and there is no other; I am God, and there is none like Me."

—*(Isaiah 46:9)*

Recently I corresponded about God with a college classmate, who is an avid sailor. His view of God seemed to rest on Exodus 3:14, in which God told Moses, "I am who I am." My friend seemed to think that all we can or should know about God is that he exists, and that even to give God a name would limit him. Evidently that was all that he was comfortable in knowing about God.

I replied, first, that if all God wanted us to know about him was contained in this one verse of Scripture, then why did God give us the rest of Scripture, which says a great deal more about him? Then I commented that, as a sailor, my friend needs to know more about winds and ocean currents than just that they exist. He needs to know when it will be high tide at a particular location, what currents to expect at various points in the harbor at various tides, when an off-shore or on-shore breeze is likely to arise, what various markings and wave formations in the water mean, what various cloud formations mean, what the signs are of an impending squall, what a rising and falling barometer mean, how much wind his sails can safely handle before they should be reefed or taken down, and much more. If he does not know and understand these things, he may lose his boat and even his life. Similarly, if we are to function effectively in the universe God has created, we need to know as much about God as we can.

There are many people today who say that they believe in God. If you ask, you find that some of them have a very vague idea of who or what God is. They may speak of "something bigger than I," or "a universal force or energy." Some say that everything is God. Some say, "I am God." Some say that "all gods are the same." All of these views of God are demonstrably contrary to what Scripture says about him. Scripture is a direct revelation from God. (See Chapter 2.) Therefore, we had better base our ideas about God on what Scripture says and not on human speculation.

God is too big for us to understand fully. He is beyond any words we can use to describe him. Our limited human minds and vocabularies are too small to comprehend him fully. There is nothing to which we can compare him (Isaiah 40:18). But in his Scripture, God has told us a great deal about himself, and we need to understand clearly what he has told us.

One of our essential tasks as Christians is to know God, to know what his will is for us, to know what pleases him, and to live a life that is pleasing to him. There are many ideas about God that may seem appealing but that rest on a false concept of God. In order not to be deceived by them, we need to have a clear and true concept of who God is. Our life, as Christians, should be centered on God. "In him we live and move and have our being" (Acts 17:28). We had better be sure that we are focussed on the true God.

If we do not have a correct concept of God, all our other thinking is apt to be skewed.

There is also a view that is current that there is no such thing as truth. All truth is said to be relative (i.e., what is true for me may not be true for you). Such a view is totally contrary to Scripture. Scripture asserts that there is truth that applies to all people at all times, and that it is to be found in Scripture. God's word is truth (John 17:17). All God's words are true (Psalm 119:160). Jesus is the truth (John 14:6). If we follow Jesus' words, we will know the truth and the truth will set us free (John 8:31-32). God's truth is eternal; it is true for all time. "The word of our God stands forever" (Isaiah 40:8). (Also see Psalm 119:89; Matthew 24:35.)

In this chapter, I want to identify briefly some of the essential things Scripture tells us about God, and contrast them with some false conceptions that are current. Other chapters in this book will reveal more of God's character and attributes. As always, I urge you to read the Scripture passages in context, reflect on them, pray about them, and ask the Holy Spirit to guide you. The study of God is a lifetime activity. I can only give a few basic ideas.

GOD'S NATURE

There is so much that could be said about God that I hesitate even to undertake the task of writing about him. The God of Scripture is endlessly fascinating.

We can never begin to know all about him. But perhaps I can be helpful by dispelling some fairly common misconceptions about God.

God Is a Person

Scripture always refers to God as a person. God speaks in the first person singular, "I." He identified himself as "I AM" (Exodus 3:14). Jesus referred to him as "Abba," the term a child would use for his Daddy. Jesus told us to pray to God as "Our Father." Paul wrote, "I know whom I have believed" (2 Timothy 1:12). **Whom**, not **what**. Paul's belief is in a person. Our belief should be in a person.

God teaches us and guides us. He acts in our lives, and in history. He raises up nations and brings them down. He created the nation of Israel, brought them out of captivity in Egypt, and enabled them to conquer Canaan. When they persistently refused to obey him, God raised up the Assyrians and Babylonians to conquer them, and then brought some of his people back from Babylon. When the time was fulfilled, he sent his only Son to earth for our salvation. "And we know that in all things God works for the good of those who love him, who have been called according to his purpose" (Romans 8:28 NIV).

God is not a force, an energy, an intelligence. He is not a "something bigger." He is a very definite, clearly delineated, person. God is not an IT. God is a HE.

We see this all through Scripture. God has emotions; he feels. He loves. He has mercy. He has compassion. He longs. He seeks our company. He can be pleased and take delight. He is grieved. He is angry. He has great wrath.

God has repeatedly entered into covenant, into a formal agreement, with his people. A typical covenant is, "I will be their God, and they shall be My people" (Jeremiah 31:33). One of the essential truths of both the Old and the New Testaments is that we are a covenant people. A covenant is a contractual relationship between persons. A thing cannot enter into a covenant.

God loves us. His greatest commandment is that we love him, with all our heart, mind, soul and strength. A thing cannot love or be loved. Love is a personal relationship between persons. You cannot love, and be loved by, an IT.

An IT cannot give us words which have the power to change our lives.

Why is it important to understand all this?

Christianity is about a relationship. It is not primarily about doctrines, or rituals, or intellectual beliefs. It is about a personal relationship with a personal God. You can have a relationship with a personal God. You can't have a relationship with an impersonal energy or force. We are responsible, accountable, to a personal God.

God is a person. Any view of God that denies or ignores that fact is unscriptural. It denies the very essence of God.

God Is Creator

Scripture tells us that God created the physical universe.

There may be room for differences of opinion as to how God created, or the time schedule on which he created, but the fact that he is the Creator is stated all through Scripture.

"In the beginning God created the heavens and the earth" (Genesis 1:1). "He commanded and they were created" (Psalm 148:5). (Also see Psalms 24:1-2, 33:6-9, 102:25, 121:2, 146:6; Isaiah 40:28, 42:5, 45:12, 51:13.) "All things were made through Him" (John 1:3). (Also see Colossians 1:16; Hebrews 1:2; 2 Peter 3:5.) Throughout Scripture, we see the theme that God is to be praised because he is the Creator. "You are worthy, O Lord, to receive glory and honor and power; for You created all things, and by Your will they exist and were created" (Revelation 4:11).

There are some who say that God created everything and then went off and left it to run by itself. This is not Scriptural. God not only created all things, he sustains everything by his word (Hebrews 1:3). He holds it all together (Colossians 1:17). Scripture shows a God who is constantly active in men's lives. "The eyes of the LORD run to and fro throughout the whole earth, to show Himself strong in behalf of those whose heart is loyal to Him" (2 Chronicles 16:9). "He will not let your foot slip—he who watches over you will not slumber; indeed, he who watches over Israel will neither slumber nor sleep" (Psalm 121:3-4 NIV). Jesus said, "My Father is always at his work to this very day…" (John 5:17 NIV). (Some of these passages refer to Jesus Christ, but Jesus Christ is also God. See Chapters 6 and 7.)

Because God is the Creator, everything on earth belongs to him. "The earth is the LORD's and everything in it, the world, and all who live in it" (Psalm 24:1 NIV). We are his. "Know that the LORD, He is God. It is He who made us, and not we ourselves; we are His people and the sheep of His pasture" (Psalm 100:3). "Who has ever given to God, that God should repay him? For from him and to him and through him are all things. To him be the glory forever! Amen" (Romans 11:35-36 NIV).

God Is Separate From His Creation

A common idea about God, today, is that he is in everything. Some would say that God is everything and everything is God. This is called pantheism.

This is contrary to Scripture. God is separate from his creation. His presence is everywhere, but he is still separate from his creation. God existed before anything was created, and he will exist even if everything physical is destroyed.

We find this beautifully expressed in Psalm 102:25-27 (NIV): "In the beginning you laid the foundations of the earth, and the heavens are the work of your hands. They will perish, but you remain; they will all wear out like a garment. Like clothing you will change them and they will be discarded. But you remain the same and your years will never end." To God, the earth, the sun, and all the millions of stars, which scientists say extend over millions of light years, are like a garment. God wears them for a time, but then he discards them and puts on a new garment.

An episode in the life of the prophet Elijah is also suggestive. When Elijah had gone to Mt. Sinai to escape the wrath of Jezebel, God spoke to him. The Scripture says that there was a powerful wind, "but the LORD was not in the wind." Then there was an earthquake, "but the LORD was not in the earthquake." Then there was a fire, "but the LORD was not in the fire." Finally there came a gentle whisper, and that was the voice of the Lord (1 Kings 19:11-13).

One of God's essential attributes (characteristics) is that he is holy (1 Peter 1:16). To be holy is to be separated, set apart. There is evil and sin in the world. "Through one man [Adam] sin entered the world, and death through sin" (Romans 5:12). God cannot be part of evil or sin.

God Is Unique

Another common assertion, today, is that all gods are the same and all religions the same. From this it is argued that (1) it does not matter what god you say you serve, or what concept of god you have, and (2) it should be possible to develop a single one-world religion into which all existing religions can be blended. Even some people who call themselves Christians have been attracted by this idea of a one-world religion.

Scripture denies this. Jesus declared that his Father is "the only true God" (John 17:3). He said, "I am the way, the truth, and the life. No man comes to the Father except through Me" (John 14:6). Paul said that there is no God but one (1

Corinthians 8:4). God declared, "I am the LORD and there is no other; there is no God besides Me" (Isaiah 45:5).

God warned his people over and over not to serve other gods, and to worship him alone. (See, for example, Deuteronomy 7:1-6, 11:16, 13:1-18.) Jesus said that no one can serve two masters (Matthew 6:24). Paul spoke of the pagan gods of his day as "demons" (1 Corinthians 10:20-21), and warned Christians to have nothing to do with them (2 Corinthians 6:14-18). He warned us not to follow "...a different gospel—which is really no gospel at all..." (Galatians 1:6-7 NIV).

Paul repeatedly warned Christians not to try to combine the gospel of Jesus Christ with other beliefs. In Galatians he warned against adding to the Christian gospel many requirements of the Jewish law. In Colossians he warned against combining the Christian gospel with a number of gnostic (or pre-gnostic) beliefs and practices. He insisted that Christ is all we need.

These warnings are just as applicable today as they ever were. We must not water down the power of our Christian faith in an effort to blend it with other religions that do not come from the one true God.

God Does Not Change

Some people say that the God of the Old Testament is a harsh, vengeful God, and the God of the New Testament is a loving God. This is not true. God has not changed. "I am the LORD, I do not change" (Malachi 3:6). In God "there is no variation or shadow of turning" (James 1:17). (Also see Hebrews 6:17.) Jesus Christ (who is God, see Chapter 6) "is the same yesterday, today and forever" (Hebrews 13:8).

Actually the Old Testament is full of the love of God. One of the great Old Testament words is *chesed*, variously translated as "love, lovingkindness, mercy." *Chesed* appears 240 times in the Old Testament. God is "abounding in love" (Psalm 103:8 NIV). Every verse of Psalm 136 ends, "His mercy endureth forever" (KJV). "Because of the LORD's great love we are not consumed, for his compassions never fail" (Lamentations 3:22 NIV). Many more examples could be given.

On the other hand, the New Testament speaks often of God's wrath. (See, for example, Romans 1:18, Ephesians 5:6; 2 Thessalonians 1:7-9; Revelation 6:16.) It also speaks of judgment and eternal punishment. (See, for example, Matthew 13:42, 25:31-46; Mark 9:43-48; John 5:29.)

God Acts in Our Lives

Some have a conception of God as a remote, distant figure who plays no part in our daily lives. Such a conception is contrary to Scripture. It is contrary to the God I have experienced in my life as a Christian.

God has said to us, "I will instruct you and teach you in the way you should go; I will guide you with My eye" (Psalm 32:8). (Also see Proverbs 3:5-6.) God is like a voice behind us saying, "This is the way; walk in it" (Isaiah 30:21). To those who commit themselves fully to him, Scripture says, "He shall give his angels charge over you, to keep you in all your ways" (Psalm 91:11). God's power is always at work in us (Ephesians 3:20). (Also see Ephesians 1:19; Philippians 2:13.) It is because he is constantly at work in the lives of believers that he is "able to keep you from stumbling, and to present you faultless before the presence of His glory with exceeding joy" (Jude 24).

As I look back over my own life, and that of many others, I am amazed to see how God has worked in each of us to develop the character qualities he wants, and to use us for his purposes. My experience is that God is continually acting in our lives, whether we recognize it or not.

We Are Not God

There are some New Agers today who declare, "I am God." They seek the "god within" or the "goddess within" as their source of guidance and strength. This is contrary to Scripture. Anyone who thinks he is God either is incredibly arrogant, or totally fails to comprehend the greatness of God, or both. Scripture clearly condemns anyone who would exalt himself against the true God and claim to be God. That was the source of Adam's fall; the serpent (satan) told him that he would be like God (Genesis 3:5) and Adam believed the serpent. Aiming to be equal to God was the source of satan's downfall. (See Isaiah 14:12-15, Ezekiel 28:13-19.)

We need to be very clear here, because, without careful understanding, there is room for confusion.

When anyone receives Jesus Christ as his Lord and Savior, the Holy Spirit of God comes to dwell in him (John 14:17). The Holy Spirit teaches him, guides him and empowers him. In this sense, we who believe in Jesus can partake in the divine nature (2 Peter 1:4). We believers can have God in us. (See Chapter 11.) But Jesus said, "Remain in me and I will remain in you…apart from me you can do nothing" (John 15:4, 5 NIV). Of ourselves we can do nothing. Whatever of

God's character and power we may possess is ours only because we have submitted ourselves to, and continue to submit ourselves to, Jesus Christ.

GOD'S CHARACTER

The important thing to remember about God's character is that it has many aspects. God is loving, compassionate, merciful, forgiving, and kind. He is amazingly patient with us. He also disciplines those he loves. He is holy, righteous, and just. He cannot tolerate evil. He can be a God of terrible wrath. He is a God of judgment.

God has all wisdom and all knowledge. He is faithful; he keeps his promises. He reaches out to us and desires our companionship. He wants us to know him personally. But he is also a great and powerful God. He is awesome in the original and true meaning of that word.

I could go on and list many more aspects of God's character. It would take a whole book to begin to deal with them adequately. But the point I want to emphasize is that we need to deal with every aspect of God's character. One of the great sources of error in our thinking about God is that we sometimes put so much emphasis on certain aspects of his character that we neglect the others and arrive at a distorted picture. We need to know and follow the whole teaching of Scripture about God, and not just parts of it. Let me illustrate this by just one example.

The Kindness and Severity of God

Paul wrote, "Therefore consider the goodness and severity of God" (Romans 11:22). (The NIV says "...kindness and sternness...")

God is a loving God. "God is love" (1 John 4:16). "God so loved the world that He gave His only begotten Son, that whoever believes in Him should not perish but have eternal life" (John 3:16). God is merciful and patient with us. "The LORD longs to be gracious to you..." (Isaiah 30:18 NIV). He lavishes his grace—his unmerited favor—on those who love him.

But he is also a just God and a holy God. He will not forever tolerate evil and sin. He is capable of great wrath. He is a God of judgment. "...we will all stand before God's judgment seat" (Romans 14:10 NIV). (Also see John 5:28-29.)

Scripture tells us to love God, and also to fear God. I believe that word "fear" means "fear," and not just awe or reverence. The Greek word can mean "fear exceedingly." Some of the Old Testament texts speak of "dread." Hebrews 10:31

(NIV) says, "It is a dreadful thing to fall into the hands of the living God." I think we need to take the word "fear" in its original meaning as "fear," whether we like to deal with that meaning or not.

How can we do both? How can we both love God and fear him? A simple example may help. A young child loves his daddy. But he also fears him, especially when his daddy finds it necessary to discipline him physically.

We need always to be aware of these two aspects of God.

In the past, there have been those who put such emphasis on God's severity—on his wrath and judgment—that we tended to lose sight of his love and mercy. Today there are some who put such emphasis on God's love and mercy that we tend to lose sight of his wrath and judgment. Either view is incomplete. Either view, without the other, is a distortion of God's character.

THE GREATNESS OF GOD

God is "the great God, mighty and awesome" (Deuteronomy 10:17). (Also see Deuteronomy 7:21; 2 Samuel 7:22; Nehemiah 1:5, 9:32; Daniel 9:4; Titus 2:13.) "O LORD my God, You are very great: You are clothed with honor and majesty" (Psalm 104:1). (Also see Psalms 48:1, 95:3.) "Great is the LORD and most worthy of praise; his greatness no one can fathom" (Psalm 145:3 NIV). To get some sense of God's greatness, I suggest reading Isaiah, chapter 40, and Revelation, chapters 4 and 5. Even they do not give the whole picture.

God created the earth, the sun, the moon, our solar system, and millions upon millions of stars, most of which are larger than our sun. He created a physical universe that extends, so our scientists tell us, for a huge number of light years—distances that most of us cannot begin to grasp. And he is greater than his creation!

We cannot begin to conceive the full measure of God's greatness, his splendor, his majesty, his power. He has given us, in his Scriptures, some remarkable visions of him; but they are incomplete and partial. God lives "in unapproachable light, whom no man has seen or can see" (1 Timothy 6:16).

Part of God's greatness is that he is all-powerful. God is the Almighty. That is his nature. That is what it is to be God. God's power is incomparably great (Ephesians 1:19). He can do all things. Nothing is impossible for him (Job 42:2; Matthew 19:26; Luke 1:37; Genesis 18:14). God's purpose and plans will prevail; nothing can thwart or defeat them (Psalm 33:1; Isaiah 14:24; 37:9; 46:10; Job 42:2).

My daughter's poem expresses God's greatness in a different way.

MIGHTY GOD

Heaven is your throne, the earth is your footstool.
Glorious in holiness, fearful in praises,
Doing wonders, mighty God!

You stretched out the heavens with your powerful hand.
You created all things with a word of command.
You decree a thing and it comes to pass.
Our world will fail—your Word will last.

Angels and saints cry, "Holy! Holy!"
Glorious in holiness, fearful in praises,
Doing wonders, mighty God!

I think that a major problem with the Christian church today is that, as a whole, we are not sufficiently aware of God's greatness. We need constantly to be aware of God's greatness.

The Fear of the Lord

Because God is so great, we should fear him. "The fear of the LORD is the beginning of wisdom" (Psalm 111:10). (Also see, for example, Psalms 19:9, 34:9; 90:11, Proverbs 1:7; 2 Corinthians 7:1; Philippians 2:12.)

What does it mean, to fear God? I think it means that we recognize God's tremendous power, and his potential for wrath against things that are ungodly. God is not mocked. There is no such thing as cheap grace. We need constantly to keep watch over how we live.

It means that we do not presume on God. "Keep back your servant from presumptuous sins…and I shall be innocent of great transgressions" (Psalm 19:13). What are presumptuous sins? We presume on God when we take him for granted, or seek to manipulate him. We presume on God when we put him to the test. (See Matthew 4:7.) Jesus would have presumed on God if he had thrown himself from the Temple when God did not tell him to do so. We presume on God whenever we think we can obligate him to give us something or to do something on our behalf. God does not owe anything to anybody; he is not obligated to anybody. (See Romans 11:35.) God is not a heavenly vending machine in which you put in a prayer and get whatever you have asked for. God is sovereign. And note that the Psalmist refers to presumptuous sins as "great transgression."

It means that we recognize that we cannot hide anything from God. God knows us completely (Psalm 139:1-6). He knows our every thought and action. And we cannot escape from him (Psalm 139:7-12). Even those who deny the existence of God will ultimately have to deal with him.

It means that we are serious about our faith. God wants a total commitment of our lives to him. (See Chapter 16.)

It means that we take his Scriptures seriously. We don't just ignore them, or give them lip service, or construe them in a way that waters down their clear meaning. It means that we act on them and live by them.

Some do not like to consider God's greatness because it makes them feel small. That is where God wants us. Scripture tells us to humble ourselves before God (1 Peter 5:6; James 4:10). This is part of the fear of God, that we recognize how much greater he is than we are.

Again, my daughter has put it well.

KNOWING GOD

The fear of the Lord is
Beginning of wisdom.
The fear of the Lord gives us
Knowledge and strength.

God's love is amazing,
His mercy astounding:
To know Him we need
The fear of the Lord.

Confidence in God

God's greatness also means that, by his incomparably great power working within us, we can conquer whatever problems and difficulties we may have to face. God is bigger. He is bigger than anything we have to deal with. Nothing is impossible for him. In him we can overcome trials and difficulties. (See Chapter 11.) It is wonderful to be able to trust in such a great God.

Freedom From Fear

To put it another way, if we fear God, we do not need to fear anything else. If we do not fear God, then we will fear everything else.

CONCLUSION

I have said a few things about who God is and who he is not. Much more could be said. But I want to emphasize one thing, that applies to much of what I have written in this book.

When we think of God we can make two kinds of errors. One is to think that we know nothing about God. The other is to think that we know everything about God.

Scripture tells us a great deal about God and his ways of dealing with men. It tells us many very specific, definite things. The created universe also tells us about him (Psalm 19:1). (Also see Isaiah 40:21; Romans 1:19-20.) Our own experience of God tells us about him. "His [God's] divine power has given us everything we need for life and godliness, through our knowledge of him who called us by his own glory and goodness" (2 Peter 1:3 NIV). God has given us all that we need to know about him.

But we must also remember that, while here on earth, we perceive everything imperfectly and incompletely (1 Corinthians 13:12). Paul, the most learned and intellectual of the New Testament writers, wrote, "Oh, the depth of the riches both of the wisdom and knowledge of God! How unsearchable are His judgments and His ways past finding out" (Romans 11:33). Isaiah, the greatest of the Old Testament writing prophets, said that no one can fathom God's understanding (Isaiah 40:28). God has told us, "'For My thoughts are not your thoughts, nor are your ways My ways,' says the LORD. 'For as the heavens are higher than the earth, so are My ways higher than your ways and My thoughts higher than your thoughts'" (Isaiah 55:8-9). With God there is always an element of mystery. There is always much more than we think we see or understand. I think we can see several aspects to this, which I shall try to sketch.

- We humans live in a world limited by space and time. God lives in infinity and eternity. He is not bound by space and time. He sees things differently than we do.
- "God is spirit" (John 4:24). He lives in the world of the spirit, while we live in a material world. Translating ideas and concepts from one of these

worlds to the other is difficult. Our language and our minds do not have the words or the concepts to understand fully and adequately what God would tell us about spiritual things.

- God is infinitely great and magnificent. We simply do not have words or concepts adequate to express his greatness. We have nothing to compare him to. (See Isaiah 40:18, 25.)
- God is life; he is the source of life. We analyze him and discuss him in intellectual terms, and this is useful. But we must be careful that our intellectual constructs do not blind us to the life behind them. Paul wrote, "The letter kills, but the Spirit gives life" (2 Corinthians 3:6).

In everything I have written, I have used prosaic words because they are the means of communication I am familiar with. But such words are quite inadequate to express the truth about God. I hope that somehow those who read this will be able at least to glimpse the reality that lies behind the words. We need not only to read about God, but to experience him in our lives. I hope also that you will keep aware of the sense of mystery that surrounds everything we may try to say about God. And I hope that you will recognize that one of the most important and necessary things a Christian can do is to come to know God better. This is a lifetime occupation.

My words are inadequate to convey the greatness and majesty of God. Hopefully my wife's poem will give another perspective.

I SAW YOU SEATED

Through the prophet's eye
I saw You seated
focus to explosions of jewelled light
and thundering flashings
coupled with the rushing sounds of waters
causing prophet's tongue to stumble,
causing trembling knees to seek in weakness
the humbling fact of earth.

O holy, holy, holi-ness,
crowns of gold, tossing, tossing;
clouds of saints adoring.

Holy, holy, holi-ness;
flashes of Ox, of Eagle;
flashes of Man and Lion.

Holy, holy, holi-ness;
the flow of gold-transparent
flowing from the throne.

O holy, holy, holi-ness
    angels hovering, angels singing,
    prayers as incense rising, rising.
Holy, holy, holi-ness.

And we, O Lord, not prophets of old but saints of now
straddling earth and heaven,
embrace Your Cross, exultantly;
trust in You,
obedient,
and give assent for all that is to be.

6

Jesus Christ

o o o o o o o o o o o o o o o o o o o o o o o o o o o o o o o

"At the name of Jesus every knee should bow, of those in heaven, and of those on earth, and of those under the earth, and that every tongue should confess that Jesus Christ is Lord, to the glory of God the Father."

—*(Philippians 2:10-11)*

Our Christian faith is based on a person, Jesus Christ. Our life, as Christians, centers on him. He is our Lord as well as our Savior (Romans 10:9). We are told to bring "every thought into captivity to the obedience of Christ" (2 Corinthians 10:5). Scripture uses powerful images to describe the closeness of our relationship with him. We are in Christ (2 Corinthians 5:17) and Christ is in us (Colossians 1:27). We have clothed ourselves with Christ (Galatians 3:27). Paul wrote, "I have been crucified with Christ; it is no longer I who live, but Christ lives in me" (Galatians 2:20). He wrote that he was "in the pains of childbirth until Christ is formed in you" (Galatians 4:19 NIV).

Hence it is very important to be quite clear who Jesus Christ is and who he is not. Jesus has warned us, "Take heed that no one deceives you. For many will come in My name, saying, 'I am the Christ,' and will deceive many" (Matthew 24:4-5). Again he said that, in the end times, "false Christs and false prophets will rise and show great signs and wonders to deceive, if possible, even the elect. See, I have told you beforehand" (Matthew 24:24-25). I believe that we are close to, if not in, the end times, and that we are seeing a number of false Christs and false concepts of Christ. We need to know clearly who the true Jesus Christ is in order that we not be deceived by the false ones.

Scripture tells us quite a bit about Jesus Christ. This chapter will try to sketch some of what the Bible says about him, and to refute some false concepts of Jesus Christ that have been expressed by some people.

JESUS CHRIST IS GOD

Jesus Christ is God, who once came down to earth and lived in the form of a man. Scripture makes this very clear. His name is "'...Immanuel'—which means 'God with us'" (Matthew 1:23 NIV). (Also see Luke 19:44.) Jesus is the Word, the *logos,* who "was in the beginning with God." Jesus "was God," and he "became flesh and dwelt among us" (John 1:1, 2, 14). Paul says the same thing in a different way. "Being in the form of God" Jesus was "found in appearance as a man" (Philippians 2:6, 8). (Also see Romans 8:3.) I don't see how anything could be clearer. Jesus was and is God, who came down to earth and took on human form.

Other Scriptures confirm this. He is "our great God and Savior, Jesus Christ" (Titus 2:13). He is "over all, the eternally blessed God" (Romans 9:5). When Thomas worshiped him as "My Lord and my God," Jesus commended him, saying, "Because you have seen Me, you have believed" (John 20:28-29).

Jesus has the attributes of God. He is eternal. Like the Father, he is the First and the Last (Revelation 1:17). He was with God in the beginning, before the physical universe was created (John 1:1; 8:58; 17:5). He took part in the creation; nothing was created without him (John 1:3; Colossians 1:16; Hebrews 1:2). He holds the universe together (Colossians 1:17; Hebrews 1:3). He lives forever (Hebrews 7:23). He is "alive forevermore" (Revelation 1:18).

Jesus is one with the Father. He said, "I and My Father are one" (John 10:30). "He who has seen Me has seen the Father" (John 14:9). (Also see John 8:19; 10:38; 12:45; 14:11.) He said, "All that belongs to the Father is mine..." (John 16:15 NIV). "For in Christ all the fullness of the Deity lives in bodily form" (Colossians 2:9 NIV). (Also see Colossians 1:19.)

In John's great vision, we see "every creature which is in heaven and on the earth and under the earth and such as are in the sea, and all that are in them" worshiping the Father and the Son together, and singing, "Blessing and honor and glory and power be to Him who sits on the throne, and to the Lamb [Jesus] for ever and ever!" (Revelation 5:13).

There are some who assert that Jesus never claimed to be God. They assert that the claim that he is God is something invented by the human authors of Scripture years after his death. This is simply false. A number of the Scripture references quoted in this chapter are the words of Jesus. Many of the things Jesus said about himself could only be said of God.[16]

Some Scriptures refer to Jesus as the Son of God. (See John 3:16.) This in no sense takes away from the fact that Jesus is God. It merely shows the unity between Father and Son.

We need to be very clear that Jesus is God. There are many who speak of him as a great moral teacher, a great example, a great prophet, etc. He was all of these. But he was much more. He was God who took human form. Because he was God, he was able to make atonement for us, and break the power of sin. There have been many humans who were fine teachers and examples, and some of them sacrificed their lives, but only Jesus could break the power of sin in the world. "For what the law was powerless to do in that it was weakened by the sinful nature, God did by sending his own Son in the likeness of sinful man to be a sin offering…" (Romans 8:3 NIV). "Salvation is found in no one else, for there is no other name under heaven given to men by which we must be saved" (Acts 4:12 NIV).

JESUS CHRIST IS SUPREME

Scripture tells us very clearly that Jesus Christ is supreme. He has "all authority" in heaven and on earth (Matthew 28:18). He is "…far above all rule and authority, power and dominion, and every title that can be given, not only in the present age but also in the one to come. And God placed all things under his feet…" (Ephesians 1:21-22 NIV). In everything he has the supremacy (Colossians 1:17-18). "At the name of Jesus every knee should bow, of those in heaven and of those on earth, and of those under the earth, and that every tongue should confess that Jesus Christ is Lord, to the glory of God the Father" (Philippians 2:10-11).

Jesus Christ is above, and greater than, every evil spirit, including satan himself. "By Him [Jesus] all things were created that are in heaven and that are on earth, visible and invisible, whether thrones or dominions or principalities or powers. All things were created through Him and for Him" (Colossians 1:16-17). Jesus Christ is above all spiritual forces of wickedness, including satan. They are created beings; he is their Creator. They must bow the knee to him.

Some New Agers speak of Jesus as one among a number of "Ascended Masters" or as one member of a hierarchy of ruling spirits—a spirit of the earth, of the solar system, of the galaxy, etc. Some Hindus recognize him as one of many "gods." Muslims recognize him as a prophet. Scripture rejects every such concept.

Jesus Christ is not one of many. He is unique. He is supreme in everything. He is above every spiritual power, except the Father himself.

JESUS CHRIST IS ALL-POWERFUL

Because he is God, and is Supreme, it follows that Jesus is all-powerful. Nothing can stand against him. Nothing is impossible for him. We tend often to sentimentalize him, particularly in some of what passes for religious art. Jesus could be very gentle, but it was a gentleness that came from great strength. The disciple John knew Jesus well. He was with Jesus at the Mount of Transfiguration, and he saw the Resurrection and the Ascension, but when he had a vision of Jesus in his glory, he "fell at his feet as though dead" (Revelation 1:17). Revelation speaks of the kings of the earth and other powerful men who hid in caves for fear of the "wrath of the Lamb [Jesus]" (Revelation 6:16). It shows Jesus as a rider on a white horse, leading the armies of heaven, and ruling the nations with an iron scepter. (See Revelation 19:11-16.) We must never sentimentalize Jesus.

JESUS CHRIST IS OUR SAVIOR

Jesus, and only Jesus, saves us from our sin. Jesus, and only Jesus, gives us eternal life with God if we believe in him.

Jesus is the "Lamb of God who takes away the sin of the world" (John 1:29). The angel said of him, "He will save His people from their sins" (Matthew 1:21). It is through belief in Jesus that we can have eternal life with God (John 3:16). God has reconciled us to himself by Jesus Christ (Colossians 1:20-22). "Now, once at the end of the ages, He [Christ] has appeared to put away sin by the sacrifice of Himself" (Hebrews 9:26). (Also see Hebrews 9:28, 10:10.) God "sent His Son to be the propitiation for our sins" (1 John 4:10). He "sent the Son as Savior of the world" (1 John 4:14).

Scripture declares that salvation is found in no one other than Jesus, and that there is no other name under heaven given to men by which we can be saved (Acts 4:12). No one comes to the Father except through Jesus (John 14:6). We are justified "through the redemption that is in Christ Jesus" (Romans 3:24). Jesus, and only Jesus, was the atonement for our sins (Romans 3:25). We were reconciled to God by the death of his Son (Romans 5:10). (Also see Romans 8:3; 2 Corinthians 5:18; Colossians 1:20, 22.) It is through belief in Jesus, and only through belief in Jesus, that we obtain eternal life (John 3:16). Jesus, and only Jesus, is the second Adam who brought justification that brings life to all who will accept it (Romans 5:12-19). "There is one God and one Mediator between God and men, the Man Christ Jesus" (1 Timothy 2:5). In John's great vision, Jesus, the Lamb, was the only one who was found worthy to open the scroll (Revelation 5:5, 9).

We find this in the Old Testament also. "There is no Savior besides me" (Hosea 13:4). (Also see Isaiah 43:11.) God is the only Savior. There is no one else alongside him. From the New Testament we learn that Jesus is God. No one else (except the Holy Spirit) is God.

It is because Jesus is God that he could be our Savior. Jesus warned us that there would be "false Christs" (Matthew 24:24). Any attempt to elevate any person to a status even close to being equal to Jesus is totally unscriptural. It is elevating a human to the status of God.

Some New Agers speak of a "Christ consciousness," which they define as an awareness of one's unity with god. This vague "consciousness" of one's unity with an unidentified "god" has nothing to do with the Scriptural Jesus Christ, whom God the Father sent to earth to be the atoning sacrifice for our sins and to reconcile us to him.

IS CHRISTIANITY EXCLUSIVE?

Jesus declared that his Father is the only true God (John 17:3) and that he is the only way to the Father (John 14:6). Peter said that there is no other name by which we can be saved (Acts 4:12).

From this, some assert that Christianity is "exclusive" and hence narrow, bigoted, ungenerous, intolerant, etc. I do not think the accusation is justified.

The promises of Christianity are open to everyone who will receive them. God "desires all men to be saved and to come to the knowledge of the truth" (1 Timothy 2:4). He is "not willing that any should perish but that all should come to repentance" (2 Peter 3:9). (Also see Titus 2:11.)

But, like any promises, we have to accept them on the giver's terms. If I offer $500 to anyone who stops smoking for six months, then only those who have actually stopped smoking for six months can receive the $500. Similarly, we can receive the promises of Christianity only if we are willing to accept them on the terms on which they are offered. Among those terms are these: that we believe in the Father as the only true God, and that we believe in and commit our lives to his son Jesus Christ. Anyone who is willing to meet the conditions set by God can receive the promises of Christianity. Christianity will not work for anyone who does not accept God's terms.

OTHER ASPECTS OF JESUS

Incarnation

Scripture makes it absolutely clear that Jesus did not have an earthly father. He was conceived by having the Holy Spirit overshadow a young woman named Mary. When Mary asked how she could have a child, since she was a virgin, the angel told her, "The Holy Spirit will come upon you, and the power of the Highest will overshadow you" (Luke 1:35). Another angel told Joseph, "do not be afraid to take to you Mary your wife, for that which is conceived in her is of the Holy Spirit" (Matthew 1:20). Joseph took her as his wife, but he "did not know her [have sexual relations with her] till she had brought forth her firstborn Son," who was Jesus (Matthew 1:25).

There is no record, in Scripture or elsewhere, of any other person who was so conceived. Because of it, Jesus was and is wholly man and wholly God. There is no other person of whom that can be said.

Some may say, "This couldn't happen." It is true that it has never happened before or since. It is unique. But that does not mean it could not happen. With God all things are possible. God's creation of both Adam and Eve were unique, one-of-a-kind, events. Who is to say that he could not create the man Jesus Christ by another unique event?

My mind cannot comprehend the Incarnation. I can't understand how the Creator of the universe could become a helpless baby in the womb of one of his creations. I can't understand how Almighty God could be an infant in a human mother's arms. But I don't have to understand it to believe it. I have no right to try to limit what God does to those things that my imperfect mind can understand. Scripture declares unequivocally that this is what happened, and I shall simply accept what Scripture says.

Life Without Sin

Jesus "was in all points tempted as we are, yet without sin" (Hebrews 4:15). There is no one else of whom that can be said. "All have sinned and fall short of the glory of God" (Romans 3:23). It is because Jesus was totally sinless that he, and he alone, was able to make atonement for our sins.

Crucifixion

Jesus' Crucifixion is described in each of the four gospels, and referred to many times in the epistles. There can be no doubt that it occurred and that it was incredibly painful.

I want to make one thing clear about the Crucifixion. Jesus went through it voluntarily. He said, "I lay down My life that I may take it again. No one takes it from Me, but I lay it down of Myself" (John 10:17-18). Jesus knew that Judas Iscariot would betray him, yet he let him go. Then Jesus went to his accustomed place where Judas was apt to find him. As he was being arrested, he said, "Do you think I cannot call on my Father, and he will at once put at my disposal more than twelve legions of angels? But how then would the Scriptures be fulfilled that say it must happen in this way?" (Matthew 26:53-54 NIV). John's gospel says that when the High Priest's men came to arrest him, Jesus spoke and "they drew back and fell to the ground" (John 18:6). Jesus simply stood there, and let them get up and arrest him. Jesus could have avoided the Crucifixion. I believe he could have stopped it at any time. But he chose not to because of his astonishing love for us.

It is hard for us to imagine the love that could enable Jesus to endure being scourged (flogged with a whip that had sharp things in it to tear the flesh), being nailed to the Cross, and hanging on the Cross in agony for six hours, when he could have stopped it at any time. "While we were still sinners, Christ died for us" (Romans 5:8). Jesus knew what he was doing. He predicted the Crucifixion many times. He said that he came "to give his life a ransom for many" (Matthew 20:28). He did it willingly. It is also hard to imagine the love of God for us men, such that he could send his beloved son on such a mission and could watch as his son suffered so intensely. God's love for us "...surpasses knowledge..." (Ephesians 3:19 NIV). We will never fully understand it or grasp its greatness.

Resurrection

There are some who deny that Jesus was resurrected. However, the Scriptural evidence for his Resurrection is overwhelming.

- Jesus predicted several times that he would be resurrected.
- The Resurrection is described in all four gospels. While there are some differences in the accounts, as one might expect, they all agree that after his Crucifixion he was buried in a stone tomb, that three days later the

tomb was found empty and angelic figures said that Jesus had risen, and that after that Jesus appeared to the disciples and others, and spoke with them. Luke says that he ate food with them. Jesus stayed with the disciples for forty days, teaching them about the kingdom of God (Acts 1:3).

- The preaching of the apostles, recorded in the Book of Acts, places primary reliance on the fact of the Resurrection as establishing who Jesus was. They boldly confronted the Jewish leaders with it. Peter spoke to them of "Jesus Christ of Nazareth, whom you crucified, whom God raised from the dead" (Acts 4:10). (Also see Acts 2:23-24.) The Jewish leaders tried unsuccessfully to stop the disciples from talking about the Resurrection (Acts 4:18-21), but they could not prove that it did not occur.
- The epistles, written over a period of about 15 to 35 years after Jesus' death, refer repeatedly to the Resurrection as a well-established fact.
- The Sanhedrin (Jewish leaders) had strong motives for trying to disprove the Resurrection. They were never able to produce the body of Jesus or to discredit accounts of his Resurrection.

The Resurrection is absolutely central to much of the teaching in the epistles. Paul declared, "And if Christ has not been raised, our preaching is useless and so is your faith" (1 Corinthians 15:14 NIV). (Also see verse 17.) I believe that a fair reading of Paul's epistles demonstrates over and over how central the Resurrection was to his thinking. (See, for example, Romans 6:1-14; 1 Corinthians 15:1-34; 2 Corinthians 1:9; Ephesians 1:19-23; Colossians 2:20-3:3; 2 Timothy 2:8.) Paul wrote that belief in the Resurrection is necessary for salvation. "If you confess with your mouth the Lord Jesus and believe in your heart that God has raised him from the dead, you will be saved" (Romans 10:9). Peter wrote that God "has begotten us again to a living hope through the resurrection of Jesus Christ from the dead" (1 Peter 1:3). (Also see Hebrews 13:20.) The Crucifixion and Resurrection go together; without the Resurrection there is no victory.

I believe it can be said that there are few facts of ancient history that are as well documented as the Resurrection of Jesus Christ.[17]

Ascension

Forty days after his Resurrection, Jesus was physically taken up into heaven while the disciples watched (Acts 1:9). He is not the only one to whom this occurred. Elijah was taken up bodily into heaven while Elisha watched (2 Kings, chapter 2). Apparently Enoch was also taken up into heaven (Genesis 5:24).

I don't understand how either the Resurrection or the Ascension could have occurred. But God's truth is not limited by my inadequate understanding. Scripture says that they happened, and that should be enough.

Living in Heaven

Jesus now lives with God in heaven. He said, "But from now on, the Son of Man will be seated at the right hand of the mighty God" (Luke 22:69 NIV). Stephen "gazed into heaven and saw the glory of God, and Jesus standing at the right hand of God" (Acts 7:55). John had a tremendous vision of Jesus in which Jesus said, "Behold, I am alive forevermore" (Revelation 1:18). Scripture tells us that Jesus always lives to intercede for believers (Hebrews 7:25).

Second Coming

Jesus said that he would come again to earth (Matthew 24:30, 25:31, 26:64). His coming will be very conspicuous. "All the tribes of the earth" will see "the Son of Man [his name for himself] coming on the clouds of heaven with power and great glory," with angels, and with a loud trumpet call (Matthew 24:30-31). It will be like lightning, which lights up the entire sky (Luke 17:24). At his Ascension, the angels said, "This same Jesus, who was taken up from you into heaven, will so come back in like manner as you saw Him go into heaven" (Acts 1:11). Paul wrote, "The Lord himself will descend from heaven with a shout, with the voice of an archangel, and with the trumpet of God" (1 Thessalonians 4:16). (Also see 2 Thessalonians 1:7.)

There are some today who say that Christ has returned and is living on earth, unnoticed. Sun Myung Moon, of the Unification Church, claims to be Jesus Christ returned. There are others who make similar claims. Some say that Christ will not return in the flesh; his return will simply be an increase in his spirit in men. None of these assertions fit the Biblical account. Jesus Christ will return, as an adult, in great glory and in a very conspicuous manner.

Judgment

Jesus said that, when he returns in glory, all nations will be gathered before him and he will judge the people (Matthew 25:31-46). Elsewhere he said that

God had entrusted all judgment to him, and that a time was coming when he would judge all those who are in their graves (John 5:22-30). (He will also judge the living, 2 Timothy 4:1.) At the end of the age, Jesus will send out his angels. They will "...weed out of his kingdom everything that causes sin and all who do evil. They will throw them into the fiery furnace, where there will be weeping and gnashing of teeth. Then the righteous will shine like the sun in the kingdom of their Father..." (Matthew 13:41-43 NIV). (Also see verses 49-50.)

There are many who do not like the idea of judgment, and of eternal punishment for those who do not believe in Jesus Christ. But Scripture speaks of it repeatedly. It is all through the New Testament. If we would believe Scripture, we must accept the fact that we are responsible to God and will be judged. We should be thankful that God has warned us in advance, and has told us what we need to do to obtain eternal life. The Gospel is very good news for those who believe in Jesus Christ—and very bad news for those who refuse to accept Jesus Christ.

There is much more that could be said about Jesus Christ—his love, his compassion, his gentleness and also his wrath. We can spend a lifetime studying his life as recorded in Scripture, and seeking to become like him. These eight points that I have listed in this section are things that we must accept and believe if we would call ourselves followers of Jesus Christ.

CONCLUSION

Our salvation, and our eternal life with God, depend on our faith in Jesus Christ. Hence it is extremely important that we have a clear and accurate concept of who Jesus Christ is. There are many false Christs, and Jesus warns us not to be deceived by them. Belief in a false Christ will not save us. Only the true Christ described and identified in Scripture will do that. When Scripture makes it so clear who Jesus Christ is, we ignore or reject its words at our peril.

7

The Trinity

o o o o o o o o o o o o o o o o o o o o o o o o o o o o o o o o o o o

"May the grace of the Lord Jesus Christ, and the love of God, and the fellowship of the Holy Spirit be with you all."

—*(2 Corinthians 13:14 NIV)*

Scripture indicates that God is both one and three. There are three separate persons. And yet the three are also one. There is only one God. Christianity is monotheistic.

This is puzzling to many people. It is hard to understand and accept. Sometimes, in an effort to explain it or make it understandable, people say things that Scripture does not support. Because it is a stumbling-block to many, I want to deal with it.

It is not surprising that some people find the concept puzzling or difficult. We humans approach any new concept by trying to compare it to something we already know. But God is unique. He cannot be compared to anything we know because he is not like anything we know.

What we need to do is to recognize that we are dealing with something totally unique, and outside of our normal experience, and simply accept whatever Scripture says about the Trinity as true without trying to compare it to, or test it against, anything in our normal experience. We need also to be careful not to go beyond what is written in Scripture, and to recognize that our human logic and experience is inadequate to give us a full comprehension of this mystery.

THE TRINITY IS SCRIPTURAL

Contrary to what is sometimes asserted, the concept of the Trinity is clearly expressed in Scripture. The word "Trinity" is not used, but there are many references in Scripture to the three members of the Trinity, and quite a bit is said about their relationship. The following are some examples. Each of these passages speaks of three persons—the Father, the Son (Jesus), and the Holy Spirit—and treats them as equal in status. This is the basic concept of the Trinity.

- Jesus told his disciples to "make disciples of all nations, baptizing them in the name of the Father and of the Son and of the Holy Spirit" (Matthew 28:19).
- Paul ended his second letter to the people of Corinth, "The grace of the Lord Jesus Christ, and the love of God, and the communion of the Holy Spirit be with you all" (2 Corinthians 13:14).
- Paul also wrote, "There are diversities of gifts, but the same Spirit. There are differences of ministries, but the same Lord. And there are diversities of activities, but it is the same God who works all in all" (1 Corinthians 12:4-6).
- Paul wrote, "through Him [Jesus] we both have access by one Spirit to the Father" (Ephesians 2:18).
- Peter speaks of those "who have been chosen according to the foreknowledge of God the Father, through the sanctifying work of the Spirit, for obedience to Jesus Christ..." (1 Peter 1:2 NIV).

We see this even in the Old Testament. Isaiah 61:1 says, "The Spirit of the Lord GOD is upon me, because the LORD has anointed me to preach good tidings to the poor..." In Luke 4:21, Jesus specifically identified himself with the speaker of this passage. Jesus is the "anointed one" (which is what the words "Messiah" and "Christ" mean). So God (the Father) has anointed Jesus (the Son) and the Holy Spirit is upon him. Similarly in Isaiah 48:16 we read, "And now the Lord GOD and His Spirit have sent Me." The Father and the Spirit sent the Son. All three are present.

The following are some more Scriptural examples in which we see each of the three members of the Trinity clearly present and separate from each other:

THE BAPTISM OF JESUS—At Jesus' baptism, the Son is baptized in the Jordan river; the "Spirit of God" descends on him in the form of a dove; and the voice of the Father from heaven says, "This is my beloved Son, in whom I am well pleased" (Matthew 3:16-17). The Son is in the Jordan River, the Spirit descends from heaven and alights on him, and the Father speaks from heaven. Father, Son and Holy Spirit are all present and all clearly separate. Acts 10:38 is similar; it says that "God anointed Jesus of Nazareth with the Holy Spirit and with power."

JESUS ASKED THE FATHER TO SEND US THE HOLY SPIRIT—In John 14:16-17, Jesus says, "I will pray the Father, and He will give you another Helper, that He may abide with you forever—the Spirit of Truth." The whole context of John chapters 14 to 16 makes it clear that this Helper is the Holy Spirit. The Son will ask the Father to send the Holy Spirit. All three persons are present.

PENTECOST—On the Day of Pentecost, when the Holy Spirit descended in power, Peter said that Jesus "…has received from the Father the promised Holy Spirit and has poured out what you now see and hear" (Acts 2:33 NIV). Again, we see the three members of the Trinity as separate and distinct.

CREATION—We even see all three members of the Trinity at the Creation. "In the beginning God created the heavens and the earth" (Genesis 1:1). But the Son was with the Father at the Creation. "All things were made through Him [Jesus], and without Him nothing was made that was made" (John 1:3). (Also see Colossians 1:16; Hebrews 1:2.) And, at the very beginning, "the Spirit of God was hovering over the face of the waters" (Genesis 1:2). Father, Son and Holy Spirit were all present at the creation. It is significant that the word that Genesis, chapter 1, uses for God, *Elohim,* is in the plural. The Creator is plural. He is both one and three.

In the rest of this chapter, I shall refer to other Scriptures that speak of the three persons of the Trinity and tell us about their nature, characteristics and relationship. Everything in this chapter will demonstrate that the concept of the Trinity is Scriptural.

THE MEMBERS OF THE TRINITY ARE SEPARATE PERSONS

Scripture makes it clear that the three members of the Trinity are separate persons, and that each is God. The three members of the Trinity are not different aspects or facets of God, or different ways of looking at God, or different ways in which God manifests himself. They are always spoken of as three separate persons, each of whom is God. Our minds may find this hard to grasp, but this is what Scripture says. As I have already noted, sometimes we see these three separate persons acting, in total unity, but as separate individuals. The Father speaks from heaven, while the Son is being baptized and the Holy Spirit descends upon him. All three are present and are clearly separate.

The Father

God the Father is a person. (See Chapter 5.)

The Son

Jesus Christ, the Son of God, is also God. (See Chapter 6.)

Jesus is a person who is separate from God the Father. This was obviously so when he was here on earth, but let us look at Scriptures dealing with his position in heaven. Jesus "had come from God and was going to God" (John 13:3). In other words, he was with the Father in heaven; the Father sent him to earth (Jesus often spoke of himself as having been sent); and he returned to heaven. In heaven now he is "at the right hand of God" (Romans 8:34). (Also see Acts 7:55-56; Matthew 26:64; Ephesians 1:20.) In Revelation, chapter 5, he appears as the Lamb who comes to the throne of God, who takes the scroll with the seven seals from the hand of God, and who then is praised and worshiped together with God the Father. In Daniel's vision, Jesus ("One like the Son of Man") approaches the "Ancient of Days" (God) who is seated on a throne (Daniel 7:13-14). He is with the Father but separate from the Father.

The Holy Spirit

The Holy Spirit is a person. He is not just an essence or a quality. Scripture refers to him as "he." He speaks (Acts 13:2, 20:22, 21:10). The Holy Spirit has gifts, and he distributes them as he wishes (1 Corinthians 12:11). "...the Spirit himself intercedes for us with groans that words cannot express" (Romans 8:26 NIV). The Holy Spirit can be grieved (Ephesians 4:30).

The Holy Spirit is God. He is referred to as the Holy Spirit of God (Ephesians 4:30). (Also see Matthew 10:20; Romans 8:14; 1 Corinthians 2:11, 3:16, 6:11; 2 Corinthians 1:22, 3:16.) He is also referred to as the Spirit of Jesus Christ (Philippians 1:19). (Also see Romans 8:9; Acts 16:7; Galatians 4:6.) He comes from God and is sent by God (John 14:16). (Also see Luke 11:13; John 3:34; Acts 2:33, 38; 5:32; Romans 5:5.) We "...worship by the Spirit of God..." (Philippians 3:3 NIV).

In a number of passages, we see an equivalence between the Holy Spirit and the Father or the Son. 2 Timothy 3:16 says that "all Scripture is given by inspiration of God." But 2 Peter 1:21 says that the prophets "spoke as they were moved by the Holy Spirit." (Also see Hebrews 10:15.) Scripture speaks of David as speaking by the Spirit (Matthew 22:43). (Also see Acts 1:16, 4:25.) Men preach the gospel "by the Holy Spirit sent from heaven" (1 Peter 1:12). (Also see 1 Thessalonians 1:5.) Scripture speaks of the "sword of the Spirit, which is the word of God" (Ephesians 6:17). It is the Holy Spirit who "will tell you things to come" (John 16:13). (Also see 1 Timothy 4:1.) So the Scriptures are inspired by God and inspired by the Holy Spirit. Is not this saying that God and the Holy Spirit are equivalent? Is not this saying that the Holy Spirit is God?

We receive eternal life by believing in Jesus Christ (John 3:16). But Scripture also says that the Holy Spirit gives us eternal life. "The one who sows to please his sinful nature, from that nature will reap destruction; the one who sows to please the Spirit, from the Spirit will reap eternal life" (Galatians 6:8 NIV). (Also see Romans 8:4-14.) Jesus said, "unless one is born of water and the Spirit, he cannot enter the kingdom of God" (John 3:5). The Spirit gives life (John 6:63). We are "made alive by the Spirit" (1 Peter 3:18). So the Spirit and Jesus Christ are equivalent. Since Jesus is God, does not this mean that the Holy Spirit is also God? There is no conflict here. There is never a conflict between members of the Trinity. We receive eternal life only by believing in Jesus Christ. But when we believe in Jesus Christ, we can receive the Holy Spirit, whom God gives to those who obey him (Acts 5:32). And it is by sowing to please the Spirit, by living a life controlled by the Spirit, by being born again of the Spirit, that we can appropriate this eternal life.

We are sanctified by God (John 17:17). But Scripture also speaks of the "...sanctifying work of the Spirit..." (2 Thessalonians 2:13 NIV). (Also see 1 Peter 1:2.) It says, "but you were washed, but you were sanctified, but you were justified in the name of the Lord Jesus Christ and by the Spirit of our God" (1 Corinthians 6:11). God "saved us, through the washing of regeneration and renewing of the Holy Spirit" (Titus 3:5).

It is Jesus who has given us access to the Father (Hebrews 4:14-16). He said, "no one comes to the Father except through me" (John 14:6). But the Holy Spirit also plays a part in that access. Scripture says that "through Him [Jesus] we both have access by one Spirit to the Father" (Ephesians 2:18). We are told to "...pray in the Spirit on all occasions..." (Ephesians 6:18 NIV).

Before Pentecost, Jesus told his disciples, "You shall receive power [*dunamis*] when the Holy Spirit has come upon you" (Acts 1:8). In Ephesians, Paul talks about the power (*dunamis*) of God which works in us (Ephesians 1:19, 3:20, 6:10). I believe this is the same power. The Holy Spirit has given to believers the power of God.

When Ananias and Sapphira lied, Peter said, "why has Satan filled your heart to lie to the Holy Spirit" and "you have not lied to men but to God" (Acts 5:3, 4). Lying to the Holy Spirit is considered the same as lying to God. Indeed, Jesus made the remarkable statement that the one sin that could never be forgiven was the blasphemy of the Holy Spirit (Matthew 12:32).

Hebrews 10:29 (NIV) says, "How much more severely do you think a man deserves to be punished who has trampled the Son of God under foot, who has treated as an unholy thing the blood of the covenant that sanctified him, and who has insulted the Spirit of grace?" Trampling the Son under foot and insulting the Holy Spirit are treated as parallel and equal in severity.

Is it not clear that the Father, the Son and the Holy Spirit are each God?

THE MEMBERS OF THE TRINITY ARE ONE

Our Faith Is Monotheistic

One of the striking features of the Judeo-Christian faith is its radical monotheism. Historically this has stood out in sharp contrast to the polytheism of many Near Eastern religions, and the polytheism of Greece, Rome and the Norse religion. Today it stands out in sharp contrast to the polytheism of Hinduism, of the pagan religious revival, and of the many animist religions. And the fact that our God is a personal God stands out in sharp contrast to the pantheism of the New Age movement.

Deuteronomy 6:4 declares, "Hear, O Israel, the LORD our God, the LORD is one!" This became a prayer, which was and is recited daily by practicing Jews. Jesus repeated these words in Mark 12:29.

Throughout Scripture we find a reiteration of this concept that God is one. Moses told the people of Israel, "Know this day, and consider it in your heart that the LORD Himself is God in heaven above and on the earth beneath; there is no other" (Deuteronomy 4:39). David declared, "O LORD, there is none like You, nor is there any God besides You" (1 Chronicles 17:20). Solomon declared that "the LORD is God; there is no other" (1 Kings 8:60). God declared through Isaiah, "I am the LORD and there is no other; there is no God besides Me" (Isaiah 45:5). (Also see Isaiah 45:21, 46:9.) Jesus declared that God the Father is "the only true God" (John 17:3). Paul said, "God is one" (Galatians 3:20). There is "one God and Father of all, who is above all and through all and in you all" (Ephesians 4:6).

How can we reconcile these statements that there is only one God with the statements that Father, Son and Holy Spirit are separate persons and each of them is God? Apparently Jesus saw no inconsistency between them. Nor did Paul. The answer that Scripture gives is that the members of the Trinity are three and yet they are also one. If that is what Scripture says, then we should accept it, even though it does not fit our logic or our earthly conceptions. God is God, and our understanding of who and what he is should be based solely on what he has revealed in Scripture. If what Scripture says about him does not fit our preconceptions, then we need to realign our thinking with Scripture.

Jesus declared that the first and greatest commandment was "Love the Lord your God with all your heart, with all your soul, with all your mind, and with all your strength" (Mark 12:30). In a polytheism, men cannot love (or serve, or worship, or fear) one "god" with "all" their heart, soul, mind and strength, because their devotion to one "god" takes away from, or conflicts with, their devotion to another "god." But with the Trinity, there is no such conflict. To love the Father is to love the Son and the Holy Spirit. To worship the Father is to worship the Son and the Holy Spirit. We see this in Revelation, chapter 5, where both the Father and the Son (the Lamb) are worshiped together with no sense of conflict or of one detracting from the other. "Blessing and honor and glory and power be to Him who sits on the throne, and to the Lamb, forever and ever" (Revelation 5:13). There is no conflict because when we praise the Son, we are praising the Father, and when we praise the Father, we are praising the Son. We see this expressed in John 5:23, "that all should honor the Son just as they honor the Father. He who does not honor the Son does not honor the Father who sent Him." 1 John 2:23 tells us, "Whoever denies the Son does not have the Father either; he who acknowledges the Son has the Father also."

In the polytheisms with which we are somewhat familiar, such as the Greek, Roman and Norse polytheisms, we see different "gods" working at cross-purposes with each other, opposing each other, playing tricks on each other. There is nothing remotely like that in the Trinity. Scripture gives us a historical record going back some 6,000 years. During all that time, there is no record of any conflict or disagreement among the members of the Trinity. We cannot conceive of such unity. We humans have never experienced anything like it. We have never heard of individuals who are so united that they never disagree, never quarrel, never feel angry or resentful towards each other, never work at cross purposes, never even entertain thoughts that disagree. But with God all things are possible.

To know the Son is to know the Father. Jesus said, "This is eternal life, that they may know You, the only true God, and Jesus Christ whom You have sent" (John 17:3). "If you had known Me, you would have known My Father also" (John 8:19). (Also see John 14:7.)

We find this unity expressed in various ways. Jesus said, "I and My Father are one" (John 10:30). While on earth, he did only what he saw the Father doing, and spoke only the words that the Father gave him (John 5:19, 8:28, 12:49-50, 15:15). He said, "I do not seek My own will but the will of the Father who sent Me" (John 5:30). "I always do those things that please Him" (John 8:29). Again, Jesus said of the Holy Spirit, "He will guide you into all truth; for He will not speak on His own authority, but whatever He hears He will speak; and He will tell you of things to come. He will glorify Me, for He will take of what is Mine and declare it to you. All things that the Father has are Mine. Therefore I said that He will take of Mine and declare it to you" (John 16:13-15).

Although God is three persons, God is also one.

A Common Misconception

Scripture says that Jesus Christ forever makes intercession for us (Hebrews 7:25; Romans 8:34). (It also says that the Holy Spirit intercedes for us. Romans 8:27.) Some picture this as a loving and merciful Jesus pleading with a harsh Father for mercy for us humans. Such a concept is contrary to the character of God and contrary to the concept of unity expressed in Scripture. Consider the following:

JESUS WILL JUDGE US—It is Jesus who will judge all men. The Father "has committed all judgment to the Son" (John 5:22). (Also see Matthew 25:31-46, 13:40-43, 7:23.)

JESUS AND THE FATHER ARE BOTH LOVING AND JUST—There is no difference in character between Jesus and God. Jesus is loving, but so is God. God is love (1 John 4:16). God did an extraordinary act of love in sending his Son to die on the Cross (John 3:16). God "desires all men to be saved" (1 Timothy 2:4). (Also see 2 Peter 3:9.) On the other hand, Jesus is holy and just, and capable of great wrath (2 Thessalonians 1:7-10; Revelation 6:16-17).

THE FATHER WANTS ALL PEOPLE TO BE SAVED—There is no need to beg the Father for salvation for men. The work of salvation was done on the

Cross. Those who believe in Jesus are already saved. Jesus has already paid the price. The righteousness that comes from faith in Jesus (Romans 3:21-26) has already been imputed to those who believe in Jesus. God wants all men to be saved. The problem lies with man, not with God. It is man's unwillingness to believe in and accept Jesus that prevents him from being saved.[18]

JESUS TAUGHT US TO PRAY FOR THE FATHER'S WILL TO BE DONE—Jesus taught us to pray, "[God's] will be done, on earth as it is in heaven" (Matthew 6:10). He prayed, "not as I will, but as You will" (Matthew 26:39). He always sought to do his Father's will. There is no record anywhere of his pleading with the Father to manipulate his Father's actions or decisions. In John, chapter 17, Jesus gave us a model of an intercessory prayer. In that great prayer there is no hint of pleading or imploring for mercy. He prays that God will protect and sanctify the disciples and give them joy, and he prays for unity among all believers. He prays, not to change the Father's will, but to reinforce what is already the Father's will for us.

I believe that when Jesus is making intercession for us—that is, for those who believe in him—he is praying that God's will be done in our lives. He is praying that we will fulfill the purpose God has for us, that we will be sanctified and grow into spiritual maturity, that we will be transformed by the renewing of our minds, that we will have the strength to overcome strongholds and obstacles, that we will not turn away or fall away from God, and the like. In other words, by his intercession, he is adding his mighty strength to our feeble strength to enable us to become the people God wants us to be. It is by his intercession that Jesus is imparting to us God's "...incomparably great power for us who believe..." (Ephesians 1:19 NIV). He is praying to reinforce what is already God's will for us.

Further Illustrations of Unity

There are passages in which some might find inconsistency as to which member of the Trinity is operating. I believe there is no inconsistency, and that what these passages are saying is that God is at work, and it really does not matter whether we speak of him as the Father, the Son, the Holy Spirit, or all three.

For example, God the Father is in us (1 John 4:12-16). Christ is also in us (Colossians 1:27; Galatians 2:20; John 15:4 KJV). And the Holy Spirit is in us (John 14:16-17; 1 Corinthians 3:16, 6:19). We can say, as some Scriptures do, that it is by the Holy Spirit that both the Father and the Son live in us (1 John 3:24, 4:13; Ephesians 2:18, 22), and I believe this is true. But a simpler way of looking at it is to say that God is in us, and it does not really matter whether we see him as the Father, the Son, the Holy Spirit, or all three, because all three are God. The point is that God is in us.

In the same way, we speak of God's power in us (Ephesians 1:19). (Also see Ephesians 3:20, 6:10.) But Jesus Christ is also the source of our power, for he said, "without Me you can do nothing" (John 15:5). And Acts 1:8 says, "you shall receive power when the Holy Spirit has come upon you." Again I suggest that it does not really matter whether we think of the power as coming from the Father, the Son, or the Holy Spirit. It is all God's power.

The Father's word is truth (John 17:17). Jesus is the truth (John 14:6). The Holy Spirit is the Spirit of truth (John 14:16). (Also see 1 John 5:6.) Father, Son and Holy Spirit are all the truth.

Some Christians disagree as to whether we should pray to the Father or to the Son. I believe a proper understanding of the Trinity indicates that we pray to God, and whether we address our prayers specifically to the Father, the Son, or the Holy Spirit makes little difference. They are all prayers to God.

CONCLUSION

What Scripture says about the Trinity is quite clear. God is three. He is also one. There are three separate persons. Yet they are one God. We cannot expect fully to understand this mystery, nor do we have anything in our experience with which we can compare it. All we can do is to accept and believe what Scripture so clearly tells us.

8

Good and Evil

o o o o o o o o o o o o o o o o o o o o o o o o o o o o o o

"Woe to those who call evil good, and good evil; who put darkness for light, and light for darkness; who put bitter for sweet, and sweet for bitter!"

—(Isaiah 5:20)

Today's educational system teaches moral relativity. Many of our public school children and college students are taught that there are no enduring moral standards, that there is no such thing as good and evil, and that it is wrong to make any judgment that something is good or evil. In our criminal system, inability to tell good from evil is considered a sign of criminal insanity. Are we deliberately training our young people to be unable to tell good from evil, and thus to be criminally insane?

Scripture emphatically rejects the idea that good and evil are relative, or that they do not exist. In what follows I have, as usual, quoted or referred to quite a lot of Scripture, even though it is only a small sample of what is in the Bible. I ask that you read these and other Scriptures, think about them, pray about them, and ask the Holy Spirit to show you what they mean and how you need to apply them in your life. This is one issue that we must understand. We must always be willing to defend God's truth. We must never let God's truth be watered down by facile euphemisms, double talk, or Orwellian "newspeak." Scripture compares God's word to gold refined in the fire. (See Psalm 19:10.) Let us not adulterate the truth of God's word by twisting it or ignoring it.

My wife's poem expresses this well.

NIGHT vs. DAY

Truth and Beauty
like deep wells
slake the thirsty
seeking light.

◆ ◆ ◆

But Truth distorted,
twisted in complexity,
pollutes already itching ears
generating Blight.

Truth polluted,
contagious in its plight,
generates false energy
causing Death and Night.

◆ ◆ ◆

Holy Fear,
springing from God's source of Love
unlocks Discernment,
separating Dark from Light.

Clarity and simplicity,
distilled in depth of thought,
carry truth unhindered
marking Day from Night.

Burdens carried steadily
on the Shepherd's shoulders,
rest the weary spirit
freeing Life, and human might.

Music,
flowing from the Heart,
lifts up pulsing Truth,
soaring in its flight.

BIBLICAL MORALITY

Scripture is full of words like "good," "evil," "sin," "righteous," "unrighteous," "wicked." Many, today, reject such concepts. They use a variety of arguments, but basically I think it comes down to one thing. They do not want to be held accountable by a higher authority. I would assert that to reject the concept of good and evil is to reject the Bible and to reject God.

There is so much said about this in Scripture that I cannot begin to do justice to it. I can only give some highlights. Good and evil are foundational concepts of Scripture.

Two Spiritual Forces

A common New Age concept is that everything is one. Scripture rejects this. It tells us, very clearly, that there are two spiritual forces operating in the world. There is God, who is good (Matthew 19:17). "God is light and in Him there is no darkness at all" (1 John 1:5). And there is the devil, or satan, who is evil. Scripture calls him the evil one (Matthew 6:13) and the enemy (Luke 10:19). It says that he comes to "steal, and to kill, and to destroy" (John 10:10). (Also see John 8:44.) The devil, or satan, is the spirit behind the evil that men do. One reason Jesus came to earth in human form was "that He might destroy the works of the devil" (1 John 3:8). (Also see Hebrews 2:14.)

These forces are not equal. God is Creator and satan is a created being. Jesus is far above every spiritual force of wickedness. But satan does have considerable power to deceive us and lead us astray, if we are not careful.

The conflict between God and satan is so intense that the Bible refers to it as being a "war in heaven" with satan and his angels fighting against God and his angels (Revelation 12:7-9). Because we belong to God, satan is also at war against us. (See Chapter 12 of this book.) He is a fierce enemy who "deceives the whole world" (Revelation 12:9), he is a liar and a murderer (John 8:44), and his goal is to destroy us in any way that he can (John 10:10).

When I was in a New Age organization, I noticed a strong tendency, which I think is typical of much of the New Age movement, to consider that everything "spiritual" is good. This is not what the Bible says. There are "spiritual hosts of wickedness in the heavenly places" (Ephesians 6:12). There is a "...spirit who is now at work in those who are disobedient" (Ephesians 2:2 NIV), a "spirit of the Antichrist" (1 John 4:3). There are evil spirits, and Jesus and his disciples cast them out of people. John tells us, "do not believe every spirit, but test the spirits, whether they are of God" (1 John 4:1).

Scripture tells us that there are two kingdoms in this world, a kingdom of darkness, and the kingdom of Jesus Christ (Colossians 1:13). (Also see 1 Peter 2:9.) It tells us that there are two kinds of people, "children of God" and "children of the devil" (1 John 3:10).

Do Not Tolerate Evil

In today's world, it would seem that, for many, the greatest virtue is "tolerance." We are told to tolerate everything and condemn nothing. This is not God's way. God never tolerates evil or falsehood. "Your eyes are too pure to look on evil; you cannot tolerate wrong" (Habakkuk 1:13 NIV). God says, "...Take your evil deeds out of my sight..." (Isaiah 1:16 NIV). God's wrath comes on those who persist in doing evil, and his wrath is terrible.

Many, today, do not like to think of God's wrath. But it is in Scripture, over and over, and we have to deal with it. Following are a few examples. "Doing wickedly in the sight of the LORD, to provoke Him to anger" (Deuteronomy 9:18). "The LORD was very angry with Israel, and removed them from His sight" (2 Kings 17:18). "Your iniquities have separated you from your God" (Isaiah 59:2). "The wrath of God is being revealed from heaven against all the godlessness and wickedness of men who suppress the truth by their wickedness" (Romans 1:18 NIV). Paul listed various evil deeds and said, "...because of such things God's wrath comes on those who are disobedient" (Ephesians 5:6 NIV). (Also see Colossians 3:6.)

Jesus did not tolerate evil. He "...gave himself for us to redeem us from all wickedness..." (Titus 2:14 NIV). He denounced the religious leaders of his time as hypocrites and children of the devil (Matthew, chapter 23; John 8:48). When a woman who had committed adultery was brought before him, he said that he did not condemn her, but then he said, "Go and sin no more" (John 8:11). "He [Jesus] will punish those who do not know God and do not obey the gospel of our Lord Christ. They will be punished with everlasting destruction..." (2 Thessalonians 1:8-9 NIV). Scripture tells us of the "wrath of the Lamb [Jesus]" and asks who can stand against it (Revelation 6:16-17).

Scripture tells us, over and over, to love good and hate evil. "Hate evil, love good" (Amos 5:15). "Abhor what is evil. Cling to what is good" (Romans 12:9). "Turn away from evil and do good" (1 Peter 3:11, quoting Psalm 34:14). "Cease to do evil, Learn to do good" (Isaiah 1:16-17). "You who love the LORD, hate evil" (Psalm 97:10). "The fear of the LORD is to hate evil" (Proverbs 8:13). We should be "...eager to do what is good" (Titus 2:14 NIV). "Blessed is the man who walks not in the counsel of the ungodly, nor stands in the path of sinners, nor sits in the seat of the scornful...For the LORD knows the way of the righteous, but the way of the ungodly shall perish" (Psalm 1:1, 6).

Hate? We should hate? That is totally contrary to today's exaltation of "tolerance" as the greatest virtue. But it is Scriptural. God hates evil and he expects us to hate evil. We need to hate it, we need to feel strongly about it, in order to be willing to make the effort to get it out of our lives. God is never tolerant of evil and we should not be. We can love people even though they do evil things, but we must hate the evil. We can hate the sin and love the sinner.

Scripture tells us to avoid every kind of evil. "...I will have nothing to do with evil" (Psalm 101:4 NIV). "...because I consider all your precepts right, I hate every wrong path" (Psalm 119:128 NIV). "Fear the LORD and depart from evil" (Proverbs 3:7). "Do not enter the path of the wicked, and do not walk in the way of evil." (Proverbs 4:14). "Turn from your evil ways" (2 Kings 17:13). "...Turn now, each of you, from your evil ways and your evil practices..." (Jeremiah 25:5 NIV).

Mature Christians are those "...who by constant use have trained themselves to distinguish good from evil" (Hebrews 5:14 NIV). "Test all things; hold fast what is good. Abstain from every form of evil" (1 Thessalonians 5:21-22). "...be wise about what is good, and innocent about what is evil" (Romans 16:19 NIV). Believers should "...learn to devote themselves to doing what is good" (Titus 3:14 NIV). "...train yourself to be godly" (1 Timothy 4:7 NIV).

We must be very careful never to confuse the two. "Woe to those who call evil good, and good evil; who put darkness for light, and light for darkness" (Isaiah 5:20).

What We Sow, We Shall Reap

There is a spiritual principle of sowing and reaping. What we sow, we shall reap. If we sow good, we shall reap good; if we sow evil, we shall reap evil. "Say to the righteous that it shall be well with them, for they shall eat the fruit of their doings. Woe to the wicked! It shall be ill with him, for the reward of his hands shall be given him" (Isaiah 3:10-11). (Also see Psalm 1; Jeremiah 17:5-8.) "Do not be deceived: God cannot be mocked. A man reaps what he sows. The one who sows to please his sinful nature, from that nature will reap destruction; the one who sows to please the [Holy] Spirit, from the Spirit will reap eternal life" (Galatians 6:7-8 NIV). "For if you live according to the sinful nature, you will die, but if by the [Holy] Spirit you put to death the misdeeds of the body, you will live." (Romans 8:13 NIV). "Seek good and not evil, that you may live" (Amos 5:14).

We see this expressed very clearly in Deuteronomy, chapter 28, where God spelled out for his people, in great detail, the blessings that would follow if they obeyed him, and the terrible curses that would follow if they turned away from him and disobeyed him. Then in Deuteronomy 30:19 he said, "I call heaven and earth to record this day against you, that I have set before you life and death, blessing and cursing; therefore choose life that both you and your descendants may live." This same theme is repeated often in Scripture.

What Is Evil?

How does Scripture define good and evil? Much could be written about this. My sense is that the essence of it comes down to something pretty simple. Good is to accept God, to serve him, to obey his words and his commands, and to seek to please him. Evil is to reject God and to disobey him. Beyond that, we need to keep studying what Scripture says, and keep checking against Scripture everything that we are doing and saying and thinking. Our test, for all that we think and say and do, and for all that we are tempted by, is the test of Scripture. How does this match up with what God has told us? If it matches Scripture, we can feel safe with it. If it does not match Scripture, we had better reject it. What I am speaking of is not just a mechanical match against a "proof text." We need to match things against the whole counsel of Scripture, as best we understand it.

Another way to gauge good and evil is to ask ourselves some questions that help us see things from a different perspective. For example: "How would I feel if Jesus Christ walked into the room while I was doing this?" "Would I be uncomfortable or embarrassed if Jesus was sitting next to me while I was watching this movie?" "How would I feel if somebody videotaped what I am doing right now, and showed the video to the people I love?" "Would Jesus want to look at this website?" "Would I want my daughter to behave like the people I am watching on this TV show?"

CONCLUSION

One of the themes of this book is growth to spiritual maturity. We need to become mature Christians who can stand on our own feet and who can support and strengthen others. Scripture tells us that one of the marks of a mature Christian is that he has trained himself, by constant repetition, to distinguish evil from good (Hebrews 5:14). I believe that this is a very important passage. It means that good and evil exist and can be distinguished from each other. It means that we can and must train ourselves to distinguish between them. It means that we train ourselves by constant use, by doing it again and again. Another Scripture tells us how to do this: "Test everything. Hold on to the good. Avoid every kind of evil" (1 Thessalonians 5:21-22 NIV). Everything we do and think needs to be tested by Scripture. If it conforms to Scriptural teaching, if Scripture says it is good, we hold on to it. We keep doing it. If it does not conform to what Scripture says, we reject it, we stop doing it. If we have done it, we repent of it and renounce it. It is by this constant process of testing, and adjusting our thinking and actions accordingly, that we learn how to distinguish good from evil. As we keep doing this, we become more and more sensitive to the presence of evil.

The modern gospel of moral relativism is totally false. It is evil, and it leads people to tolerate evil and to do evil. It is the kind of thing that Paul was speaking of when he wrote, "See to it that no one takes you captive through hollow and deceptive philosophy, which depends on human tradition and the basic principles of this world rather than on Christ" (Colossians 2:8 NIV). Again, Paul warns us that we need to become mature in our faith so that "we should no longer be infants, tossed to and fro and carried about with every wind of doctrine, by the trickery of men, in the cunning craftiness of deceitful plotting, but, speaking the truth in love, may grow up in all things into Him who is the head—Christ" (Ephesians 4:14-15).

The stakes are very great. To follow good leads to joy and satisfaction in this life, and to eternal life with God. To follow evil leads to misery in this life, and to eternal torment. We need to know which we are doing.

9

Man's Relationship to God

o o o o o o o o o o o o o o o o o o o o o o o o o o o o o o

"What is man that You are mindful of him?"

—*(Psalm 8:4)*

Many people (especially college students) spend years trying to "find themselves." The best way to find out who we are is to see what the Bible has to say about us, and then live by Biblical principles. In this chapter I shall very briefly summarize a few basics. The rest of this book deals with other aspects of our relationship with God.

MAN IS A CREATED BEING

Man is a created being; God is the Creator (Genesis 1:27). This basic fact has many consequences.

WE ARE NOT EQUAL TO GOD—We should never think of ourselves as equal to God. This was the reason for satan's fall; satan said, "I will be like the Most High" (Isaiah 14:14). (Also see Ezekiel 28:13-19.) Satan tempted Adam and Eve by saying that if they ate of the forbidden fruit, they would be like God (Genesis 3:5).

WE BELONG TO GOD—Everything that lives on earth belongs to God (Palm 33:11). "We are His people and the sheep of His pasture" (Psalm 100:3).

WE TRUST IN GOD AND NOT OURSELVES—"Trust in the LORD with all your heart, and lean not on your own understanding" (Proverbs 3:5). Our understanding is always incomplete, and often false. "Cursed is the man who trusts in man and makes flesh his strength, whose heart departs from the LORD" (Jeremiah 17:5).

WE SHOULD NOT TALK BACK TO GOD—"Woe to him who quarrels with his Maker..." (Isaiah 45:9 NIV). "...Concerning things to come, do you question me about my children, or give me orders about the work of my hands" (Isaiah 45:11 NIV). God said to Job, "Would you condemn Me that you may be justified?" (Job 40:8).

We should also not try to edit or rewrite God's Scripture. Some modern theologians have attempted this. They have said that modern man cannot accept miracles or other supernatural events. Therefore, in order to make the Bible acceptable to modern man, they would "demythologize" the Bible by removing from it all references to miracles and the supernatural. In effect, they are saying to the Holy Spirit of God, "You made a serious mistake when you inspired the words of the Bible. Fortunately we are here to correct the mistake you made." This is a form of presumption that men should not indulge in.

GOD'S STRENGTH—When our strength is inadequate, God provides his strength to enable us to do what we need to do. (See Chapter 11.)

JESUS CHRIST HAS REDEEMED US FROM OUR SINS

Originally God created man in God's own image. But when Adam and Eve made the wrong choice in the Garden of Eden, evil came into the world. As the result, all men are afflicted with the rebellious condition of Adam and Eve. "All have sinned and fall short of the glory of God" (Romans 3:23). Our sins separate us from God (Isaiah 59:2; Colossians 1:21).

So God, in an extraordinary act of love, sent Jesus Christ to earth to die for us and redeem us from our sins. (See Chapter 6.) Only Jesus, the sinless Son of God, could have accomplished this. The result is that those who believe in Jesus Christ are saved. We are justified—made right—not by our own righteousness, but by the righteousness of Jesus. Our sins are forgiven and our relationship with God is restored. "Once you were alienated from God and were enemies in your minds because of your evil behavior. But now he has reconciled you by Christ's physical body through death to present you holy in his sight, without blemish and free from accusation—if you continue in your faith, established and firm, not moved from the hope held out in the gospel…" (Colossians 1:21-22 NIV). (Also see Romans 5:15-19.)

Those who believe in Jesus are saved by grace. It is an undeserved gift of God (Ephesians 2:8-9). As a result, our sins are forgiven, the power of sin over our lives is broken, and we receive eternal life with God. We also receive an abundant life on earth, and we can overcome any difficulties. (See Chapter 11.)

There is much more that could be said about our salvation, but I think this is enough for now. Let me close this section with a poem by my wife, which communicates in a different way what I have been trying to say.

SALVATION

Since the days
when Adam was walking with God
in the cool of the evening;

since the angels erected a fiery wall
with Adam cast out for his sin,

no man has been perfect without and within,
excepting for Christ.

(Cain, son of Adam,
erupted in murder.
Sin has been hounding us all.)

> *Do not fret; do not weep;*
> *do not mourn hobbled childhood:*
>
> *Let your Father be God,*
> *his children your Family.*
>
> *Christ gave us the Way:*
> *Acknowledge his Lordship:*

Be redeemed
from the Fall!

GOD WANTS A CLOSE RELATIONSHIP WITH US

One of the extraordinary aspects of Christianity is that God seeks us. In most religions, men are seen as seeking their god. But the one true God seeks us. "We love because he first loved us" (1 John 4:19 NIV). He sent his only Son to give us salvation. "This is love: not that we loved God, but that he loved us and sent his Son as an atoning sacrifice for our sins" (1 John 4: 10 NIV). "Yet the LORD longs to be gracious to you; he rises to show you compassion..." (Isaiah 30:18 NIV). This sense of God longing for us, yearning for us, is all through Scripture. (See, for example Luke 15:7, 10, 20; Matthew 9:13, 23:37.)

OUR ETERNAL LIFE

Although our physical body dies, our spirit exists into eternity. Those who believe in and follow Jesus will live in heaven with God. Those who do not believe will suffer in hell, separated from God forever.

Heaven and hell are very real places. Scripture does not tell us a great deal about either, but some things seem reasonably clear.

Hell is a place of eternal torment. It is a place of "everlasting punishment" (Matthew 25:46). It is better to lose an arm, a leg or an eye than to "go to hell, into the fire that shall never be quenched" (Mark 9:43). Jesus speaks of it as "a furnace of fire" (Matthew 13:42). He gives us a vivid picture of a man being continually tormented by fire in hell (Luke 16:23-31). I think the pain will be unimaginably great. It never ends. There is no relief from it.

Heaven is a place of amazing glory, magnificence, praise and worship. (See Revelation, chapter 4.) Some speak of eternal rest, or picture us as sitting on clouds playing the harp. My sense is that we will probably be very active. God is constantly working. The angels are in heaven, and the picture we get of them from Scripture is that they are quite busy. We are told that some of us will rule on earth with Christ for 1,000 years (Revelation 20:4, 6). I rather expect that those people will be quite busy preparing for this task. So I picture life in heaven as one of activity, but an activity that is perfectly in tune with the will of God.

I see the life of believers here on earth as preparation for this life in heaven. The more we mature in Christ, the closer a relationship we develop with God, the more equipped we will be when we enter heaven. Jesus tells us, "Lay up for yourselves treasures in heaven" (Matthew 6:20). The greatest treasure we can lay up is a character that is in accord with God's will.

There seem to be different levels of reward in heaven, depending on how a believer conducted himself on earth. Those who built a lasting work will receive a reward; those whose work did not last will suffer loss but will still be saved (1 Corinthians 3:12-15). Jesus speaks of those who will receive a great reward in heaven (Matthew 5:12). (Also see verse 19.) He says that "in My Father's house are many mansions" (John 14:2), which seems to imply that different people will be treated differently. "The Lord will give to everyone according to what his life and work show forth. Surely it is a challenge to all of us to live every day as servants of the Lord, and to be as ready as possible when he returns."[19]

PART IV

GROWING TO CHRISTIAN MATURITY

10

The Importance of Maturity

o o o o o o o o o o o o o o o o o o o o o o o o o o o o o o

"...so that the body of Christ may be built up until we all reach unity in the faith and in the knowledge of the Son of God and become mature, attaining to the whole measure of the fullness of Christ."

—*(Ephesians 4:12-13 NIV)*

When we accept Jesus Christ as Lord and Savior, we begin a life-long process of growth and change.

Some Christians don't see it that way, or don't act as if they see it that way. Perhaps some may view their salvation simply as a ticket to heaven, or an insurance policy against hell. Some may see church, and Christian fellowship, as a pleasant social club, or a tradition that they enjoy holding on to. Some want to fit in as much as they can to a world that is increasingly becoming non-Christian. Some have found an easy, comfortable level in their Christian life and don't want to move out of their comfort zone.

But Scripture makes it clear that growth and change are a major part of the Christian life. I shall develop this in some detail, because it is so essential to understand it.

Paul's epistle to the Romans is the most comprehensive and systematic exposition he wrote of his basic teaching to believers. Near the end, as he usually does, he turns to practical principles of Christian living. One of the first things he says is, "Do not be conformed to this world, but be transformed by the renewing of your mind" (Romans 12:2). I believe this transformation is an absolutely essential part of Christian life. Its purpose is nothing less than to have us become like God in character! (I discuss this in chapter 14.)

As someone has put it, "God loves us as we are, but he also loves us too much to let us stay the way we are."

This process of change is also a process of growth. We see this powerfully expressed in many passages of Scripture. I quote at some length, in order to give the full flavor of what they are saying. I ask you to consider each word and phrase thoughtfully and prayerfully. In Ephesians, Paul wrote,

> "It was he [Christ] who gave some to be apostles, some to be prophets, some to be evangelists, and some to be pastors and teachers, to **prepare God's people for works of service**, so that the body of Christ may be **built up** until we all reach unity in the faith and in the knowledge of the Son of God and **become mature, attaining to the whole measure of the fullness of Christ**. Then we **will no longer be infants**, tossed back and forth by the waves, and blown here and there by every wind of teaching and by the cunning and craftiness of men in their deceitful scheming. Instead, speaking the truth in love, we will in all things **grow up** into him who is the Head, that is, Christ. From him the whole body, joined and held together by every supporting ligament, **grows and builds itself up** in love, **as each part does its work**" (Ephesians 4:11-16 NIV).

Much could be said about this remarkable passage, but for now I simply want to emphasize that it says, over and over, that we believers in Christ need to grow. We must be built up, become mature, cease being spiritual infants, and grow up.

Peter writes this,

> "His [God's] divine power has given us everything we need for life and godliness through our knowledge of him who called us by his own glory and goodness. Through these he has given us his very great and precious promises, so that through them you may participate in the divine nature and escape the corruption in the world caused by evil desires.
>
> "For this very reason, **make every effort to add** to your faith goodness; and to goodness, knowledge; and to knowledge, self-control; and to self-control, perseverance; and to perseverance, godliness; and to godliness, brotherly kindness; and to brotherly kindness, love. For if you possess these qualities **in increasing measure, they will keep you from being ineffective and unproductive** in your knowledge of our Lord Jesus Christ. But if anyone does not have them, he is nearsighted and blind, and has forgotten that he has been cleansed from his past sins. Therefore, my brothers, **be all the more eager** to make your calling and election sure. For if you do these

things, you will never fall, and you will receive a rich welcome into the eternal kingdom of our Lord and Savior Jesus Christ" (2 Peter 1:3-11 NIV).

This is one of my favorite passages in Scripture. I keep finding new things in it. For the present, I would simply emphasize two things.

- Peter, writing to believers, tells us to make every effort to add a number of qualities to our faith. He tells us to possess these qualities in increasing measure, and to be eager to do so. He is telling us to grow. If we will think about each of the qualities he mentions, it is obvious that a lifetime is not sufficient to grow in them as much as we would want to. He is setting quite a challenge before us!
- Peter says that God has given us all we need. Then he says that, **for this reason**, we should make every effort. The gifts that God gives us are not for us just to sit back and enjoy. They are for us to appropriate, to make our own and to apply and use. The more we receive, the more is expected of us (Luke 12:48). It is **because** God has equipped us so completely that we need to make every effort to grow and mature.

James writes, "Consider it pure joy, my brothers, when you encounter trials of many kinds, because you know that the testing of your faith develops perseverance. Perseverance must finish its work so that you may **be mature and complete, not lacking anything**" (James 1:3-4 NIV).

Again we see the call to become mature and complete. But James adds some new thoughts. (1) Very often it is trials, difficulties, testings, and suffering that mature us. The maturing process can be painful and difficult. (I discuss this more fully in Chapter 19.) Maturing is seldom easy. (2) Maturing involves a testing of our faith. (3) Maturing typically requires perseverance. Perseverance—hanging in there in the face of difficulties, keeping going when things seems impossible—is an essential quality that we Christians need. In today's "fast food," "quick fix" society, it is not easy to persevere, but it is necessary. To stand firm to the end when others are turning away means to persevere.

Paul says, "...stand firm in all the will of God, mature and fully assured..." (Colossians 4:12 NIV). It requires maturity to be able to stand firm.

The author of Hebrews gives us another perspective about growth:

> "Endure hardship as discipline; God is treating you as sons. For what son is not disciplined by his father? If you are not disciplined (and everyone undergoes discipline), then you are illegitimate children and not true sons...Our fathers disciplined us for a little while as they thought best; but **God disci-**

> **plines us for our good**, that we may share in his holiness. No discipline seems pleasant at the time, but painful. Later on, however, it **produces a harvest of righteousness and peace for those who have been trained by it. Therefore, strengthen your feeble arms and weak knees.** 'Make level paths for your feet,' so that the lame may not be disabled, but rather healed" (Hebrews 12:7-8, 10-13 NIV).

We tend, today, to think of "discipline" as punishment. It can have that meaning. However, according to Strong's *Dictionary of the Greek Bible*, the Greek word translated "discipline" in this passage has as its root a word meaning education or training, and it is sometimes translated "instruction, nurture." Today, one of the accepted meanings of the word is to train or develop by instruction and exercise.

Other Scriptures also talk about our need for training. We train ourselves to tell good from evil (Hebrews 5:14). We train ourselves to be godly (1 Timothy 4:7). (Also see 2 Timothy 2:15.) We train ourselves to be righteous (2 Timothy 3:16).

Maturity is necessary to enable us to understand the full message of Scripture. Scripture expresses this in the image of food. Elementary teaching is described as milk; more advanced teaching as solid food. The spiritually immature can only handle milk. The spiritually mature are able to receive the solid food of Scripture (Hebrews 5:12-14; 1 Corinthians 3:1-2).

Other Scriptures mention some specific areas in which we need to grow. Paul prayed that our **love** would "abound still more and more in knowledge and all discernment" (Philippians 1:9), that we would be able to understand and "know the love of Christ which passes [surpasses] knowledge" (Ephesians 3:19), and that our love for each other would increase and overflow (1 Thessalonians 3:12, 4:10). He prayed that we would grow in the **knowledge of God** and be strengthened with all power (Colossians 1:10-11). Peter urged us to "grow in the grace and knowledge of our Lord and Savior Jesus Christ" (2 Peter 3:18). Our **faith** needs to grow more and more (2 Thessalonians 1:3). The disciples asked, "Increase our faith" (Luke 17:5). Paul urges us "to abound more and more" in our **ability to please God** (1 Thessalonians 4:1). Jude tells us to build ourselves up in our faith (Jude 20). Paul urges us to "become **complete**" (2 Corinthians 13:11). We need to grow in every aspect of our life. Jesus told us to "be perfect, just as your Father in heaven is perfect" (Matthew 5:48). The Greek word for "perfect" includes the meanings of complete, mature, adult, of full age.[20]

We need to grow in both knowledge and character. The process never stops. Paul, near the end of his life, wrote that he had not yet achieved what he aimed at, "...But one thing I do: Forgetting what is behind and straining towards what is ahead, I press on toward the goal..." (Philippians 3:13-14 NIV).

Scripture is full of vigorous, energetic images such as straining, pressing on, making every effort, and being eager. One senses that we, as believers, are not to sit back and watch someone else do it all. We are to apply ourselves vigorously and energetically to whatever needs to be done. The process of growth doesn't just happen; it requires a good deal of energy and determination. We are to pursue, with all vigor, the things that will help us be transformed—training, discipline, spending time with God (in prayer, Scripture, praise and the like). We are to throw off everything that hinders (Hebrews 12:1). We don't just let go of it; we hurl it as far from us as we can! We are to capture every thought so as to make it obey Christ (2 Corinthians 10:5)—a military image of considerable force! And, as I shall point out in chapter 12, the devil will resist all of this at every turn.

My pastor likes to say that his job is to "comfort the afflicted and afflict the comfortable." I'm afraid we Christians in the United States today have tended to allow ourselves to become too comfortable.

The rest of this book deals with various aspects of the process of growth and change. I would like to make a few general comments about the process.

What is needed, as I see it, is growth both in knowledge and in character. One aspect that I have had much difficulty with is that of getting knowledge down from the head level to the heart level. Intellectual knowledge, while useful, is not enough. If I want knowledge that I can stand firm on in the face of great difficulties, it has to be knowledge and faith that I am deeply convinced of in my heart and my inmost being. Indeed, I cannot effectively communicate it to others unless it is deeply rooted within me. What I have written in this book is based on study of Scripture, but it is also based on deep conviction.

One reason we need to become mature is, as Ephesians 4:14 says, so that we will not be easily deceived. Jesus, in his great end-time prophecy, warned us, "Take heed that no one deceives you" (Matthew 24:4). Paul warns that "some will depart from the faith, giving heed to deceiving spirits and doctrines of demons" (1 Timothy 4:1). There are a great many things being said and taught in the world today which may have some surface plausibility, but which are spiritually false. The best safeguard against every kind of deception is to grow to maturity in Christ. Then we will know beyond question what we believe, and will have the faith and character to stand firm in it despite heavy pressure.

Another reason is that we all have a part to play. Ephesians 4:16 (NIV) says, "...as each part does its work." We find the same thought in 1 Corinthians 12:12-30 and Romans 12:3-8. Just as every part of the human body has its function, so every believer has a function in the body of Christ. Ephesians also says that the task of leadership is to equip the saints (all believers) "for the work of ministry" (Ephesians 4:12). "For we are God's workmanship, created in Christ Jesus to do good works, which God prepared in advance for us to do" (Ephesians 2:10 NIV). We, the whole body of God's people, are "a royal priesthood" (1 Peter 2:9). God has a calling, a function, for each one of us, and we need to be prepared to do that function to the best of our ability. This calls for maturity, sound knowledge, and strong character.

Satan is waging war against us. (See Chapter 12.) In a time of such war, children are greatly at risk because they often don't know how to protect themselves. If we fail to become mature Christians, then we endanger ourselves and the people who depend on us.

We need to keep a balance in this process. Growth to maturity is a gradual process; it doesn't happen all at once. Sometimes it cannot be hurried. The process is never completed on this side of heaven. As my pastor says, "I'm not where I need to be, but thank God I'm not where I used to be." We don't have to work on every aspect of growth at once. Work on whatever the Holy Spirit prods you to work on. Sometimes we find that when we have dealt with one area, we have improved in another area also that we didn't think we were working on.

But at the same time, we need to have a sense of urgency. The times we now live in are difficult and challenging. They could become much more so, rather quickly. We should not wait until the difficulties are greater. We need to work **now** on increasing our maturity, so as to be ready for whatever may come. As Jesus said in a different context, "I must work the works of Him who sent Me while it is day; the night is coming when no one can work" (John 9:4). Paul wrote, "Be very careful, then, how you live—not as unwise but as wise, making the most of every opportunity, because the days are evil" (Ephesians 5:15-16 NIV). Growing to maturity needs to be a top priority.

I could go on. But I think it clear that one of the central things we need, in order to be able to stand firm against opposition, is to become so mature in our faith and our Christian life that we cannot be shaken. We need to be able to persist, to endure, to persevere, to hang in there. Jesus tells us that the one whose faith is not firmly rooted will not endure when difficulties and persecution come (Mark 4:17). Our faith needs to be so sure, and so solidly rooted, that difficulties merely serve to make our faith stronger. When other things are being shaken, our faith needs to be unshakeable. (See Hebrews 12:26-29.) In the rest of this book I shall deal with further aspects of spiritual maturity.

11

Our Position in Christ

o o o o o o o o o o o o o o o o o o o o o o o o o o o o o o

"If anyone acknowledges that Jesus is the Son of God, God lives in him and he in God."

—*(1 John 4:15 NIV)*

When we accept Jesus Christ as our Savior and Lord, our sins are covered over, and we become justified by Jesus Christ's righteousness. As a result, we receive eternal life in heaven with God. This is a tremendous, unmerited gift from God!

But there is more to salvation than that. Our salvation has a great impact on our life here on earth. Jesus promises, to those who believe in him and accept him as their Lord, an abundant life here on this earth (John 10:10 KJV). It is that abundant life here on earth that I want to talk about in this chapter.

Scripture tells us that when we are in Christ, we become a new creation (2 Corinthians 5:17). We are born again, or born from above (John 3:3, 5). (Also see 1 Peter 1:3.) We become children of God (John 1:12; Romans 8:16; 1 John 3:10). We partake in the divine nature (2 Peter 1:4). We become a new person. (See Chapter 14.)

This is a tremendous change. The change usually does not happen all at once, but continues throughout our life as Christians. It sometimes occurs so gradually that we hardly perceive it. But it is tremendous.

Christians are called to overcome every problem and difficulty that the world presents (1 John 5:4-5). (Also see John 16:33; Romans 8:35-37, 12:21; Philippians 4:10-13; 1 John 2:13-14.) But most of us seldom act like overcomers. God "...has given us everything we need for life and godliness..." (2 Peter 1:3 NIV), but most of us often allow ourselves to feel defeated by circumstances or by our own inadequacies. I think much of the reason is that we have not fully understood or accepted what our position in Christ really is. We have not made it our own. We have not lived up to it. We have not really believed it. In this chapter, I want to sketch out at least some aspects of that position, as we find it described in Scripture.

As I reflect on the Scriptures dealing with our position in Christ, I find many of them to be truly astonishing. I believe them in my mind, but I have found it hard to really believe them in my heart. It is not always easy to believe that I am an overcomer when the medical evidence tells me that I have advanced cancer in my body; but I need to believe it, because it is true. I have written this chapter for my own benefit as much as for anyone else's, and I think I am becoming more able really to believe the Scriptural truths I have tried to express in it.

I think we have to start simply with faith in what the Scriptures say. Whose report will we believe? Will we believe the eternal truths that God has revealed in his Scriptures? Or will we believe our own feelings, impressions and ideas?

Then we need to reflect on these Scriptures, to chew on them, to let them sink into our inmost being. As the word of God becomes engrafted in us (James 1:21 KJV), it is able to work in us (1 Thessalonians 1:13) and change us. The word of God is living and active. We need to hear the word, believe it and not doubt, and then act on it. It is by our actions that we show what we really believe.

And so I invite everyone who reads this chapter to ask God to "open my eyes that I may see wondrous things from Your law" (Psalm 119:18). With Paul I pray, for myself as well as for you, "that the God of our Lord Jesus Christ, the Father of glory, may give to you the spirit of wisdom and revelation in the knowledge of Him, the eyes of your understanding being enlightened; that you may know what is the hope of His calling, what are the riches of the glory of His inheritance in the saints, and what is the exceeding greatness of His power toward us who believe" (Ephesians 1:17-18).

As we consider these extraordinary promises of Scripture, let us also remember that "Eye has not seen, nor ear heard, nor have entered into the heart of man the things which God has prepared for those who love Him" (1 Corinthians 2:9).

Fasten your seat belts and here we go!

WE ARE BECOMING UNITED WITH GOD

We find this unity expressed in Scripture in a number of ways. The unity is not perfect. Nothing on this earth is perfect. But there is a unity, and it is far more real than many of us have recognized.

God Lives in Us

To say that God lives in us seems astonishing, but it is Biblically true. From it flow a number of very important consequences.

"…if we love one another God lives in us…" (1 John 4:12 NIV). "We know that we live in him [God] and he in us, because he has given us of his Spirit" (1 John 4:13 NIV). "If anyone acknowledges that Jesus is the Son of God, God lives in him and he in God" (1 John 4:15 NIV). "…Whoever lives in love lives in God, and God in him" (1 John 4:16 NIV).

The Holy Spirit is one member of the Trinity. He is God. And he lives in us. Jesus said that we will know him "for He dwells with you and will be in you" (John 14:17). Paul wrote, "Do you not know that your body is a temple of the Holy Spirit who is in you, whom you have from God" (1 Corinthians 6:19). (Also see 1 Corinthians 3:16.)

Christ also lives in us. If we will abide (live) in him, he will abide (live) in us (John 15:4 KJV). God has made known to those who believe in him this mystery, "which is Christ in you, the hope of glory" (Colossians 1:27). Paul wrote, "I have been crucified with Christ; it is no longer I who live, but Christ lives in me" (Galatians 2:20).

Paul wrote, "You, however, are controlled not by the sinful nature but by the Spirit, if the Spirit of God lives in you. And if anyone does not have the Spirit of Christ, he does not belong to Christ. But if Christ is in you, your body is dead because of sin, yet your spirit is alive because of righteousness. And if the Spirit of him who raised Jesus from the dead is living in you, he who raised Christ from the dead will also give life to your mortal bodies through his Spirit, who lives in you" (Romans 8:9-11 NIV). (I believe that "if" in this passage really means "when." Paul is saying that God does live in those who believe in Jesus Christ and are controlled by the Holy Spirit.)

Notice how Paul speaks of the one who lives in us as "the Spirit of God," "the Spirit of Christ," "Christ," and "the Spirit of him who raised Jesus from the dead" (that is, the Spirit of the Father). While we usually speak of the one who lives in us as the Holy Spirit, it is really all three members of the Trinity. It is God who lives in us, as John's epistle says.

This is absolutely astonishing. Almighty God created the physical universe by his word, and sustains the universe by the word of his power. He is truly awesome (in the original sense of that overused word). Scripture tells us that "no one has seen God at any time" (John 1:18), and that God lives "in unapproachable light" (1 Timothy 6:16). Scripture gives us some magnificent visions of God, but even they do not begin to show his full glory. God's ways and his thoughts are far higher than ours (Isaiah 55:8-9). He is beyond our understanding (Romans 11:33-34). "His greatness is unsearchable" (Psalm 145:3).

And yet this same awesome God lives in me! He lives in each individual who has accepted Jesus Christ and received the Holy Spirit! The concept is so staggering that it is difficult to grasp, but it is what Scripture says. It does not matter whether we feel his presence or not. According to Scripture, he is there. It may be good to pray for a greater awareness of his presence, but we already have his presence.

When Solomon built a magnificent Temple to God, he prayed, "But will God indeed dwell with men on the earth? Behold, heaven and the heaven of heavens cannot contain You. How much less this temple which I have built!" (2 Chronicles 6:18). But now God lives in each believer. My body, your body (if you are a believer), is a temple in which Almighty God dwells!

In the Temple in Jerusalem, there was a holy of holies where God was thought to dwell. Only the High Priest could enter it, and he did so only once a year. Because of Christ's sacrifice on the Cross, the curtain of the Temple has been torn in two (Matthew 27:51) and we can all approach God boldly (Hebrews 4:16). But it goes beyond that. We now **are** the temple. God is **in us**. We have him with us continuously. We do not need to seek his presence, because he is **already** here. He is with us always.

All too often, in our Christian life, some of us tend to pray earnestly, and cry out, for what we already have. For example, some people pray for God's presence to be with them. According to Scripture, if they are Christians, then God abides (lives) in them. How can he be more present than that?

Jesus said, "Where two or three are gathered together in My name, I am there in the midst of them" (Matthew 18:20). There is strength and power in gathering together in his name. But if I read correctly the Scriptures about God's presence within us, they are saying that we don't have to have two or three gathering together. God is with us when we are alone. This is very important to know. If we are bed-ridden and cannot get to church, God is still with us. If we are persecuted and in prison, perhaps in solitary confinement, God is still with us. I once read of an American general who was captured by Italian terrorists. For over a year they kept him isolated. They kept earphones on his head and required him to listen to hard rock music for 24 hours a day. He found that, even under these circumstances, he could feel the presence of God, and he could pray and communicate with God. Nothing, except our own willfulness, can separate us from the presence of God. (See Romans 8:35-39.)

To avoid any possible misunderstanding, I want to make one thing clear. I am not saying that we are gods, or equal to God. We have God living in us, but that does not make us gods. The God who is in us is the only true God, who has existed for all eternity, and who is separate from his creation. God is the Creator. We humans are created beings. God is omnipotent. We humans can exercise such power as God chooses to give us, and for only as long as he chooses to give it to us. Apart from God, we can do nothing. (See John 15:5.) The New Age picture of someone tramping an ocean beach shouting, "I am God, I am God" is both ridiculous and blasphemous. But having said that, I go on to say that God has given extraordinary things to those who believe in Jesus Christ and continue to abide in him.

We Are Part of Christ's Body

Scripture expresses this unity with God in another way. We are part of Christ's body. We are as closely related to Jesus Christ, through whom the universe was created, as our neck or arms are related to our head!

All believers were baptized by one Spirit into one body (1 Corinthians 12:13). Paul compares this body of believers to the human body. We are part of each other, just as the hand, the foot, the eye, the ear, the kidneys and the liver are part of each other (1 Corinthians 12:12-26). Then Paul says something amazing, "Now you are the body of Christ, and each one of you is a part of it" (1 Corinthians 12:27 NIV). "Do you not know that your bodies are members of Christ himself?..." (1 Corinthians 6:15 NIV). We are part of Christ's body! We are part of the body of Almighty God!

"...in Christ we who are many form one body, and each member belongs to all the others" (Romans 12:5 NIV). "Speaking the truth in love, [we] may grow up in all things into Him who is the head—Christ—from whom the whole body, joined and knit together by what every joint supplies, according to the effective working by which every part does its share, causes growth of the body for the edifying [building up] of itself in love" (Ephesians 4:15-16). "For we are members of His [Christ's] body, of His flesh and of His bones" (Ephesians 5:30). (Also see Colossians 2:19.)

On the night before he was crucified, Jesus prayed for all who would believe in Him, "that they all may be one, as you, Father, are in Me, and I in You; that they also may be one in Us, that the world may believe that you sent Me. And the glory which you gave Me I have given them, that they may be one just as We are one: I in them and you in Me" (John 17:21-23). All who believe in Jesus Christ are to be unified because we are in Jesus Christ and in God.

What does this mean? Just as the human body is formed of many parts, which are bound together in many ways and form part of a single body, so we who believe in Jesus Christ form a single body, closely bound together. But this is not just our body; it is the body of Christ. Christ is the head; we are the arms, legs, hands, feet, internal organs, etc. We are as closely joined to Jesus Christ as our neck is joined to our head. We and he are part of one body. Not only is God in us; we are in God!

We often speak of wanting to have a closer relationship with God. These Scriptures say that we **already** have it. How can you have a closer relationship than that of the different parts of the human body? What we need to do is to recognize, appropriate, and live, this relationship that we already have.

Scripture uses another image to express this unity. We who believe are to become the bride of Christ (Matthew 9:15, 25:1-13; Revelation 19:7, 22:17). Scripture tells us that in marriage "'a man shall leave his father and mother and be joined to his wife, and the two shall become one flesh.' This is a great mystery, but I speak concerning Christ and the church" (Ephesians 5:31-32). So we, as the bride of Christ, will be united with him.

How can human beings, created objects, be joined so closely to Almighty God? Paul calls it a mystery, and I suggest that it is almost as great a mystery as the fact that Jesus Christ is fully God and fully man. But Scripture declares that it will happen, and we can only give thanks that God has chosen to so unify us with his Son.

We Become Children of God

Another way of expressing this unity is to say that we are children of God.

"But as many as received Him, to them he gave the right to become children of God, to those who believe in His name" (John 1:12). "For as many as are led by the Spirit of God, these are sons of God. For you did not receive the spirit of bondage again to fear, but you received the Spirit of adoption by whom we cry out 'Abba, Father.' The Spirit Himself bears witness with our spirit that we are children of God, and if children, then heirs—heirs of God and joint heirs with Christ" (Romans 8:14-17). "Behold what manner of love the Father has bestowed on us that we should be called children of God!" (1 John 3:1). (Also see verse 10.)

What does it mean to say that we are children of God?

It means that we can have a close and personal relationship with God. It means that we can pray to him as our Father, and call him *abba*, the term a little child would use for his Daddy. It means that we can expect God to love us, provide for us and care for us as a father would his child. It means that we are joint heirs with Christ—and I shall not attempt here to explore the meaning of that expression. It means that when we meet up with other Christians, we can greet them as family.

God is not a remote, stern, forbidding personage, as some visualize him. He is our father, our Daddy, and he loves us as a father loves his children. Regardless of what our relationship may have been with our earthly father, God is what a father should be, what we have always wanted a father to be.

We Become Part of the Kingdom of God

When we accepted our salvation, God "delivered us from the power of darkness" and "translated us into the kingdom of his dear Son" (Colossians 1:13 KJV). He picked us up out of one kingdom and put us into a different kingdom.

Jesus taught often about the kingdom of God; it was central to his teaching. Much has been written about it since. At the risk of great over-simplification, let me say that, with Jesus' coming, there are now two kingdoms on earth, a kingdom of darkness (or of the evil one), and the kingdom of God.[21] These are not physical locations, but they express where a person's loyalty is. All those who have committed themselves to God and seek genuinely to serve him become part of the kingdom of God.

What does it mean to say that we are part of the kingdom of God? It has nothing to do with physical location. It is a matter of loyalty. To say that we are in the kingdom of God is to say that our loyalty, our allegiance, is to God. It also means that we are under God's protection and we get the benefit of all the promises he has made to those who truly serve him.

SOME CONSEQUENCES OF THIS UNITY

We Can Become More Like God in Character

We are to be transformed by the renewing of our mind (Romans 12:2). "If anyone is in Christ, he is a new creation; old things have passed away; behold, all things have become new" (2 Corinthians 5:17). Scripture tells us what this new creation is. "And we, who with unveiled faces all reflect the Lord's glory, are being transformed into his likeness with ever-increasing glory, which comes from the Lord, who is the Spirit" (2 Corinthians 3:18 NIV). We are being transformed into God's likeness in character. (See Chapter 14.)

Originally, God created mankind in his own image (Genesis 1:27). With the Fall in Eden, man lost much of this image. Now, as a result of Jesus' sacrifice on the Cross, the image of God, in which we were originally created, has been restored for those who believe in Jesus Christ. We are transformed into God's "likeness," into the "image" of our Creator. We can, increasingly, have his mind and participate in his nature. He must increase and my old self must decrease. (See John 3:30.)

Paul emphasizes the magnitude of this change by referring to Adam as the first Adam and to Jesus Christ as the second (or last) Adam (1 Corinthians 15:45-49). (Note that the name, "Adam," means "a human being," "mankind.") With the coming of the second Adam, the ground lost by the first Adam has been retaken.

I think it is not overstating it to say that Jesus Christ's sacrificial atonement on the Cross has resulted in a new species. Those who believe in Jesus Christ are a new creation. We are born from above. We become children of God, born of God.

God Works in Us

God is working in us to carry out his purposes for us. "The LORD will perfect that which concerns me" (Psalm 138:8). "...he who began a good work in you will carry it on to completion until the day of Christ Jesus" (Philippians 1:6 NIV). God is "working in you what is pleasing in his sight" (Hebrews 13:21). "Work out your own salvation with fear and trembling; for it is God who works in you both to will and to do for his good pleasure" (Philippians 2:12-13). The word of God "effectively works in you who believe" (1 Thessalonians 2:13). God was at work in the ministries of Peter and Paul (Galatians 2:8). Paul said, "...I labor, struggling with all his energy, which so powerfully works in me" (Colossians 1:29 NIV). God's word penetrates us and judges our thoughts and attitudes (Hebrews 4:12). We are made holy by the sanctifying work of the Holy Spirit (2 Thessalonians 2:13; 1 Peter 1:2). God is working in us.

Part of the way God works in us is by enabling us to live by the Holy Spirit. (See Chapter 15.) The Holy Spirit lives in our spirit. He wants to be able to control our soul and flesh as well. It is only as we learn to live according to the Spirit and to be controlled by the Spirit that we can find peace and please God. I believe it is because the Holy Spirit lives within us that he is able to work in us to bring us into obedience, so that we will live by the Spirit.

God Strengthens and Empowers Us

Paul prayed that the Ephesians would have the eyes of their heart enlightened so that they might know God's "...incomparably great power for us who believe" (Ephesians 1:19 NIV). (Also see Ephesians 3:20.) God's incomparably great power is at work within us. We may not feel it, but Scripture says that it is there.

"Be strong in the Lord and in the power of His might" (Ephesians 6:10). God wants us to live every aspect of our life in his strength and his mighty power. "In Him we live and move and have our being" (Acts 17:28). We should do everything in his great power. Apart from him, we can do nothing (John 15:5). In all things we can draw on the mighty power of the God who lives in us and in whom we have our being.

Paul wrote, "I can do all things through Christ who strengthens me" (Philippians 4:13). He wrote, "I will rather boast in my infirmities, that the power of Christ may rest upon me" (2 Corinthians 12:9). He prayed that the Colossians would be "strengthened with all might according to [God's] glorious power" (Colossians 1:11). When David was greatly distressed, he "strengthened himself in the LORD his God" (1 Samuel 30:6). (Also see 2 Samuel 22:33; Psalms 28:7, 46:1, 119:28.)

While on earth, Jesus Christ ministered in the power of the Holy Spirit (Luke 4:14). He told his disciples, "you shall receive power when the Holy Spirit has come upon you" (Acts 1:8). This occurred on the Day of Pentecost, and from then on they ministered in great power (Acts 4:33). Peter made it clear that the promise of this power is "...for all whom the Lord our God will call" (Acts 2:39 NIV).

This includes the power to love people who seem unlovable, to forgive those who have wronged us deeply, to get rid of all bitterness, to cast off everything that hinders (Hebrews 12:1), to persevere in the face of great obstacles, to live by the Spirit, to show the fruit of the Spirit, to minister in love to others, and much more. It is God's power to become what we could never become on our own. Grace came through Jesus Christ (John 1:17), and part of the definition of grace is God's influence working in us.[22] It is only by God's power working in us that we can possibly hope to become like God in character and to have the mind of Christ.

I find all this astonishing. Of ourselves we are weak and fallible. Of ourselves we can do nothing. But the Almighty God, who created and sustains the universe, has enabled us to be strong in the Lord and in his mighty power. By the mighty power of God working in us, we can overcome the world's temptations and pressures, and we can surmount every difficulty and problem we may face. Whatever our problems or difficulties may be, the one who lives in us is greater. We need to learn to believe this, to feel it, and to act on it.

WE HAVE HOPE

With God there is always hope. He is "the God of hope" (Romans 15:13). (Also see 1 Timothy 1:1, 4:10.) "Happy is he…whose hope is in the LORD his God" (Psalm 146:5). (Also see Psalms 33:20, 37:9, 39:7, 62:5, 130:7, 147:11; Jeremiah 14:22.) Those who believe in God will always have hope (Psalm 71:14). Part of standing firm in the faith is to "…hold unswervingly to the hope we profess…" (Hebrews 10:23 NIV). We need to "…continue in your faith, established and firm, not moved from the hope held out in the gospel" (Colossians 1:23 NIV). "This hope we have as an anchor of the soul, both sure and steadfast" (Hebrews 6:19).

God "…has given us new birth into a living hope…" (1 Peter 1:3 NIV). Peter is there talking about the hope of eternal life, but with God there is hope in this world also. "Those who hope in the Lord will renew their strength. They will soar on wings like eagles; they will run and not be weary; they will walk and not faint" (Isaiah 40:31 NIV). Abraham in hope believed God's promise that he and Sarah could have a son, and their hope was realized (Romans 4:18-22). The Psalmist wrote, "I hope in Your word" (Psalm 119:81). (Also see verse 147.) He wrote, "Why are you cast down, O my soul? And why are you disquieted within me? Hope in God, for I shall yet praise Him" (Psalm 42:5). (Also see Psalms 42:11, 43:5.) Whenever we find ourselves getting discouraged, the answer is to put our hope in God.

Those who are without God are without hope (Ephesians 2:12). "Brothers, we do not want you to…grieve like the rest of men, who have no hope" (1 Thessalonians 4:13 NIV). (Also see Hebrews 2:15; Job 27:8; Proverbs 24:20.)

Christian hope is not wishful thinking. It is "confident expectation".[23] As Christians we can be "…sure of what we hope for…" (Hebrews 11:1 NIV). "…those who hope in me will not be disappointed" (Isaiah 49:23 NIV). "Hope does not disappoint" (Romans 5:5). Our confidence is based on who God is. We know, without any doubt, that God is far greater than any problem or concern we may have, that he is a good and loving God, and that he is faithful to keep his promises. We know that "...in all things God works for the good of those who love him, who are called according to his purposes" (Romans 8:28 NIV).

One of the remarkable things about our position in Christ is that so often we find ourselves in a win-win situation. However it comes out, we will be winners. Paul gives us one example. He wrote that God's power is made perfect in weakness, and therefore Paul delighted in his weaknesses, because when he is weak (in himself) then he is strong (in God's power) (2 Corinthians 12:9-10). So whether Paul feels strong or weak, it all works out for good. I can give an example in my own life. If I should die soon of this cancer, then I will go to be with the Lord. That is a very good place to be! And if I go, I am sure that God will continue to take care of my family. On the other hand, if, as I hope and desire, God heals me of this cancer, then I will have more time to serve him here on earth. So I cannot lose. Whatever happens, God works it out for good.

Because of our position in Christ, we can know that, no matter how difficult the outward circumstances may seem, we can, in God's strength, be overcomers. And so we can be "rejoicing in hope" (Romans 12:12).

WE CAN OVERCOME ANY ADVERSITY

God enables his people to overcome evil. "His divine power has given to us all things that pertain to life and godliness" (2 Peter 1:3). Therefore, we can overcome trials and tribulations, and we can conquer the temptations of the world, the flesh and the devil.

Jesus said, "In the world you will have tribulation; but be of good cheer, I have overcome the world" (John 16:33). But then Scripture says that **we** can overcome the world. "For whatever is born of God overcomes the world. And this is the victory that has overcome the world—our faith. Who is he who overcomes the world, but he who believes that Jesus is the Son of God?" (1 John 5:4-5). When Scripture says that we can overcome the world, I believe this means that no matter what our problem or difficulty, the power of God is greater.

Paul was an overcomer. He had "...learned the secret of being content in any and every situation..." (Philippians 4:12 NIV). (See verses 11-13.) He was no longer at the mercy of his circumstances.

We are more than conquerors because nothing can separate us from the love of Christ (Romans 8:35-39). We can see this with Stephen. An angry mob stoned him to death, but Stephen saw the glory of God and he died praying for his enemies. They conquered him physically, but Stephen was more than a conqueror.

The mob couldn't destroy his relationship with Jesus Christ or his godly character. (See Acts 7:54-60.) We have "...authority...to overcome all the power of the enemy..." (Luke 10:19 NIV). We can overcome every evil influence because "He who is in you is greater than he who is in the world" (1 John 4:4).

CONCLUSION

I think I have said enough to indicate that, as believers, our position in Christ is extraordinary. The problem is that many of us do not act as if we believe it. We do not act as if we are overcomers. We do not act as if God's power is working in us. We do not act as if we have God's character. We do not act as if we believe that God is in us. We have these wonderful words of Scripture, but we have not been able to appropriate them and make them our own. We have not been able to live by them.

I think a major part of the problem is unbelief. We read these astonishing scriptures. Our mind accepts them. But in our hearts, in our guts, we can't quite believe they are really true. We need to recognize our unbelief and deal with it. We need to pray, "I do believe. Help me overcome my unbelief." We need to think about these Scriptures, chew on them, make them a part of us, let them work in us. We need to see evidence that they do, indeed, work, and let that evidence strengthen our faith. We need to decide that we will trust God's eternal word rather than our momentary feelings.

Another part of the problem may be our pride. We like to think, "I can handle this. I don't need any help." We need to get to the point that Paul had arrived at when he said that he rejoiced in his weakness, because then God could act in and through him, so that when he was weak (in himself) he was strong (in God) (2 Corinthians 12:9-11). "God resists the proud, but gives grace to the humble" (James 4:6).

This is one of the main reasons for prayer. We do not need to inform God of our problems; he already knows them. He knows all things. But we need to come to him and say, "Lord, I need your help with this." We need to humble ourselves and say, "I can't handle this. I need you." When we come to that point, we are ready to receive what God has for us.

We need to know, to believe with all our hearts, all the time, that in all things we can be overcomers, because we have one in us who is greater than he that is in the world, greater than any obstacle or difficulty we may face. The God who is in us is greater than anything we may face, whether it be physical or mental illness, habits or addictions, financial difficulties, problems with relationships, bitterness, unforgiveness, faulty mindsets, or whatever. God knows our needs. If we put him first, if we seek his kingdom and trust in his power, we can overcome whatever problems and difficulties we may face. Just as God "...will not let you be tempted beyond what you can bear..." (1 Corinthians 10:13 NIV) so, I believe, he will not allow us to be burdened beyond what we can bear, and he will, in every situation, give us the strength to overcome trials and difficulties.

In dealing with any troubles, obstacles or problems we may encounter, we operate from a position of strength. We have Almighty God in us, and he is greater than any difficulty we may encounter. He gives us his mighty strength and his incomparably great power. We are made in his image and partake in his nature. Therefore, we can overcome any adversity.

David faced and defeated a giant. He did not look at how big and powerful the giant was; he looked at how much bigger God was. "You come to me with a sword, with a spear, and with a javelin. But I come to you in the name of the LORD of hosts, the God of the armies of Israel, whom you have defied...for the battle is the LORD's, and He will give you into our hands" (1 Samuel 17:45, 47).

When we face our own giants (adversities that seem overwhelming), we need to know who we are in Christ. It is to stir up an awareness of our position in Christ that I have written this chapter. In reading everything that follows, I ask you to keep constantly in mind these truths about our position in Christ. They are basic to an understanding of everything else I have written.

Having said all this, I want to mention one of the "it is also writtens" of Scripture. In all things, we need to have the whole counsel of Scripture. Jesus appointed 70 of his followers to go out two by two to preach the gospel (Luke 10:1-20). They returned and said, "Lord, even the demons are subject to us in Your name." Jesus replied, "Nevertheless do not rejoice in this, that the spirits are subject to you, but rather **rejoice because your names are written in heaven**" (Luke 10:17, 20). The most important thing about our position in Christ is that we are, in fact, in Christ. We are children of God. Jesus saved us from eternal death. He saved us from our sins and gave us eternal life. We must never become so focussed on other things that we lose the joy of our salvation. (See Psalm 51:12.)

12

Our Conflict With the Devil

o o o o o o o o o o o o o o o o o o o o o o o o o o o o o o

"Be sober, be vigilant; because your enemy the devil walks about like a roaring lion, seeking whom he may devour. Resist him, steadfast in the faith."

—(1 Peter 5:8-9)

One reason why it is important to understand our position in Christ is that the devil seeks, in every way that he can, to keep us from growing into spiritual maturity. He wants to destroy us. Dealing with this is so intense and so strenuous that Scripture describes it as fighting a man-eating lion or waging warfare against an enemy. The devil is a liar (John 8:44), a deceiver (Revelation 12:9), a tempter (Matthew 4:1-11). He comes to kill, steal and destroy (John 10:10). He has a number of names: the devil, satan, the enemy, the evil one, the prince of this world, the god of this world, Lucifer, Beelzebub. Jesus came to "destroy the works of the devil" (1 John 3:8), "to destroy him who has the power of death, that is the devil" (Hebrews 2:14). He taught his disciples to do the same.

Some Christians use the term "spiritual warfare" to describe the conflict we have with the devil and his demons. Other Christians, and many non-Christians, may find the term puzzling and confusing. In particular, they may read into that term a suggestion of the religious wars in Europe that killed so many people. That is **not** what Scripture says about it. This fight is not against flesh and blood, not against humans. It is against evil spirits. (See Ephesians 6:12.) Our weapons are not physical weapons; they are truth, righteousness, the gospel of peace, faith, salvation, the word of God, and prayer (Ephesians 6:10-18). However, to avoid any possibility of misunderstanding, I shall not use the term.

It is important to understand the existence of this conflict with the devil, but also not to overemphasize it. The devil is a defeated enemy. He still has the capacity to cause a lot of damage, but he is defeated and his ultimate destruction is sure.

SPIRITUAL CONFLICT EXISTS

There Are Evil Spirits

Scripture makes it clear that there are good and evil spirits. There is God, and his ministering angels. (See Psalms 34:7, 91:11-12.) There is satan, and his evil spirits. (See 2 Corinthians 11:14-15.) There are "rulers of the darkness of this world," and "spiritual wickedness in high places" (Ephesians 6:12 KJV). There is "…the spirit who is now at work in those who are disobedient" (Ephesians 2:2 NIV). John warns, "Do not believe every spirit, but test the spirits, whether they are of God" (1 John 4:1).

Scripture does not tell us a great deal about these evil spirits, but it tells us enough to give us a good idea of what we have to deal with. Jesus told his disciples, "I saw Satan fall like lightning from heaven" (Luke 10:19). Revelation 12:9 shows satan being cast out of heaven. "Satan himself transforms himself into an angel of light" (2 Corinthians 11:14). From these and other Scriptures, many believe that satan was an angel who rebelled against God, and that his demons are also fallen angels. As such, they are spirits.

There are some who doubt or deny that the devil exists. The Scriptures I have already referred to, and shall refer to later in this chapter, make it very clear that he does exist. Following are some additional references for those who want to pursue the issue further: Job 1:6-12, 2:1-7; Matthew 13:38-39; 2 Corinthians 2:11, 12:7; 1 Timothy 4:1.

Do evil spirits actually exist today? I have absolutely no doubt that they do. Scripture says clearly that they do exist, and Scripture speaks for all time.

One thing that Scripture makes clear is that God and the devil are not equal. God is the Creator of all things. The devil is a created being. (See Colossians 1:16.) So God has power over the devil. (See Ephesians 1:21-22.) This is shown clearly in Job, chapters 1 and 2, where God gave satan permission to harm Job, but God set limits on what satan could do to Job. (Also see Luke 22:31.)

There Is Conflict Between These Spirits

There is conflict between these good and evil spirits. Scripture gives us glimpses of it. God is the Lord of hosts, the Lord mighty in battle. (See, for example, Psalm 24:8-10.) Joshua had an encounter with one who identified himself as "Commander of the army of the LORD" (Joshua 5:14). Scripture speaks of the "armies in heaven" (Revelation 19:14). It tells us that "War broke out in heaven: Michael and his angels fought with the dragon [satan]; and the dragon and his angels fought" (Revelation 12:7). Jesus came to earth to "destroy the works of the devil" (1 John 3:8). (Also see Hebrews 2:14; Colossians 2:15.) Daniel tells of a time when an angel from God was delayed 21 days by "the prince of the kingdom of Persia" until the powerful archangel Michael came to his aid (Daniel 10:12-13). Evidently this "prince" (literally, ruler) was a spiritual power. What human could resist God's angel for 21 days?

We Humans Are Involved in This Conflict

Consider carefully the following Scriptures that describe our ongoing conflict with the devil and his demons:

> "Submit yourselves, then, to God. Resist the devil, and he will flee from you" (James 4:7 NIV).

> "Be self-controlled and alert. Your enemy the devil prowls around like a roaring lion, looking for someone to devour. Resist him, standing firm in the faith…" (1 Peter 5:8-9 NIV).

> "Finally, be strong in the Lord and in his mighty power. Put on the full armor of God so that you can take your stand against the devil's schemes. For our struggle is not against flesh and blood, but against the rulers, against the authorities, against the powers of this dark world and against the spiritual forces of evil in the heavenly realms. Therefore put on the full armor of God, so that when the day of evil comes you may be able to stand your ground, and after you have done everything, to stand. Stand firm then, with the belt of truth buckled around your waist, with the breastplate of righteousness in place, and with your feet fitted with the readiness that comes from the gospel of peace. In addition to all this, take up the shield of faith, with which you can extinguish all the flaming arrows of the evil one. Take the helmet of salvation and the sword of the Spirit, which is the word of God. And pray in the Spirit on all occasions with all kinds of prayers and requests…" (Ephesians 6:10-18 NIV).

> "For though we live in the world, we do not wage war as the world does. The weapons we fight with are not the weapons of the world. On the contrary

> they have divine power to demolish strongholds. We demolish arguments and every pretension that sets itself up against the knowledge of God, and we take captive every thought to make it obedient to Christ" (2 Corinthians 10:3-5 NIV).
>
> "...in the hope that God will grant them repentance leading them to a knowledge of the truth and that they will come to their senses and escape from the trap of the devil, who has taken them captive to do his will" (2 Timothy 2:25-26 NIV).

(Also see Romans 7:22-23; Galatians 5:17; Colossians 2:14-15; 1 Peter 2:11; 1 John 4:4. And see Chapter 8 of this book.)

There are some who say that, because Jesus triumphed over evil forces on the Cross, we have no more conflict with them. The short answer to this is that most of the Scriptures quoted above are from letters written to believers 15 to 30 years **after** Jesus' Crucifixion, Resurrection and Ascension. Evidently James, Peter and Paul did not consider that conflict with evil spirits had ended. Satan will not meet his final doom until he is thrown into the lake of burning fire, after Jesus' Second Coming. Until then, although basically defeated, he still has power to do much harm.

Scripture shows us that we Christians are involved in an ongoing conflict with evil spirits.

- The first time that we see spiritual conflict in the New Testament is when satan tempted Jesus in the wilderness. If Jesus, who was sinless, was not immune to being attacked by the devil, then neither are we.
- 2 Corinthians 10:3-5 speaks of arguments and pretentious thoughts that are raised up against the knowledge of God. These thoughts, feelings, and imaginations make it difficult for us to comprehend God's nature and character. This undermines our trust in God, which makes it more difficult for us to love him. It can result in doubt and confusion. It can also undermine our determination to resist temptation.
- The Scriptures quoted above were written to believers. Thus, 1 Peter was written to God's elect (1 Peter 1:1). Ephesians is written to those who have been saved by grace (Ephesians 1:7, 2:8). The Corinthian church had been enriched by God in every way and did not lack any spiritual gift (1 Corinthians 1:5-7). Indeed, Paul speaks of **"our"** struggle, and of the weapons **"we"** fight with (Ephesians 6:12, 2 Corinthians 10:4). Thus Paul identifies himself, with other believers, as being engaged in warfare against evil spirits.

Some have suggested that the "roaring lion" of 1 Peter 5:8 is a toothless lion incapable of doing harm. That is not Peter's simile. Peter speaks of a lion who seeks to, and does, devour people.

In the face of the Scriptures quoted above, I do not see how anyone who believes in Scripture can deny that conflict with evil spirits exists here on earth now, and needs to be taken seriously, and that believing Christians are involved in it.

When we are in a state of conflict, we have two choices. We can deal with it, or we can shut our eyes to it and let ourselves be beaten up. The devil is a ruthless and determined enemy. There can be no compromise with him. A policy of appeasement will not work. He will not go away just because we don't want him there.

THE DEVIL'S PURPOSES AND TACTICS

God's desire is that his will shall be done on earth as it is in heaven (Matthew 6:10). The devil's desire is exactly the opposite. He opposes God's will on earth in every way that he can.

God "desires all men to be saved and to come to a knowledge of the truth" (1 Timothy 2:4). (Also see 2 Peter 3:10.) The devil seeks to prevent men from coming to salvation. If they are saved, then he seeks one or more of several things: (1) to lead them into error so that they will cause harm to the body of Christ, (2) to render them ineffective, or (3) to cause them to backslide and abandon their faith. He comes to "kill, and to steal, and to destroy" (John 10:10).

The devil has a variety of tactics. He uses both doubt and fear to attack our faith. He tempts us to do ungodly things. He lies and deceives. He uses discouragement, confusion and apathy to try to make us ineffective.[24]

One thing clear is that the devil never lets up, except for his own tactical purposes. Paul says we "wrestle" (KJV) against evil spirits. Wrestling has no time outs, no breaks. Greek athletes often wrestled to the death.

It is a mistake to think that the devil causes every set-back that we suffer. We are tempted by the devil (Matthew 4:1-11, 6:13), but we are also tempted by our own desires (James 1:14). Some illnesses are caused by the devil (Luke 9:37-43, 13:16), but many others have natural causes. Some accidents may be caused by the devil; others are caused by our own carelessness or by circumstances beyond our control. Some trials may be caused by the devil; others are caused or allowed by God to teach, discipline and strengthen us. (See Chapter 19.) But whatever their cause, the devil will try to use them for his purposes. But if we love God, then God will make these things work out for our long-range good (Romans 8:28).

Some Scriptures speak in terms of a direct frontal attack by the devil or his evil spirits. (See Ephesians 6:10-18; James 4:7; and 1 Peter 5:8-9.) The enemy makes a frontal attack and we stand against him.

There are other times when we find ourselves hit by a mental stronghold, or mindset, or blind spot, that has been there all along. Perhaps we did not know it was there, or perhaps we thought we had dealt with it, only to find it coming back. This is what 2 Corinthians 10:3-5 is dealing with. It does not speak of demons or evil spirits. It speaks of things in our mind—strongholds, arguments, and pretentious thoughts that hinder us from knowing God. Our object is to make every thought obey Christ. Mindsets, strongholds, thought patterns and the like have been set up inside us by our own flesh and by the world system. Satan will use these to make us ineffective, or to lead us into error, unless we uproot and demolish them.

Note one other difference between these two types of conflict. We cannot destroy evil spirits. We can only resist them. But we are told to destroy our internal strongholds.

HOW DO WE STAND OUR GROUND AGAINST THE DEVIL AND HIS DEMONS?

Stand Firm

When the devil attacks, we "resist him, standing firm in the faith" (1 Peter 5:9 NIV). "Resist the devil and he will flee from you" (James 4:7). "Stand your ground, and after you have done everything, to stand. Stand firm then..." (Ephesians 6:13-14 NIV).

These Scriptures tell us not to compromise with, or negotiate with, or try to appease the devil. If we stand our ground against him, then he will go away. He may try to come back again, but if we continue to stand firm, he will go away. This is an important aspect of our standing firm in the faith.

Stand in God's Power

When dealing with the devil, we stand in God's power, and not our own. "Be strong in the Lord and in the power of his might" (Ephesians 6:10). We take up all the spiritual weapons that God has given us (Ephesians 6:13). We fight with spiritual weapons that have divine power (2 Corinthians 2:4). God provides his incomparably great power for those who believe (Ephesians 1:19). Of ourselves, without God's power working within us, we cannot expect to prevail. Apart from Jesus, we can do nothing (John 15:5). But in God's power, we can and will prevail.

One of the devil's schemes is to try to discourage us and make us feel weak and helpless. When this happens, we need to do as David did. When things looked very bleak, he "strengthened himself in the LORD his God" (1 Samuel 30:6). Again he cried out, "Why are you cast down, O my soul? And why are you disquieted within me? Hope in God, for I shall yet praise Him, for the help of His countenance" (Psalm 42:5). (Also see Psalms 42:11, 43:5.) When we are feeling downcast, discouraged, weak, we need to make a conscious effort to fix our minds on God and his mighty power. A Scottish evangelist I knew has said, "Whenever you're feeling downhearted, read about the glory of God!" It's good advice. It works.

Submit Ourselves to God

"Submit to God. Resist the devil and he will flee from you" (James 4:7). To submit, *hupotasso* (from *hupo*, under and *tasso*, to arrange), means to subordinate, to obey, to be under obedience. It implies a military type of discipline. Paul expresses this clearly in Romans, chapter 6. "Do not offer the parts of your body to sin as instruments of wickedness, but rather offer yourselves to God, as those who have been brought from death to life; and offer the parts of your body to him as instruments of righteousness" (Romans 6:13 NIV). (The word translated "instruments" is *hoplon*, which literally means "weapons.") "…you are slaves to the one whom you obey—whether you are slaves to sin, which leads to death, or to obedience, which leads to righteousness" (Romans 6:16 NIV). (See Chapters 16 and 17.) It is when we are submitted to God that we can stand against the devil in God's power.

Scripture warns us not to give the devil a foothold (Ephesians 4:27). When Jesus was about to be arrested, he said, "…the prince of this world [the devil] is coming. He has no hold on me" (John 14:30 NIV). We need to make every effort to avoid giving the devil anything he can grab hold of. An image will convey the thought. We can think of the devil as having Velcro. If we allow sin in our lives, then we have Velcro that he can attach to. It was because Jesus was sinless that he could say that the devil had no hold on him. There was nothing in

Jesus to which the devil could attach himself. This is part of being submitted to God.

Be Watchful and Alert

"Be self-controlled and alert" (1 Peter 5:8 NIV). "Watch and pray, lest you enter into temptation" (Matthew 26:41). "Take heed that no one deceives you" (Matthew 24:4). In a state of conflict, alertness and watchfulness are necessary.

The devil often works by deception and trickery. He slides in a little insinuation, and then tries to build on it. (See, for example, Genesis 3:1.) We need to be alert and watchful to catch this kind of thing quickly, to nip it in the bud.

Guard Our Minds and Hearts

"Do not believe every spirit, but test the spirits whether they are from God" (1 John 4:1). The devil is a liar and the father of lies. Lying is his natural language. There is no truth in him (John 8:44). He is constantly trying to place false and lying thoughts in our minds, and to take advantage of any false thoughts we may have.

Sometimes we say that we believe God's word, and we do believe it in our mind, but in our heart we may actually believe something quite different.

We need, therefore, to keep constant watch over our thoughts and our words, so that we do not fall into the devil's lies and deception. The U.S. Constitution defines "treason" as "giving aid and comfort to the enemy." We do not want to commit spiritual treason by accepting and believing the devil's lies and deception, thereby giving aid and comfort to our spiritual enemy, the devil. We need to check our thoughts and words against Scripture, and reject those which are not Scriptural. When we catch ourselves thinking or saying something that is contrary to Scripture, we need immediately to renounce it and repent of it, and to declare the truth of God's word. Using God's spiritual weapons of divine power, "we demolish arguments and every pretension that sets itself up against the knowledge of God, and we take captive every thought to make it obedient to Christ" (2 Corinthians 10:5 NIV). This process of taking our thoughts captive to obey Jesus Christ is a never-ending one. It continues throughout our Christian life. It is part of being watchful and alert.

This is one reason why it is so important to spend time reading and studying Scripture, and allowing it to become a very part of ourselves. It is when we know and understand Scripture, and have engrafted it into ourselves, that we are able to discern, and take authority over, any thoughts and words that are not Scriptural.

Don't Blame God

Jesus said, "Blessed is he who is not offended because of Me" (Matthew 11:6; Luke 7:23). The Greek word for "offend" is *skandalizo.* According to Strong's *Dictionary of the Greek Bible*, it means "to entrap, i.e. trip up...entice to sin, apostasy or displeasure". He said that in the end times, many would be offended (Matthew 24:10). Therefore, we need to be on guard against taking offense. Jesus knew that we would go through trials that might tempt us to blame him instead of dealing with those trials according to Scriptural principles. (For a Scriptural understanding of pain and suffering, and how to deal with it, see Chapter 19.)

One of the devil's goals is to try to put a wedge between us and God; so he will try to tempt us to become offended with, or angry at, God. If he can pry us away from God, then we become weak and vulnerable. If we continue to let the gap between us and God grow wider and wider, it can cause us to turn away from, and reject God, and can lead to our spiritual destruction. Jesus said, "Abide in Me, and I in you. As the branch cannot bear fruit of itself, unless it abides in the vine, neither can you, unless you abide in Me. I am the vine, you are the branches. **He who abides in Me, and I in him, bears much fruit; for without Me you can do nothing. If anyone does not abide in Me, he is cast out as a branch and is withered: and they gather them and throw them into the fire, and they are burned**" (John 15:5-7).

In our modern American culture, blaming has become a way of life. As a result, when we go through trials and difficulties, it is easy for us to fall into the trap of blaming God instead of turning to God for guidance and leaning on God for strength. This is the way of the flesh, that leads to destruction, as opposed to being led by the Holy Spirit, which leads to life. (See Chapter 15.) We first see it in the Garden of Eden when Adam told God, "The woman whom You gave to be with me, she gave me of the tree, and I ate" (Genesis 3:12). Adam first blamed God and then blamed Eve. Who knows how different our history, and our present life, would be if Adam had repented instead of blaming God?

I almost fell into this way of blaming in my situation. When I learned that my cancer had spread to the liver and lungs, I started to think, "If only I had had a colonoscopy several years ago, they would have caught this thing when it was much smaller, or even just a precancerous polyp. Why didn't my doctors recommend a colonoscopy some years ago as a routine precaution? My doctors are to blame for my having this life-threatening condition." From there it would have been a short step to saying, "God, why did you allow this to happen?"

I did not go down that road. I deliberately chose not to. If I had allowed myself to give in to that kind of thinking, I doubt if I would be alive today. If I were alive, a book written while I had that much bitterness in me towards God and my doctors would not have been of much value.

Stay Focussed

God guides us and blesses us in the real world—his world—not the world of our imagination. He gives us grace in the present moment—not the past (which is gone) or the future (which has not yet come). One of the devil's tactics is to try to get us to dwell in the past (through regret, or shame, or missing the "good old days"), or in the future (through fear or hope or wishful thinking), or in our imagination (through anxiety or daydreams). Then we are no longer focussed on God's real world, in the present moment. The devil has moved us away from the place of grace and blessing. My wife's poem expresses this well.

BLEST

O be blessed,
unruffled by clamorings of the past,
by fears for what we hold most dear.

O be blessed,
flowing by God's spirit
toward His image;
flexing to His plans—
whether shadowy or clear.

Be blessed this very moment,
the only time of touch or blessing:
for the past has fled;
but the future is not here.

Take the Initiative

The devil often tries to use discouragement or confusion to keep us from functioning effectively. When we get into a negative or discouraging frame of mind, we need consciously to shift gears so as to focus our thoughts on God. We can declare Scriptural truths that are the antidote to those feelings and the thoughts that underlie them. We can follow the example of David, who strengthened himself in the Lord (1 Samuel 30:6) and exhorted his soul to remember God's goodness and trust in him (Psalms 42:5-6, 103:1-5).

When, as happens to all of us, we find ourselves feeling "yucky," we need to say, "This is not where I need to be. I'm going to change it"—and then take ourselves to another place. As we do this, we begin to get a list of things we can do that will drive away these confusing, discouraging moods. It may be reading Scripture, listening to uplifting music, asking God to show us what the problem is, talking to or praying with a friend, changing our activity, getting some physical exercise, or whatever. We need to use whatever works for us. When we find ourselves in the wrong place spiritually, we mustn't let ourselves stay there. We need to be alert to take control and change things.

When the devil attacks, when things go badly, when we feel discouraged or confused, when we find ourselves thinking ungodly thoughts, etc., we need to take the initiative. We do not have to sit there and allow the devil to attack us. Perhaps we need to identify what our weaknesses are, what we have done to make the attack possible, and decide to do something about them. Or we may need to pray or worship. This usually calls for a conscious and deliberate change in attitude or activity. We don't just have to dig in and take it. We can do affirmative things to improve our defenses.

Use the Spiritual Weapons God Has Given Us

All too often, in our Christian life, we fail to use what God has given us. In physical warfare, our soldiers have been issued powerful and effective weapons. But those weapons will not do them any good unless they use them. A rifle, or other weapon, that remains in the soldier's backpack will not help him. Similarly, we need to use the spiritual weapons God has given us.

With these thoughts in mind, let us look further at Ephesians, chapter 6, and its list of the spiritual weapons God has given us, the "whole armor" of God.

THE BELT OF TRUTH—God's word is truth. Jesus Christ is "the truth." It is God's truth that sets us free. Spiritual conflict is primarily a truth struggle.

The devil is a liar and the father of lies (John 8:45). He is a deceiver (Revelation 20:3, 8, 10). (Also see 2 Corinthians 11:14-15.) He loves to sow confusion. Our best weapon (defensive and offensive) against his lies, deception and confusion is to stand firm on God's truth. To do this we must be well-grounded in God's truth. We must be very sure of it, and alert to detect departures from it. We need to fill ourselves with God's truth—as revealed in his Scripture—and be ready to use it at all times to confront the devil's lies and deception. We need to remind ourselves of God's truth, and reject everything that is contrary to it. We need to know Scripture well enough so that we can discern and confront the lies that the devil keeps throwing at us.

One area where this is especially important is within the church, within the body of Christ. In Jesus' parable of the wheat and the tares (Matthew 13:24-29, 37-43) the devil sowed the tares (weeds—symbol of evil) among the good wheat. He frequently sows falsity within the church, among believers. We need to be very alert to detect and confront falsity and seeds of deception within the body of Christ.

THE BREASTPLATE OF RIGHTEOUSNESS—We stand in Christ's righteousness, not our own. But at the same time we need to do all we can to become holy, as God is holy. This is part of how we get rid of any foothold the devil might seek to claim.

THE GOSPEL OF PEACE—The gospel tells us that we have been saved and are no longer under the power of sin. We are no longer in the devil's kingdom. We are no longer his children. We do not owe any allegiance to him. The gospel also tells us of our position in Christ (see Chapter 11), which is absolutely basic to our ability to fight against the devil. Part of the good news is that God is all-powerful, that the devil cannot stand against God's power, and that God has promised to protect his people.

THE SHIELD OF FAITH—Faith is essential to our Christian life. (See Chapter 18.) "All things are possible to him who believes" (Mark 9:23). Without faith in Jesus Christ, we have no salvation and no position in Christ. Without faith in God's Scripture and his promises, we would find it very difficult to stand against our spiritual enemy, the devil. When he attacks us, we stand firm in the faith (1 Peter 5:9).

The faith that stops the fiery darts of the devil is a heart-felt faith, a belief that is based on all of our heart, all of our soul, all of our mind and all of our strength. The devil attacks our faith in two ways.

- He seeks to cause fear, which is a lack of faith. Scripture says, "God is our refuge and strength, a very present help in trouble. Therefore we will not fear" (Psalm 46:1-2). "Do not be afraid; only believe" (Mark 5:36). "Be anxious for nothing" (Philippians 4:6). "God has not given us a spirit of fear" (2 Timothy 1:7). If we put our whole trust in a great God, who is far bigger than any problem or difficulty we may face, we have nothing to fear.
- He seeks to cause doubt, which destroys our faith. "He who doubts is like a wave of the sea driven and tossed by the wind. For let not that man suppose that he will receive anything from the Lord; he is a double-minded [literally, "two-souled"] man, unstable in all his ways" (James 1:6-8). Our prayer needs constantly to be, "Increase our faith" (Luke 17:5). "I do believe; help me overcome my unbelief" (Mark 9:24 NIV).

Unbelief can be a form of spiritual treason. We see this in Hebrews, where an unbelieving heart is referred to as "rebellion" and as "disobedience" (Hebrews 3:12, 16, 18, 4:11). We need to identify and reject unbelief whenever it crops up.

We must not allow the devil to undermine our faith.

THE HELMET OF SALVATION—All of our spiritual weapons depend on our salvation. It is only as we are saved, and accept Jesus Christ as our Lord and Savior, that we can claim the other spiritual weapons. It is because of our salvation, and our willingness to commit ourselves wholly to Jesus Christ, that we can have God's incomparably great power at work in us, and that we can be strong in the Lord and in his mighty power.

THE SWORD OF THE SPIRIT—One of our most powerful weapons is "the sword of the Spirit, which is the word of God" (Ephesians 6:17). "Man shall not live by bread alone, but by every word that proceeds from the mouth of God" (Matthew 4:4). The word of God is our spiritual daily bread; we need to feed on it daily.

God's word is a defensive weapon. By it we stand firm in the faith. When the devil tempted Jesus in the wilderness, Jesus stood on the word of God (Matthew 4:4, 7, 10), and the devil left him. The Psalmist, under the leading of the Holy Spirit, wrote, "Your word have I hidden in my heart, that I might not sin against

You" (Psalm 119:11). We demolish strongholds, and take every thought captive to obey Jesus Christ, by declaring the truth of God's word.

But a sword is primarily an offensive weapon. The devil cannot stand against God's word. When Jesus was tempted in the wilderness, he responded by quoting Scripture, saying, "it is written," and the devil had no answer. When we declare God's truth, as revealed in his word, the evil spirits cannot stand against it.

One of the ways we can use the word of God as a weapon of both defense and offense is to speak it out loud. When the devil seeks to get us to accept his lies, we declare the word of God. We reject the devil's lies and assert against them the truth of God's word. For example, if we are attacked with fear and doubt, we can declare that God is faithful, remind ourselves of what God has done for us and for his people, and remember that Jesus promised that he will always be with us (Matthew 28:20). We can declare that every knee must bow, and every tongue must confess, that Jesus Christ is Lord, to the glory of God the Father (Philippians 2:9-11). We demolish strongholds with Scriptural truth.

The devil cannot stand against the truth of God's word. The more we declare it, proclaim it, teach it, preach it, assert it, pray it, and live it, the more we will have victory over the father of lies.

PRAY—A very important part of the weaponry that God has given us is to "...pray in the Spirit on all occasions" (Ephesians 6:18 NIV). (Praying in the Spirit means to pray as the Holy Spirit directs, to pray under the guidance of the Holy Spirit.) Scripture tells us to pray without ceasing (1 Thessalonians 5:17).

I believe prayer is our strongest weapon against the devil. By prayer we submit ourselves to God and seek that his will be done. By prayer we line ourselves up with God's purposes for our lives. By prayer we come near to God and God comes near to us. (See James 4:8.) "...the LORD our God is near us whenever we pray to him" (Deuteronomy 4:7 NIV). The devil cannot prevail against effective prayer.

CONCLUSION

I want to close with one thought that is implicit in much of what I have said, but that needs to be made explicit. The focus of our thoughts should be on God. "Since, then, you have been raised with Christ, set your hearts on things above, where Christ is seated at the right hand of God. Set your minds on things above, not on earthly things" (Colossians 3:1-2 NIV). "Let us fix our eyes on Jesus, the author and perfecter of our faith..." (Hebrews 12:2 NIV). "Bless the LORD, O my soul; and all that is within me, bless His holy name" (Psalm 103:1). The Lord inhabits the praises of his people (Psalm 22:3 KJV). As we focus on him, and bless and praise him, we draw near to him and he to us.

When the devil attacks us, we need to deal with it. But we should not let his attacks draw our focus away from God, for "in Him we live and move and have our being" (Acts 17:28), and from him we draw our strength.

13

Dare to Be Different

o o o o o o o o o o o o o o o o o o o o o o o o o o o o o o o o o o o

"Do not conform any longer to the pattern of this world..."

—*(Romans 12:2 NIV)*

God wants his people to be radically different from others. British pastor and teacher John R.W. Stott said,

> "Insofar as the church is conformed to the world, and the two communities appear to the onlooker to be merely two versions of the same thing, the church is contradicting its true identity. No comment could be more harmful to the Christian than the words, 'But you are no different from anybody else.'
>
> "For the essential theme of the whole Bible from beginning to end is that God's historical purpose is to call out a people for himself; that God's people is a 'holy' people, set apart from the world to belong to him and to obey him; and that its vocation is to be true to its identity, that is to be 'holy' or 'different' in all its outlook and behavior."[25]

God, through Moses, told the people of Israel, "You must not do as they do in Egypt, where you used to live, and you must not do as they do in the land of Canaan, where I am bringing you. Do not follow their practices. You must obey my laws and be careful to follow my decrees. I am the LORD your God" (Leviticus 18:3-4 NIV). (Also see Leviticus 21:23; Deuteronomy 12:30-31.) Jesus told his followers, "Do not be like them" (Matthew 6:8). (Also see 2 Corinthians 6:17; 1 Peter 1:14-15.) Jesus did not want his followers to be like the heathen, or to be like the religious leaders of his time. (See, for example, Matthew 6:1-8.)

Paul told the Ephesians that they should "no longer walk as the rest of the Gentiles walk" (Ephesians 4:17).

Jesus told the religious leaders of his time, "You are of this world; I am not of this world" (John 8:23). Then he said to his Father in heaven that his disciples "...are not of the world any more than I am of the world" (John 17:14 NIV). (Also see verse 16.) The disciples were to be different. The rules of the kingdom of God are often the exact opposite of the rules of this world. That is why many people speak of the teachings of Jesus, in the Sermon on the Mount and elsewhere, as "unrealistic" or "impossible." To those who do not give their full allegiance to God, they are impossible to follow. To those who are wholeheartedly committed to God, have the Holy Spirit living in them, and God's power working in them, they are still very challenging. But as we mature as Christians, we can come fairly close to living by them.

Why is it so important for Christians to be different?

- It is the fact that we are different that challenges and draws unbelievers to God. If committed Christians are perceived as no different from anyone else, then what does Christianity have to offer to unbelievers? It is only as we are seen as having something different to offer, that people will be drawn to that something different and to God. It is only as we are perceived as being different that we can "be witnesses" to God.
- If we continue to be conformed to the pattern of this world, then our allegiance is to this world. Or else we are double-minded, with one foot in the world and one foot in the kingdom of God. In either case, we will not have the desire or the power to stand up against the ungodliness that is so prevalent in our society today.
- Most Christians spend relatively few hours a week on the things of God. The rest of the time we are bombarded—systematically, pervasively and insistently—by the things of this world. If we are to stand up against that bombardment, we need to make a deliberate effort to be radically different from the world.

Paul's letter to the Romans is the most detailed and systematic discussion that we have of Paul's teaching to believers. As in most of his letters, he starts with a discussion of basic spiritual principles, and then discusses their practical application in our lives. In Romans that discussion of application begins with chapter 12. First he tells us to give our lives to God, to commit ourselves totally to God (Romans 12:1). (I deal with this in chapter 16.)

Then he says, "Do not conform any longer to the pattern of this world, but be transformed by the renewing of your mind..." (Romans 12:2 NIV). I believe this is a key verse in Scripture. In this chapter, I deal with the first half of this sentence. In the next chapter, I shall deal with the second half. The two are closely related. They are opposite sides of the same coin. In order to be transformed into God's character, we need to reject the pattern of this world. As we become transformed, we will reject the pattern of this world. But we cannot have it both ways. Either we live by the world's rules, and to that extent reject God, or we seek to have God's character and reject the world's rules.

WHAT IS THE PATTERN OF THIS WORLD?

"World," *aion,* also translated "age," refers particularly to the prevailing thought-patterns and attitudes of the current age. Rejecting the pattern of this world does not mean that we should live in isolation, as hermits. Quite the contrary. We are called to be salt and light to the world (Matthew 5:13-14). Jesus moved about actively in the world of his day. So did Paul. But we must resist the pressure to conform to the world's ways. Scripture repeats this theme over and over, in many different ways.

Christ came to "deliver us from this present evil age" (Galatians 1:4). Jesus warns that the "cares of this world" can choke out the word of God (Matthew 13:22). Paul speaks of satan as the "god of this age" (2 Corinthians 4:4). He contrasts the wisdom of this world, or of this age, with the eternal wisdom of God, and warns against following the former (1 Corinthians 1:20-25, 2:6-8). (Also see James 3:13-18.) Paul says that we once were "dead in trespasses and sins, in which you once walked according to the course of this world, according to the prince of the power of the air, the spirit who now works in the sons of disobedience" (Ephesians 2:1-2). He says that Demas deserted him because he "loved this present world" (2 Timothy 4:10). He tells us to deny "ungodliness and worldly lusts" (Titus 2:12).

Another Greek word translated "world" is *kosmos*, which refers to the physical universe, the material in contrast to the spiritual. Scripture warns us against it, also. Jesus spoke of satan as the ruler of this world (John 12:31). He told the Jewish religious leaders, "You are of this world; I am not of this world" (John 8:23). He told his disciples, "because you are not of this world, but I chose you out of the world, therefore the world hates you" (John 15:19). (Also see John 17:14.) Paul wrote, "Now we have received, not the spirit of the world, but the Spirit who is from God, that we may know the things that have been freely given to us by God" (1 Corinthians 2:12). Paul warned, "Beware lest anyone cheat you through philosophy and empty deceit, according to the tradition of men, according to the basic principles of the world, and not according to Christ" (Colossians 2:8). He said that we have "died with Christ from the basic principles of this world" (Colossians 2:20). James tells us that pure religion is to keep oneself from being polluted by the world (James 1:27). (Also see James 4:4.) Peter warns us to escape the corruption that is in the world (2 Peter 1:4). (Also see 2:20.) John warns us not to love the world or anything in it (1 John 2:15-17). He speaks of believers as overcoming the world (1 John 5:4).

Scripture calls on us to be holy (1 Peter 1:15; Hebrews 12:14). The Greek word for "holy" is *hagios*. According to Vine's *Expository Dictionary of Biblical Words*, it "fundamentally signifies 'separated'," and hence, "separated from sin and therefore consecrated to God." In the Old Testament, the Hebrew word *quadosh* and related words also have the meaning of separated. "Come out from them and be separate, says the Lord" (2 Corinthians 6:17).

Today the pattern of this world is thrust upon us to a greater degree than ever before. From the time we get up to the time we go to bed, many of us are bombarded with sounds and visual images—from newspapers, radio, television, computers, "background" music, magazine covers, billboards, etc. Most of these sounds and images are worldly. Some encourage sexual immorality. Others contain excessive and graphic violence. There is profanity and crude language. The family (particularly fathers) is portrayed in an unfavorable light. Christian values are mocked. Lying, cynicism, hardheartedness, and sexual promiscuity are portrayed as being normal. Selfishness and greed are encouraged. Through all these, we are often exposed to the "counsel of the ungodly" (Psalm 1:1).

The world is not neutral. It is making a deliberate assault on Christian values and standards. It takes determination, and solid roots, to stand up against this assault.

Why is the world such a danger? Let me mention some, among many, reasons:

- It contains much corruption and tempts us to become corrupt.
- Our desire for material things can become a form of idolatry. The love of money, and of what money can buy, "is a root of all kinds of evil, for which some have strayed from the faith in their greediness, and have pierced themselves through with many sorrows" (1 Timothy 6:10).
- The world's ways, the world's values, are not God's ways and values.

WHY IS IT SO DIFFICULT NOT TO CONFORM?

We are dealing here with two different world-views, a secular or worldly one, and a godly one. Our world views are pervasive and deeply entrenched. We do not change them easily or quickly.

We are also dealing with mental strongholds. (See 2 Corinthians 10:4.) There is spiritual conflict going on within us. (See Chapter 15.) The devil resists strenuously our efforts to demolish the stronghold of worldliness. Often strongholds do not come down easily or quickly. It takes persistent effort.

One of the greatest temptations we face, as Christians, is the desire to please the world rather than God. Our goal should be to please God (2 Corinthians 5:9). (Also see Ephesians 5:10; Colossians 1:10.) But the temptation is always to seek to please men, or to avoid their displeasure. In an effort to be more acceptable to men, we often fall into the world's ways of thinking and acting. John's gospel speaks of religious leaders who "loved the praise of men more than the praise of God" (John 12:43). I'm afraid there are such leaders today. Jesus said, "Woe to you when all men speak well of you, for so did their fathers to the false prophets" (Luke 6:26). (This statement may seem shocking, but I think we need to take it seriously.) God said, "...Who are you that you fear mortal men, the sons of men, who are but grass, that you forget the LORD your Maker, who stretched out the heavens and laid the foundations of the earth..." (Isaiah 51:12 NIV). The social pressure to conform to the world and its standards is great, but we must resist that pressure.

I believe that one of the major causes of weakness in the body of Christ today is that many individuals, churches and denominations have tried to conform to the prevailing patterns of the world, both in thought and in conduct, and have been drawn away from God's ways and values. We have ignored Romans 12:2.

HOW CAN WE STOP CONFORMING?

Believe in the Bible

The first essential is that we must really believe in the Bible. We must consider it as authoritative and take it seriously. We must take Romans 12:2 as one of our basic rules of conduct.

Then we must check everything we say or do against what the Bible says. Our standard, for all that we think, say or do, must become, "Is this consistent with Scripture?" "Is this what God wants?"

There are quite a few Christians, and some churches and even denominations, who go along with worldly standards. Many of these are people who do not accept the Bible, the entire Bible, as authoritative. If we don't accept the Bible as authoritative, we have nothing with which to stand against the pressure to conform to worldly standards. If we stand on the truth of Scripture, we have a solid basis from which to resist worldly pressures. If we do not stand on the truth of Scripture, then there is little reason not to go along with every popular movement and teaching.

Decide

We must also make a conscious decision not to conform to the world's standards. This may take courage. It is hard to resist peer pressure. When we resist, it may lead to confrontation, to mocking and ridicule, to rejection and other unpleasant consequences. The world hated Jesus and his disciples because they were not of this world. If we would follow godly standards, we need to be willing to accept disapproval and even hatred. Whom do we want to please, people or God? There are times when you cannot do both.

Take Our Thoughts Captive to Obey Jesus Christ

Scripture tells us to take our thoughts captive to obey Jesus Christ (2 Corinthians 10:5). I would carry this further and say that we need to take our thoughts, our words, and our actions captive to obey Jesus Christ. (See Chapter 17.) This takes continual alertness. We need to notice what we are thinking, saying and doing, and compare it with Scriptural teaching. We need to catch ourselves and repent. This is not easy, but it becomes easier with time and practice.

It is when we are not consciously thinking of spiritual things that we are most apt to find ourselves conforming to the pattern of this world. During our ordinary daily life, we may find ourselves thinking thoughts, accepting attitudes, saying and doing things, that conform to the pattern of this world and not to God's will. We need to take these captive. We need to recognize them, repudiate them, and replace them with godly thoughts, attitudes and actions.

This is particularly true of what we call entertainment. When we are seeking entertainment, we tend to relax and let our guard down. There is much in the entertainment field—television, movies, music, novels, video games and the like—which is based (either openly or through underlying assumptions) on beliefs and values that are contrary to God's ways. These can instill in us (often without our awareness) a conformity to ways of this world which are in opposition to God's ways. We need to be aware of this. We need to guard what we are feeding into our hearts and minds. We must not allow ourselves to slip, unsuspectingly, into worldly ways and attitudes that can be quite destructive.

Many Americans tend to compartmentalize things, to put some things in a "religious" category, some things in a "work" category, some things in a "home life" category, and some things in a "recreation" category. But Scripture tells us to love the Lord with all of our heart, soul, mind and strength, and to pray constantly. **Everything** we think and do should be dedicated to God. This means that we should take **all** of our thoughts captive to Christ—not just "religious" ones.

Focus on the Things of God

I believe one good way to resist the pressure to conform to the pattern of this world is to make a conscious decision to focus our minds on the things of God. "Seek those things which are above, where Christ is sitting at the right hand of God. Set your mind on things above, not on things on the earth" (Colossians 3:1-2). "Look to Jesus, the author and finisher of our faith" (Hebrews 12:2). "We do not look at the things which are seen, but at the things which are not seen. For the things which are seen are temporary, but the things which are not seen are eternal" (2 Corinthinas 4:18).

This does not mean that we ignore what is going on in the world. We need to be aware of it. We may need to take a very active part in some aspects of it. But we need to balance our concern over the things of this world, by feeding our minds and spirits on the things of God. We need to feed ourselves with Scripture, prayer, praise and the like. Our primary focus needs to be on the eternal things of God.

For example, as I am doing the final editing on this manuscript, we are coming very close to a Presidential and Congressional election. My family and I care deeply about the results of the election. We spend time reading about it, discussing it, asking ourselves what we can do about it. I ran a voter registration drive in my church, and have written a letter to the editor about the Presidential election.

We pray about the election every day. Sometimes all this becomes very distressing. But then we need to come to the point of saying, "Lord, you are in charge. It will come out the way you want it, or at least the way you choose to let it. Our ultimate desire is simply to see your will be done in this election. And however this election comes out, we know that ultimately your purposes for mankind on this earth will prevail. They cannot be thwarted." So we take comfort in that knowledge. We do what we can, but ultimately it is up to God.

Also, in practical terms, we cannot fix the problems in this country. However, we can do something about getting this book published. And that, hopefully, will help some fellow Christians stand firm in their faith no matter what happens to our country. We cannot do everything, but by the grace of God, what we can do, we will do.

CONCLUSION

I cannot emphasize too much the importance of resolving not to conform to the pattern of this world. The question is, "whom will we serve?" Will we serve the world and try to please people? Or will we serve God and try to please God?

I believe that one of the principal reasons for the weakness that the Christian church as a whole has shown in resisting the growing secularization of our nation, has been the fact that many Christians have been far too willing to conform to this world.

14

Be Transformed by the Renewing of Your Mind

o o o o o o o o o o o o o o o o o o o o o o o o o o o o o o

"Do not conform any longer to the pattern of this world, but be transformed by the renewing of your mind…"

—*(Romans 12:2 NIV)*

We come now to the second part of Romans 12:2. In order not to conform, we must be transformed. This theme runs throughout the New Testament. God does not want us to stay where we are. He wants us to change, radically. Change is often difficult and can be painful. But it is what God wants and expects of us.

A RADICAL TRANSFORMATION

God expects that, when we accept Jesus Christ as our Lord and Savior, we will be radically changed, transformed. The Greek word is *metamorphoo.* This transformation is to be a metamorphosis, of a magnitude at least comparable to that by which a caterpillar becomes a butterfly. God expects us to become totally different.

Scripture uses many different images to express the change that should occur:

- We become "a new creation; old things have passed away; behold, all things have become new" (2 Corinthians 5:17). We really become a new species. Scripture speaks of the first Adam who was earthly and fell into sin, and the second Adam (Jesus Christ) who was sinless and holy (1 Corinthians 15:44-49). (Also see Romans 5:12-19.) It says that we will bear the likeness of the second Adam.

- "And we, who with unveiled faces all reflect the Lord's glory, are being transformed into his likeness with ever-increasing glory, which comes from the Lord, who is the Spirit" (2 Corinthians 3:18 NIV).
- We are "renewed in the spirit of [our] mind" (Ephesians 4:23).
- We "put off…the old man" and "put on the new man" (Ephesians 4:22, 24). (Also see Colossians 3:9-10.)
- We live by the Spirit and not by the flesh (Galatians 5:16; Romans 8:13).
- We become "instruments of righteousness" rather than "instruments of unrighteousness" (Romans 6:13).
- We have "been buried with him through baptism into death" in order that we may "walk in newness of life" (Romans 6:4).
- "I have been crucified with Christ; it is no longer I who live, but Christ lives in me" (Galatians 2:20).
- We have "been set free from sin" and have "become slaves of God" (Romans 6:22). We are no longer slaves "of sin, leading to death," but have become slaves "of obedience, leading to righteousness" (Romans 6:16).
- We are rescued ("translated" KJV) from the kingdom of darkness into the Kingdom of God's Son (Colossians 1:13). Our citizenship and our allegiance have been changed.
- We have become adopted children of God (John 1:12-13; Romans 8:15-16).
- We are born again (John 3:3, 5); born from above, of the spirit and not the flesh.

Each of these images, in a different way, emphasizes the magnitude of the change that is expected. Each is dramatic and astonishing in itself; their cumulative effect is even more powerful. We are talking about a tremendous transformation. It should be visible to others, but its internal effect should be far greater than what others can perceive.

Such a transformation is not easy to achieve. Indeed, we can only achieve it through God's mighty power working within us. We also have an enemy (satan) who will resist the transformation in every way he can. He tries to do everything he can to render us ineffective. I believe this whole area of becoming transformed is one of the major battlegrounds of our conflict with satan. (See Chapter 12.)

One of the major weaknesses among Christians today is that, often, this transformation, if it has occurred at all, is not visible to the world. Jesus said, "He that has seen Me has seen the Father" (John 14:9). I believe he expects that anyone who sees a true Christian will see in him at least something of Jesus Christ. We are expected to be "a letter from Christ…written not with ink but with the Spirit of the living God, not on tablets of stone but on tablets of human hearts" (2 Corinthians 3:3 NIV). We should be witnesses to Christ (Acts 1:8), not only by what we say, but even more by who we are. Jesus said that the world should know who his disciples are by their love for each other (John 13:35). He said of his disciples, "They are not of the world, just as I am not of the world" (John 17:16).

If a person is not significantly changed by their salvation, their acceptance of Christ as Lord and Savior, we are entitled to wonder whether their salvation was genuine.

In today's world, Christians are increasingly coming under attack. One of the grounds of attack often heard is, "You Christians are no different than anyone else. Just more hypocritical." It is distressing that such an attack can be made. We are supposed to be salt and light to the world, and to let our light shine before men (Matthew 5:13-16). We need to so live that the difference between Christians and non-Christians is inescapable. We need to stand, boldly and clearly, for what we believe.

THE GOAL OF THIS TRANSFORMATION

What is the goal of this metamorphosis? Scripture states it in a number of different ways, which overlap and can be seen as different ways of expressing the same basic concept. Scripture often does this, because our minds are inadequate to comprehend, and our language inadequate to express, the full scope of God's revelation to us.

We Become More Like God in Character

The whole concept can be summed up in the simple and astonishing statement that we are to become like God in character. Not like God in power—we should never aspire to that—but like God in character. We are to "…put on the new self, **created to be like God** in true righteousness and holiness" (Ephesians 4:24 NIV), the "…new self, which is being renewed in knowledge **in the image of its Creator**" (Colossians 3:10 NIV). "And we, who with unveiled faces all reflect the Lord's glory, are being **transformed into his likeness** with ever-increasing glory, which comes from the Lord, who is the Spirit" (2 Corinthians 3:18 NIV). God intends us "...to be **conformed to the likeness of his Son**..." (Romans 8:29 NIV). We are to "...**participate in the divine nature**..." (2 Peter 1:4 NIV). "We have **the mind of Christ**" (1 Corinthians 2:16). (Also see Philippians 2:5.)

Adam and Eve were created in the image of God (Genesis 1:26). With their Fall, much of that image was lost. But with Christ's sacrifice for us, those who accept him as Lord and Savior can be restored into God's image.

Let us look at some other ways of expressing the same concept.

We Live for the Things That Are Unseen

Two of the great statements about this transformation are:

- "...we...are being transformed into his likeness with ever-increasing glory..." (2 Corinthians 3:18 NIV).
- "If anyone is in Christ, he is a new creation" (2 Corinthians 5:17).

A look at what is said between those two statements tells us a good deal about the nature of this transformation.

In 2 Corinthians, chapters 4 and 5, Paul repeatedly contrasts the material world in which our bodies now live, and the spiritual world. He tells us that the spiritual world is the real one, on which we should focus. He says, "...we regard no one from a worldly point of view..." (2 Corinthians 5:16 NIV). Earlier he says, "The god of this age has blinded the minds of unbelievers, so that they cannot see the light of the gospel of the glory of Christ, who is the image of God" (2 Corinthians 4:4 NIV). And in 1 Corinthians 2:14, he points out that the man without the Spirit cannot understand spiritual things.

In 2 Corinthians 4:18 (NIV), Paul says, "So we fix our eyes not on what is seen, but on what is unseen. For what is seen is temporary, but what is unseen is eternal." Again, in 2 Corinthians 5:7 (NIV), he says, "We live by faith, not by sight." (Also see Hebrews 11:1 NIV, which says that faith "...is being certain of what we do not see.") Paul says much the same in Colossians 3:1-2 (NIV), "Since, then, you have been raised with Christ, set your hearts on things above, where Christ is seated at the right hand of God. Set your minds on things above, not on earthly things." God is spirit and he lives primarily in the realm of the spirit. He lived in that realm before there was any physical universe, and he will live in it even though heaven and earth pass away. (See Isaiah 51:6.) If we are to be like him, we need to learn to see things from God's perspective.

This results in a wholly different order of priorities.

First, the natural person, the untransformed person, lives primarily for material things. His priorities are those of the material world. The transformed person lives primarily in a spiritual world. He lives primarily by faith in God and in God's word, rather than by his physical senses. He regards the unseen things of faith as more real and more lasting than the material things which surround him. The transformed person is living primarily in a different world, a world in which spiritual rather than material things have primary importance.

Second, where the natural person lives only for this life, the transformed person is already living in eternity. Paul speaks of this in many ways. For Paul, tribulations and difficulties of this world become minor when compared to the glory to come. In 2 Corinthians 4:16-17 (NIV), Paul says, "Therefore we do not lose heart. Though outwardly we are wasting away, yet inwardly we are being renewed day by day. For our light and momentary troubles are achieving for us an eternal glory that far outweighs them all." (Also see 1 Peter 4:12-13; Hebrews 12:2.) He says, "So we are always confident" (2 Corinthians 5:6), because we know that when we leave this earthly body we will be with the Lord, which is better. (Also see Philippians 1:21.)

Jesus told those who believed in him that in this world they will have tribulation (John 16:33). Paul said that "We must through many tribulations enter the kingdom of God" (Acts 14:22), and that "…everyone who wants to live a godly life in Christ Jesus will be persecuted…" (2 Timothy 3:12 NIV). But we should rejoice in our troubles, because we learn and grow from them (James 1:2-4; Romans 5:3-5), and because they are far outweighed by the glory that is to come. As believers, "…we know that in all things God works for the good of those who love him, who have been called according to his purpose" (Romans 8:28 NIV).

Third, "…those who live should no longer live for themselves, but for him who died for them and was raised again" (2 Corinthians 5:15 NIV). Hence, "…we make it our goal to please him…" (2 Corinthians 5:9 NIV). We should not be like those who "loved praise from men more than praise from God" (John 12:43). (Also see Isaiah 51:12-13.) Jesus has told us, "If the world hates you, keep in mind that it hated me first. If you belonged to the world, it would love you as its own. As it is, you do not belong to the world, but I have chosen you out of the world. That is why the world hates you" (John 15:18-19 NIV).

These are all major shifts in our attitudes and priorities. Truly they require a "renewing of the mind."

These changes in priorities may help explain a passage that has long puzzled me. In Luke 10:19, Jesus said that he had given his disciples authority over all the power of our spiritual enemy (the devil) "and nothing shall by any means hurt you." Available data seems to indicate that 10 of the 12 disciples were martyred, some quite painfully. Since then, many disciples of Jesus have been martyred, beaten, or otherwise physically mistreated for their faith. This occurs today in quite a few parts of the world. How could Jesus say that nothing would hurt his disciples? Let me offer a suggestion. In spiritual terms, in eternal terms, nothing did hurt them. They went on to be with God and to receive a martyr's reward. The result of their physical pains was, in Paul's words, "an eternal glory that far outweighs them all" (2 Corinthians 4:7 NIV). Jesus was speaking in spiritual terms; he was talking of conflict with a spiritual enemy. In Luke 12:5, Jesus said, "Do not be afraid of those who kill the body and after that have no more that they can do." Was he telling his disciples that, because of the authority he had given them, they need not fear spiritual harm?

We Live by the Spirit

When we receive Jesus Christ as our Lord and Savior, God sends us the Holy Spirit to live with us and be in us (John 14:16). It is because we have the Holy Spirit living in us, and his power working in us, that we are able to be transformed. But the process is not instantaneous. The Holy Spirit inhabits our spirit, but our soul and body need to be brought under the Spirit's control. (I discuss this in chapter 15.)

We Are Yielded to God

Part of what living by the Spirit means is that we are wholly yielded to God. We are no longer slaves to sin but slaves to obedience and righteousness (Romans 6:16). We submit ourselves to God (James 4:7). (See Chapters 16 and 17.)

HOW CAN WE ACHIEVE THIS TRANSFORMATION?

The task of achieving such a transformation seems impossible. How can we humans acquire the character of God? But God always enables us to do what he calls on us to do. We can become like God in character because we have God in us. (See Chapter 11.) As we allow the Holy Spirit who is in us to control our soul and body, we can become like God in character. And God has given us the power of the Holy Spirit (Acts 1:8), the same power in which Jesus ministered while here on earth, so that we can do all things through him who strengthens us (Philippians 4:13).

We need always to keep in mind two things about this transformation. First, it is a process. It does not happen all at once. We "**are being transformed** into his likeness with **ever-increasing** glory." We spend a lifetime learning how to live by the Spirit, live a new life. We must work out, and keep on working out, our salvation with fear and trembling. We must keep making every effort to be holy (Hebrews 12:14). We must submit, and keep on submitting, to God. Over and over and over we must take our thoughts captive to obey Christ (2 Corinthians 10:5). Near the end of his life, Paul did not consider that he had arrived (Philippians 3:12).

Some of the passages do sound as if they speak of an instantaneous transformation. We can understand those passages in this way. The change in our spirit comes about immediately. But it usually takes quite a while for that change to be reflected in our soul and flesh. Also, God's time is not the same as ours. A thousand years are as a moment in his sight. 2,000 years ago, Jesus said he was coming "quickly"; we still wait for his coming. After Eli told Saul, "the LORD has torn the kingdom of Israel from you **today**, and given it to a neighbor of yours, who is better than you" (1 Samuel 15:28), it took over 20 years before David assumed the throne.

Second, we and God cooperate to bring it about. We cannot do it ourselves. And God will not usually do it without our cooperation. In this, as in so many aspects of our spiritual life, we and God are co-laborers. "We are God's fellow workers" (1 Corinthians 3:9). "…continue to work out your salvation with fear and trembling, for it is God who works in you to will and to act according to his good purpose" (Philippians 2:12-13 NIV). We work and God works. We labor together.

One aspect of this transformation is showing the "fruit of the spirit." A farmer cannot cause fruit to grow; he can create conditions favorable to its growth and protect it from parasites, diseases and other forces that seek to destroy it. In somewhat the same way, we cannot cause God's character to grow within us; only God can do that. But we can create favorable conditions for its growth—by faith, prayer, study of the word, etc.—and we can protect that growth from the devil's attacks.

What is our part in this labor? Let me suggest some aspects of it.

BELIEVE—We need to believe that God can and will transform us into his image, that this astonishing metamorphosis can and will occur. We need to consider him faithful who has made the promise (Hebrews 11:11). "Without faith we cannot please God" (Hebrews 11:6). If we do not believe that God will achieve this transformation, or if we are double-minded in our belief, we cannot expect to receive anything from God (James 1:6-8). Whenever we catch ourselves in unbelief, we must renounce it and repudiate it.

CHOOSE—We must make an act of the will. We must choose to be transformed, choose to put off the old self and put on the new self, choose to live by the Spirit, choose to submit to God, choose to be weapons of righteousness, etc. God, through Moses, told the Israelites, "I call heaven and earth as witnesses today against you, that I have set before you life and death, blessing and cursing; therefore choose life" (Deuteronomy 30:19-20). God gives us that same choice today.

STAY IN GOD'S WORD—The agent that renews our mind is the word of God. It is not enough just to read the word. We need to believe it, take it seriously, and follow it. We need to let it dwell in us, work in us, become engrafted in us, become a part of us. Scripture speaks often about the importance of meditating on the word of God (Joshua 1:8; Psalms 1:2, 119:78). The Hebrew word for meditate suggests a cow chewing its cud, working the material over and over to extract all the good from it.

GUARD OUR THOUGHTS—If we would be transformed by the renewing of our mind, be made new in the attitude of our mind, we need to guard carefully what goes into our mind. We need to think on those things that are true, noble, right, pure, etc. (Philippians 4:8). Even more important, we need to guard against our own wrong thoughts, the thoughts that come from the flesh and not the spirit. We need to take our thoughts captive to obey Christ (2 Corinthians 10:5). We need to do this, not just daily, but moment by moment. Whenever we find ourselves thinking unscriptural thoughts, we need to repudiate them, renounce them, and replace them with thoughts that are Scripturally true.

PRAY—"If any of you lacks wisdom, let him ask of God, who gives to all liberally and without reproach, and it will be given to him" (James 1:5). The same principle applies to any other quality we lack. "You do not have, because you do not ask" (James 4:2). Jesus told us, "Ask, and it will be given to you; seek, and you will find; knock, and it will be opened to you" (Matthew 7:7). The form of the verbs means "keep on asking," "keep on seeking," "keep on knocking." When we keep asking God to change us into his likeness, we unite our will with his and make it possible for him to co-labor with us.

PERSEVERE—Jesus told his disciples to persist in prayer (Luke 18:1-7, 11:5-10). We are to "...run with perseverance the race marked out for us" (Hebrews 12:1 NIV). (Also see Hebrews 6:11.) Scripture is full of words telling us to apply ourselves diligently to the task before us. We need to keep pursuing, making every effort, pressing on, continuing, standing, etc. The promises of God do not usually drop in our laps. They come to the one who persists, presses in, keeps on keeping on.

RESIST THE DEVIL—Satan does not want us to succeed. (See Chapter 12.) He does not want us to be transformed. His purpose is to steal, kill and destroy (John 10:10). If he cannot prevent us from being saved, he will try to keep us ineffective. He does not want us to take on the image of God for two reasons: (1) he hates God; (2) he knows that if we do take on the image of God, we will be more powerful opponents. So he will do everything possible to distract, discourage and defeat.

I believe this area of being transformed is one of the major areas of the conflict with satan that we face as individuals. The Spirit and the sinful nature are in conflict with each other (Galatians 5:17). Within our body, sin is at war against God's law (Romans 7:23). The sinful mind is hostile to God (Romans 8:7). The image of putting off our old self and putting on the new may sound as easy as taking off one coat and putting on another, but the devil will resist it stubbornly every step of the way.

The primary battleground is the mind. It is the mind that God wants renewed, and it is in our mind that the devil most often attacks us. Hence the paramount importance of feeding our minds on Scripture, praise and communion with God, and of learning to take every thought captive to make it obedient to Jesus Christ.

We fight the devil, not in our strength, but in God's (Ephesians 6:10). The spiritual weapons we fight with have divine power (2 Corinthians 10:3). "'Not by might nor by power, but by My Spirit,' says the LORD of Hosts" (Zechariah 4:6). Jesus has given us authority over all the power of our spiritual enemy, the devil (Luke 10:19), but it is only when we submit ourselves to God that the devil will flee from us (James 4:7). (Compare this with Acts 19:13-17.)

If we recognize the devil's work, submit ourselves to God, and stand firmly against the devil, he will not succeed. If we fail to recognize the devil, fail to submit ourselves to God, or do not take a stand against the devil, we may allow him to obstruct or defeat the transformation we seek.

KEEP THE VISION—"Where there is no vision, the people perish" (Proverbs 29:18 KJV). We need to keep hold of the vision, to keep our eyes on the promise God has given that we can be transformed into his likeness. We need to focus on the unseen promise, and not on what we perceive in the natural as our shortcomings or the seeming slowness of any progress. We need to picture what it will be like as we gradually become transformed. We need to keep reminding ourselves that all things are possible with God (Matthew 19:26), and that God "calls those things which do not exist as though they did" (Romans 4:17). Let us, then, push aside all sense of discouragement or failure, throw off everything that hinders (Hebrews 12:1), and press on toward the goal to win the prize for which God has called us (Philippians 3:14).

15

Live by the Holy Spirit

o o o o o o o o o o o o o o o o o o o o o o o o o o o o o o o

"Be very careful, then, how you live..."

—*(Ephesians 5:15 NIV)*

In the previous chapter, I have talked about the need all believers have to be radically transformed by the renewing of our minds. One major key to making this transformation is to live by the Holy Spirit (Galatians 5:16). To understand what this means, we need to take a close look at Paul's letter to the Galatians.

THREE WAYS OF LIVING

In his letter to the Galatians, Paul describes three different ways of living our lives. As I discuss these, remember that he is writing to believers, who have accepted Jesus Christ as their Lord and Savior. Only the third of these three ways will lead to the transformation that is needed. We must choose which way we will follow.

The Way of Legalism

The first way is the way of legalism. In Paul's day, this involved strict adherence to the law of Moses and to the rabbinical rules with which it was surrounded. In our day, there are other forms of legalism, but the principle is the same.

Much of Galatians, chapters 1-4, deals with this way of life. It is focussed on rules, many of which are based on human traditions, rather than on the person of Jesus. It is full of "dos" and "don'ts." It is a life based on human effort. "Are you so foolish? After beginning with the Spirit, are you now trying to attain your goal by human effort?" (Galatians 3:3 NIV). It seeks to obtain justification by our own efforts in observing the law, rather than by faith in the saving power of Jesus Christ. (See Galatians 2:15-16.) "...if righteousness could be gained through the law, Christ died for nothing" (Galatians 2:21 NIV). It is a reliance on the letter of the law, which kills, rather than on the Spirit, which gives life (2 Corinthians 3:6). Paul calls it a life "...burdened...by a yoke of slavery" (Galatians 5:1 NIV).

Paul expresses his dismay at the Galatians for following this way of life. "You who are trying to be justified by law have been alienated from Christ, you have fallen away from grace" (Galatians 5:4 NIV). "...if you let yourselves be circumcised, Christ will be of no value to you at all" (Galatians 5:2 NIV). He says they are "...turning to a different gospel—which is really no gospel at all..." (Galatians 1:6-7 NIV). "I fear for you, that somehow I have wasted my efforts on you" (Galatians 4:11 NIV). Essentially he is saying that those who rely on their own efforts in doing the works of legalism are not saved. (Also see Romans 10:2-4.)

In Romans, Paul points out that the law was unable to save men from sin. He says, "For what the law was powerless to do in that it was weakened by the sinful nature, God did by sending His own Son in the likeness of sinful man to be a sin offering..." (Romans 8:3 NIV). Those who seek to be changed into the image of God cannot succeed if they rely on their own efforts and strength.

The Way of License

In Galatians 5:1 (NIV), Paul says, "It is for freedom that Christ has set us free. Stand firm, then, and do not let yourselves be burdened again by a yoke of slavery." Then in Galatians 5:13 (NIV), he issues a warning, "You, my brothers, were called to be free. But do not use your freedom to indulge the sinful nature..." He expresses a similar thought in Romans 6:1-2, "What shall we say, then? Shall we continue in sin that grace may abound? Certainly not! How shall we who died to sin live any longer in it?" Peter says, "Live as free men, but do not use your freedom as a cover-up for evil; live as servants [literally, slaves] of God" (1 Peter 2:16 NIV).

The way of license leads to sinful acts, such as those listed in Galatians 5:19-21. It leads to "works of darkness" (Ephesians 5:11). It leads to "death," while the Spirit-led life leads to "life and peace" (Romans 8:6).

Those, today, who allow themselves to fall into this way of license, start with a valid principle—that the true believer can be sure of his salvation. But they carry it to a false place, by saying, "Well, then, once I am saved it doesn't matter what I do. I can sin repeatedly and God will always forgive. I can turn away from God and he will always receive me back." This is **not** what Scripture says.

The Spirit-Led Life

Having described two false ways of life, Paul then presents the true way. "So I say, live by the Spirit, and you will not gratify the desires of the sinful nature" (Galatians 5:16 NIV). In Romans 8:12-14, he presents the same choice.

What does it mean to live by the Spirit? It means to respond to the promptings of the Holy Spirit, to allow the Holy Spirit to guide us in all things (see John 16:13), and to allow the Holy Spirit to control all of our thoughts and actions. Paul says, "…let us keep in step with the Spirit" (Galatians 5:25 NIV). He speaks of "…the mind controlled by the Spirit…" (Romans 8:6 NIV; also see verse 9), of being "led by the Spirit of God" (Romans 8:14), of being "spiritually minded" (Romans 8:6). He speaks of being a slave of righteousness and holiness (Romans 6:16, 19).

This is not easy. It takes some doing. But it is possible. God always empowers us to do the things he calls on us to do.

This means more than just abstaining from physical (sensual) sin. It means that we trust in God with **all** our heart and acknowledge him in **all** our ways (Proverbs 3:5-6). It means living by faith and not by sight (2 Corinthians 5:7). It means seeking God's kingdom first (Matthew 6:33). It means that we set our hearts and minds on things above and not on earthly things (Colossians 3:1-2). It means that in everything we put God first.

It is by the Holy Spirit that we understand spiritual things. The natural (unspiritual) man cannot understand spiritual things; they seem foolishness to him (1 Corinthians 2:12-15). It is only as we become transformed into God's image that we can test and approve what God's will is (Romans 12:2). I believe that if we want to understand the things of God, we need to live by the Holy Spirit, and be led by the Holy Spirit.

The Spirit-led life seeks holiness. "As he who called you is holy, you also be holy in all your conduct" (1 Peter 1:15). (Also see Hebrews 12:14.) To be holy is to be set apart, to be free from sin. It relies on the sanctifying work of the Holy Spirit living within us (2 Thessalonians 2:13; 1 Peter 1:2). We must do our part. We must choose (Galatians 5:1, 16), make every effort (2 Peter 1:5; Hebrews 12:14), and pursue (1 Timothy 6:11; 2 Timothy 2:22). But without the Spirit's power and influence, we cannot hope to achieve it. It is "by the Spirit" that we "put to death the deeds of the body" (Romans 8:13).

The Spirit-led life is a disciplined life. God's discipline produces a harvest of righteousness and peace (Hebrews 12:7-11). It is a life of obedience, but the obedience arises out of and is the result of our love for God (John 14:23; 1 John 5:3). The Spirit-led life is the result of our allowing the Holy Spirit to rule our spirit, soul and body. Its goal is to become like God in character.

If we live by the Spirit, we will show the fruit of the Spirit, which is "love, joy, peace, longsuffering [patience], kindness, goodness, faithfulness, gentleness and self-control" (Galatians 5:22-23). These qualities are the result of living by the Spirit. If we desire them, our focus should be on living by the Spirit. I believe that if we seek them for themselves, without also seeking to live by the Holy Spirit, whatever we may think we receive will be weak, artificial and impermanent.

THE CONSEQUENCES OF OUR CHOICE

We must choose which of these three ways of life we will live. The consequences of our choice are extremely serious. Scripture spells them out for us in remarkable precision and detail. Evidently this is a lesson that we are not supposed to miss.

In Galatians, chapters 1-5, Paul has made it very clear that the way of legalism, which depends on the flesh rather than on the spirit of God, is no gospel at all, that it accomplishes nothing of value, and that it alienates us from Christ. To go that way, he says, is to abandon your salvation, and to make Christ's sacrifice on the Cross of no value for you. These are some pretty serious consequences!

Scripture makes even more explicit the consequences of following the way of license.

In Galatians 5:21, after listing the acts of the sinful nature, Paul says, "I tell you beforehand, just as I also told you in time past, that those who practice such things will not inherit the kingdom of God." Ephesians 5:5-7 says the same, and adds a further warning: "because of these things the wrath of God comes upon the sons of disobedience. Therefore do not be partakers with them." Colossians 3:5-6 says much the same.

Later in Galatians, Paul uses even stronger language. "Do not be deceived: God cannot be mocked. A man reaps what he sows. The one who sows to please his sinful nature, from that nature will reap destruction; the one who sows to please the Spirit, from the Spirit will reap eternal life" (Galatians 6:7-8 NIV).

In Romans, Paul again paints the contrast as one between life and death. "Those who live according to the sinful nature have their minds set on what that nature desires; but those who live in accordance with the Spirit have their minds set on what the Spirit desires. The mind of sinful man is death, but the mind controlled by the Spirit is life and peace; the sinful mind is hostile to God. It does not submit to God's law, nor can it do so. Those controlled by the sinful nature cannot please God" (Romans 8:5-8 NIV). "For if you live according to the sinful nature, you will die; but if by the Spirit you put to death the misdeeds of the body, you will live" (Romans 8:13 NIV).

In Ephesians, Paul uses the imagery of darkness and light: "For you were once darkness, but now you are light in the Lord. Walk as children of light (for the fruit of the Spirit is in all goodness, righteousness and truth), finding out what is acceptable to the Lord. And have no fellowship with the unfruitful works of darkness, but rather expose them" (Ephesians 5:8-11).

In Romans, chapter 6, he uses yet another image. "And do not present your members as instruments of unrighteousness to sin, but present yourselves to God as being alive from the dead, and your members as instruments of righteousness to God" (Romans 6:13).

Paul tells us to crucify, to put to death, the sinful nature with its passions (Galatians 5:24; Colossians 3:5).

These letters are all written to Christian believers. In them, Paul puts the choice very starkly. If we believers live according to the sinful nature, according to the desires of the flesh, we will not inherit the kingdom of heaven, we will incur the wrath of God, we will receive destruction and death, we will not be the sons of God, we will live in darkness, and we will be instruments for satan. If we live by the Holy Spirit, if we allow the Holy Spirit to control everything in us, we will have eternal life, we will be children of God, we will live in the light, we will be instruments of God, and we will become like God in character.

Scripture tells us that, if we would live by the Holy Spirit, there is an inner conflict within each of us which we must resolve. If we would live by the Spirit, it is very important that we be aware of that conflict, understand it, and resolve it. In the next section, we will consider the origin and nature of that conflict.

THE INNER CONFLICT

The Three-Fold Division

The inner conflict of which Paul is speaking is a conflict between the Holy Spirit, which has come into our spirit, and the fleshly part of us. To understand this, I believe we need to see ourselves as consisting of spirit, soul and body. (See 1 Thessalonians 5:23.) To explain adequately this three-fold division, I shall have to go into the meanings of several Greek words used in Scripture. I ask you to bear with me.

The spirit is the eternal part of us, the part that is able to receive the Holy Spirit. (The Greek word for spirit is *pneuma*, and the adjective form is *pneumatikos.*) We have access to the Father by one Spirit (Ephesians 2:18). We worship God in spirit and in truth (John 4:23). "Spirit is the element in man which gives him the ability to think of God. It is man's vertical window, while *psuche*, soul, is man's horizontal window making him conscious of his environment."[26] It is by the spirit that we understand the things of God.

The soul is the mind, the will, the emotions and other non-physical parts of us that are still tied to the fleshly nature. (The Greek word for soul is *psuche*, from which we get the English word psyche; and the adjective form is *psuchikos.*). Some Scriptures use *psuche* to apply to both soul and spirit, to all the non-physical part of us. But other Scriptures sharply distinguish between the two. Hebrews 4:12 says that the word of God pierces "even to the division of soul and spirit." 1 Corinthians 2:14 says, "The natural [*psuchikos*] man does not receive the things of the Spirit of God, for they are foolishness to him; nor can he know them, because they are spiritually [*pneumatikos*] discerned." Unless it is guided by the spirit, our soul cannot understand spiritual things. Jude 19 speaks of those who "are sensual [*psuchikos*] persons who cause divisions, not having the Spirit." James 3:15 contrasts the wisdom that comes from heaven with "wisdom" that is "earthly, sensual [*psuchikos*], demonic." 1 Corinthians 15:42-46 distinguishes between the natural (*psuchikos*) body that we now have, which is corruptible, dishonored and weak, and the spiritual (*pneumatikos*) body that we will have at the Resurrection. These Scriptures clearly identify the soul (*psuche*) with that which is natural, carnal, sensual, fleshly, worldly, unspiritual.

The body, (*soma*), is the tangible, physical body. Another Greek word for body is *sarx,* which means fleshly, carnal, or sinful. The body is often seen as sinful or as the source of sinful desires. "If you live according to the flesh [*sarx*] you will die; but if by the Spirit you put to death the deeds of the body [*soma*], you will live." (Romans 8:13). (Also see verses 10-11.) "Do not let sin reign in your mortal body [*soma*]" (Romans 6:12). (Also see verse 6.) Galatians 5:16 contrasts living by the spirit (*pneuma*) with gratifying the desires of the flesh (*sarx*). Romans 8:5-17 repeatedly makes the same distinction between living by the Spirit and living by the sinful nature. (Also see 1 Corinthians 3:1-3; Ephesians 2:3; 1 Peter 2:11; 2 Peter 2:18; Jude 7.) Paul writes, "I know that in me (that is, in my flesh [*sarx*]) nothing good dwells" (Romans 7:18).

The Inner Spiritual Conflict

When we are born again, we are born of the spirit (John 3:8). "That which is born of the flesh is flesh, and that which is born of the Spirit is spirit (John 3:6). The Holy Spirit enters into and takes control of our spirit. "He who is joined to the Lord is one in spirit with Him" (1 Corinthians 6:17). But the Holy Spirit does not immediately take control of our soul or our body. A conflict develops between the Holy Spirit of God, which is in our spirit, and the rest of us, which is unspiritual and rooted in the flesh. Scripture refers to this as "warfare."

Not even our spirit is totally free from this conflict. 2 Corinthians 7:1 (NIV) says, "…let us purify ourselves from everything that contaminates body and spirit, perfecting holiness out of reverence for God." (Also see 1 Thessalonians 5:23.) Even our spirit can be contaminated. But the primary battlefield is the soul and body, and especially the mind. That is why we must be transformed by the renewing of our mind.

Paul tells us that there is a war going on inside us. The Spirit and the fleshly nature are in conflict. "For the sinful nature desires what is contrary to the Spirit, and the Spirit what is contrary to the sinful nature. They are **in conflict** with each other, so that you do not do what you want" (Galatians 5:17 NIV). In Romans, he puts the same thought even more strongly, "I find then a law, that evil is present with me, the one who wills to do good. For I delight in the law of God according to the inward man. But I see another law in my members, **warring** against the law of my mind, and bringing me into **captivity** to the law of sin which is in my members" (Romans 7:21-23). "The carnal mind is **enmity** against God" (Romans 8:7). Peter also uses martial language, "Abstain from fleshly lusts, which **war** against the soul" (1 Peter 2:11).

Paul describes this conflict primarily in terms of the second and third ways of life, the way of license against the Spirit-filled way. But since the way of legalism also depends on the flesh, rather than the power of the Holy Spirit, the conflict he describes applies to that way of life also.

These passages speak primarily of conflict between the spirit and our fleshly desires (*sarx*), that is, our body. But I think we can see that our mind, will and emotions are part of the flesh, until they have been regenerated by the spirit. As I have pointed out above, *psuche*, soul, is often used in the sense of carnal, earthly, unspiritual. Other passages speak of our minds as fleshly or carnal. Romans 8:6-7 speaks of the "carnal" mind. Colossians 2:18 speaks of one who is "vainly puffed up by his fleshly mind."

In general, our actions originate in the soul—the mind, will and emotions—and then manifest themselves in the physical. It is our mind that must be renewed in order that we can be transformed into the image of God. Then our physical actions will follow. Romans 8:5-7 (NIV) says, "Those who live according to the sinful nature have their **minds** set on what that nature desires; but those who live in accordance with the Spirit have their **minds** set on what the Spirit desires. The **mind** of sinful man is death, but the **mind** controlled by the Spirit is life and peace; the sinful **mind** is hostile to God. It does not submit to God's law, nor can it do so."

What is our mind set on? The question is very important.

We are talking about spiritual conflict that goes on inside us. It is with this internal conflict that 2 Corinthians 10:3-5 primarily deals. Paul speaks of demolishing strongholds and arguments, and of taking thoughts captive to obey Christ. This whole passage is concerned very largely with our thought life. Each of us has internal strongholds—habits, addictions, push-button reactions, patterns of behavior and thought—that are rooted in the desires of the flesh and the soul. Each of us has mindsets—ingrained ways of thinking—that set themselves up against the knowledge of God. Each of us needs to take every thought captive to obey Jesus Christ. The battle is within us. It is in our minds, our wills and our emotions, but primarily in our minds.

God does not want us to be "double-minded" (literally, two-souled, *dipsuchos*) (James 1:8). (Also see James 4:8.) He does not want part of our soul following the Holy Spirit, and another part following our flesh. He does not want our soul bouncing back and forth between the Holy Spirit and our flesh. He desires consistency. He desires "truth in the inward parts" (Psalm 51:6 KJV). "Search me, O God, and know my heart; try me and know my thoughts: And see if there is any wicked way in me, and lead me in the way everlasting" (Psalm 139:23-24 KJV). Scripture "is a discerner of the thoughts and intents of the heart" (Hebrews 4:12). The heart, the soul, the *psuche*, is the key.

When the soul has been brought under the control of the Holy Spirit, the process continues to bring the body into complete subjection. "Now may the God of peace Himself sanctify you completely; and may your whole spirit, soul, and body be preserved blameless at the coming of our Lord Jesus Christ. He who calls you is faithful, who also will do it" (I Thessalonians 5:23-24). God is "able to keep you from stumbling, and to present you faultless before the presence of His glory with exceeding joy" (Jude 24). (Also see Hebrews 13:20-21; 1 Corinthians 1:8-9.) God is able, he is faithful, and he will do it!

This process of gradually bringing the soul and body under the control of the Spirit is the process of sanctification, of becoming holy, because the Spirit is holy (I Peter 1:16). It is achieved through "sanctification by the Spirit and belief in the truth" (2 Thessalonians 2:13). (Also see 1 Peter 1:2.) It is the process of being transformed by the renewing of our minds (Romans 12:2). It is the process of putting off the old self and putting on the new self (Ephesians 4:22-24; Colossians 3:9-10).

Another way of looking at this is to say that there are two spirits warring against each other. The unregenerate body and soul are governed by "the spirit who now works in the sons of disobedience" (Ephesians 2:2). The spirit is governed by the Holy Spirit of God. There is war between them until we yield all of ourselves to the Holy Spirit.

The resolution to this inner conflict consists in our total submission to God. (See Chapter 16.) We need to become slaves to God rather than slaves to sin (Romans 6:13, 19). We need to offer ourselves as living sacrifices to God (Romans 12:1). It is as we become totally submitted to the Holy Spirit within us that the inner conflict is finally resolved.

I want to emphasize again that this inner conflict occurs primarily **after** we have accepted Jesus as our Lord and Savior and have received the Holy Spirit in our spirit. The letters I refer to above were all written to believers, to the "saints," the sanctified ones, at various locations. They speak of a conflict going on in the life of believers. They speak of choices that must be made by believers. Indeed, it is only believers who can have this conflict, for only they have the Holy Spirit living in them.

HOW DO WE GO ABOUT LIVING BY THE SPIRIT?

I think what I have just said is the key. We need to submit ourselves to the Holy Spirit living in us. This takes a decision on our part. As Paul puts it, whose slave will we be? Will we be slaves to sin, which leads to death? Or will we be slaves to obedience, which leads to righteousness and life? (See Romans 6:16.) We cannot have it both ways. No one can serve two masters (Matthew 6:24). A double-minded man is unstable in all his ways (James 1:8). (Also see James 4:8.) There is no middle ground; it has to be one or the other.

We cannot achieve this by our own efforts. The only way we can prevail is to "be strong in the Lord and in the power of his might" (Ephesians 6:10). "The battle is not yours, but God's" (2 Chronicles 20:15). But we must do our part.

God has given us his full armor, his full weapons (Ephesians 6:11); he has given us spiritual weapons that have divine power (2 Corinthians 10:4). But we have to put on the armor and use the weapons. We do all we can (Ephesians 6:13), and then put our trust in God.

What is our part? Here are some suggestions that have impressed me as important. There are undoubtedly others that could be mentioned. Different things work better for different people, and each one has to find what works for him or her.

Choose

Which way of living will we choose? The ways of the flesh that lead to death? Or the way of the spirit that leads to life? I believe that God, speaking through Paul, has given us a clear choice. There are two ways of living that lead to death (legalism and license), and one that leads to life (living by the Holy Spirit). We must choose which one we will follow.

This process of choosing is not just a one-time thing. When we have chosen the right way of living, we then have to make a great number of specific choices. Is this action, or this thought, or this attitude, in accordance with the Holy Spirit? If not, what will we do about it?

One way of testing our decisions is to imagine Jesus Christ standing beside us and then ask ourselves, "What would he say about the things I want to do and say?" Many young people, today, wear something that says, "What would Jesus do?"

Winston Churchill said, "Character is the habit of making right decisions." If we would have godly character, we need to cultivate the habit of making godly decisions. We need to train ourselves to be godly! (See 1 Timothy 4:7-8; Hebrews 5:14.)

Seek

"Ask, and it will be given to you; seek and you will find; knock, and it will be opened to you" (Matthew 7:7). Keep on asking, keep on seeking, keep on knocking. Jesus told his disciples to persist in prayer (Luke 18:1-8; 11:5-8). God has told us, "You will seek Me, and find Me, when you search for Me with all your heart" (Jeremiah 29:13). (Also see Deuteronomy 4:29; Psalm 9:10; Psalm 119:10.) If we truly seek with all our heart to live by the Holy Spirit, if we persist and do not give up, we will be able to do it. God never asks us to do something without enabling us to do it.

We need to seek with all our heart. We need to seek fervently (Psalm 42:1-2). We need to hunger and thirst for righteousness (Matthew 5:6), to make every effort to be holy (Hebrews 12:14). God does not want us to be lukewarm or half-hearted. He wants an intensity of seeking.

Keep a Balanced View of God

I have written earlier of the need to keep a balanced view between God as a God of love and as a God of justice. (See Chapter 5.) If we focus too heavily on God's justice, we tend to fall into the way of legalism. If we focus too heavily on God's love and his unmerited favor, we can fall into the way of license. Living by the Holy Spirit requires a balanced view of God.

Respond to the Holy Spirit

God gave us his Holy Spirit to "guide you into all truth" (John 16:13). God, through his Holy Spirit, says to us, "This is the way, walk in it" (Isaiah 30:21). But we have to be attentive. We must accustom ourselves to responding to the nudges and prods of the Holy Spirit. We need to take time to shut out the noise of the world and "Be still, and know that I am God" (Psalm 46:10).

Feed the Holy Spirit

If we want to live by the Holy Spirit, we need to do all that we can to strengthen the Holy Spirit's influence within us. This means reading and meditating on Scripture, which is at work in those who believe (1 Thessalonians 2:13) and is able to save us (James 1:21). It means devoting time to praise, worship and prayer. It means thinking on those things that are good, noble, etc. (Philippians 4:8-9). It means doing all that we can to dwell in the secret place of the Most High (Psalm 91:1).

Scripture tells us, "Put on the Lord Jesus Christ" (Romans 13:14). The best protection against sinful living is to clothe ourselves with Jesus Christ. Paul wrote, "It is no longer I who live, but Christ lives in me" (Galatians 2:20). I do not yet fully understand what he means, but I think he is talking about a kind of relationship with Jesus that comes only from a radical commitment to Jesus Christ.

The goal of the Spirit-led life is to become like God in character. In order to do that, we need to spend time with God (through prayer, worship, Scripture, etc.) so that we can come to know what God is like. Unless we do that, we cannot expect to live by the Spirit.

Do Not Grieve the Holy Spirit

"Do not grieve the Holy Spirit of God" (Ephesians 4:30). "Do not quench the Spirit" (1 Thessalonians 5:19). Do not resist the Holy Spirit (Acts 7:51). I believe that we grieve the Holy Spirit, and quench the Holy Spirit, when we think, or say, or do things that are contrary to what the Holy Spirit desires. "…those who live in accordance with the Holy Spirit have their minds set on what the Spirit desires" (Romans 8:5 NIV). If we love God, we should desire to please him, and not to grieve his Holy Spirit. We need to look at everything we think, and everything we are about to say and do, and ask ourselves, "Will this please the Holy Spirit, or will it grieve him?"

We need to set our minds on what the Holy Spirit desires.

Be Alert

We need always to be alert (1 Peter 5:8). "Watch and pray, lest you enter into temptation" (Matthew 26:41). We need to be aware of the devices and schemes of the devil (2 Corinthians 2:11). We need to cut them off at an early stage, to nip them in the bud. We need to be alert to every thought and every temptation that is from the devil. The process of taking captive every thought to make it obedient to Jesus Christ begins by identifying those thoughts that are not obedient. The more alert we are to identify them quickly, the less influence they will have over us.

Guard Our Thoughts

Scripture tells us to take all of our thoughts captive to obey Christ (2 Corinthians 10:5). This is something we must do constantly. The devil is constantly putting ungodly thoughts in our mind. He wants us to believe thoughts that are contrary to God's word and God's character, to doubt God's word and his promises, and to desire things that are ungodly. If we agree with the devil, we are taking his side. This was part of Adam and Eve's sin; they agreed with what the serpent said rather than what God said. In the spiritual realm, when we accept and agree with the thoughts the devil tries to plant in us, we are giving aid and comfort to our spiritual enemy. We are committing spiritual treason. In my experience, this has been a major battleground.

We need to decide what we will think about (Romans 8:5). What have we set our minds on? What do we want to set our minds on? Where does God want us to set our minds? We need to keep asking these questions. We need consciously to decide what we will set our minds on, and then make every effort to adhere to that decision. If we find ourselves thinking about the wrong things, we need to take those thoughts captive and say, "No, that is not what I have chosen to set my mind on," and then deliberately change the focus of our thinking. I cannot emphasize this too much.

Confess Our Failures

In this battle, we will fail many times. When we slip up, that is not the end of the battle. We need to pick ourselves up, confess our failure to God and ask his forgiveness, and keep on going. Do not let the devil discourage you by your failures!

A baseball game is not lost because one error is committed. Men of courage do not give up a goal because of one setback. The important thing is not whether you have slipped up or suffered a setback. The important thing is whether, after a setback, you can pick yourself up and get going again, with a renewed determination.

Do Not Give the Devil a Place to Hold on to Us

We must not "give place to the devil" (Ephesians 4:27). Just before his arrest, Jesus said, "The ruler of this world is coming, and he has nothing in Me" (John 14:30). We need to try to be like that, and give our spiritual enemy nothing with which to grab hold of us. One can think of the devil as coming with Velcro attached to him. If we have bits of Velcro on us, he can grab us and move us as he wishes. If we are smooth, his Velcro will not attach itself to us. We need to get rid of everything that could give the devil a hold on us.

A PERSONAL APPLICATION

Perhaps I can make this more real by a personal application in my own life. I have cancer. It started in my colon, and spread to the liver and lungs. The medical prognosis is not good.

We (my wife and I) decided to do everything the doctors recommended, but to put our primary faith in God. I know that God can heal me and I believe that he will heal me. No matter what the medical data may say, God's healing power is greater. We have spent quite a bit of time in worship, praise, prayer, and listening to videos and tapes that may be helpful. Many people are praying for my healing.

I then came to realize that, if I am expecting God to heal me, I need to make more effort to live by the Holy Spirit, and to submit every aspect of my life to the Holy Spirit. I believe this illness is an attack from the devil, and, if I want the devil to flee from me, I must submit myself to God (James 4:17). In fact it has seemed to me that God may have allowed this illness in order to bring me to a higher level of faith and obedience. A Scripture that has meant a great deal to me is 1 Peter 1:7 (NIV), stating that various trials "…have come so that your faith—of greater worth than gold, which perishes even though refined by fire—may be proved genuine, and may result in praise, glory and honor when Jesus Christ is revealed."

During family prayer one evening, I realized that, at times, I was allowing myself to think thoughts that were destructive of the very faith I was relying on for my life. I would think such things as, "God is not going to heal me." "I'm of no value to him." "He has nothing more for me to do." Etc. Etc. Etc. I realized that these thoughts were contrary to God's word, and contrary to his will for me as I understand it. I realized also that these thoughts came from the devil, and that by accepting them and agreeing with them, I was giving aid and comfort to my spiritual enemy. When I allowed these thoughts to come into my mind, and agreed with them, I was not living by the Holy Spirit of God.

I resolved not to allow these thoughts any more. I found a simple device, that has worked quite well. When these and other ungodly thoughts come, I simply say, "I have set before you life and death…Now choose life." (See Deuteronomy 30:19.) And the ungodly thoughts go away. Often I reinforce this by reaffirming, out loud, my faith in God's healing power and my belief that he will heal me, quoting appropriate Scriptures. The thoughts keep coming back. We should never expect that the devil will give up easily. But they do not stay with me long. I think this is part of what it means to live by the Spirit. Some things we gradually grow in as we increasingly focus our attention on God. Other things we have to consciously identify and make a determined decision to throw off, reject, get rid of.

I also resolved to love and trust God no matter what happens, like the three young men who were thrown into the fiery furnace. (See Daniel 2:48-3:30.) So I have had to refuse to allow thoughts that undermine my confidence in God's character.

Things in our lives that are contrary to the Holy Spirit do not always go away so easily. But I believe that if we are determined to get rid of them, we shall succeed. Scripture says, "...let us throw off everything that hinders and the sin that so easily entangles..." (Hebrews 12:1 NIV). Throwing off implies vigorous action. We don't just drop it or let go of it. We throw it with all our force. When God calls on us to do something, he will enable us to do it. "I can do all things through Christ who strengthens me" (Philippians 4:13).

16

Total Commitment to God

o o o o o o o o o o o o o o o o o o o o o o o o o o o o o o o o o o o

"...offer your bodies as living sacrifices, holy and pleasing to God—this is your spiritual act of worship."

—*(Romans 12:1 NIV)*

This is an extraordinary verse of Scripture, which deserves our prayerful consideration. I want to explore in detail some of what I think it means, and calls on us to do. But first I want to look at it in the context in which Paul has placed it. I shall cross over the chapter divisions in which our modern text appears, recognizing that they are not in the original text, and sometimes lead us to make artificial divisions in our consideration of the text.

In everything in this chapter, I am speaking to myself as much as to anyone else. I have chosen to write about this because I need to hear it. If it is helpful to someone else, that's an extra benefit.

THE CONTEXT

Romans 11:33-12:2 (NIV)

11:33 Oh, the depth of the riches of the wisdom and knowledge of God! How unsearchable his judgments, and his paths beyond tracing out!

34 "Who has known the mind of the Lord? Or who has been his counselor?"

35 "Who has ever given to God, that God should repay him?"

36 For from him and through him and to him are all things. To him be the glory forever! Amen.

12:1 Therefore, I urge you, brothers, in view of God's mercy, to offer your bodies as living sacrifices, holy and pleasing to God—this is your spiritual act of worship.

2 Do not conform any longer to the pattern of this world, but be transformed by the renewing of your mind. Then you will be able to test and approve what God's will is—his good, pleasing and perfect will.

I encourage you to read this remarkable passage several times as a whole, and then look in detail at its implications. I believe much of the heart of Paul's teaching, and of what our Christian life should be, can be found in this passage.

God Is Far Greater Than Our Human Understanding of Him (Romans 11:33-34)

Paul was the best educated and most intellectually proficient of all the writers of the New Testament. Yet we find in Romans 11:33-34 the profound sense that Paul does not, and never will, fully understand the greatness of God. God's wisdom and knowledge have depths that no man can plumb. God's judgments are unsearchable and his paths beyond tracing out. This may seem a shocking statement to some, but Paul wrote it under the guidance of the Holy Spirit, and I believe it is true. We need to take it at face value and not water it down. God does, or allows, things that we just don't understand, and he doesn't owe us any explanations.

Paul expresses the same sense in many other passages. Thus he speaks of God's "…incomparably great power for us who believe…" (Ephesians 1:19 NIV), of the love of Christ "which passes knowledge" (Ephesians 3:19), of God's ability to do "exceedingly abundantly above all that we ask or think" (Ephesians 3:20), and of the peace of God "which surpasses all understanding" (Philippians 4:7). He tells us that "Eye has not seen, nor ear heard, nor have entered into the heart of man the things which God has prepared for those who love him" (1 Corinthians 2:9). He speaks of the relationship between Christ and his church as "a great mystery" (Ephesians 5:32). He says, "Behold, I tell you a mystery" (1 Corinthians 15:51). He says that in Christ "are hidden all the treasures of wisdom and knowledge" (Colossians 2:3). God is immeasurably greater than anything our limited minds can conceive. Whatever we may think or say about him, God is greater. (See Chapter 5.)

Paul also emphasizes that our knowledge and understanding of God do not come from our intellect, nor, indeed, from any attribute of ours, but from the Holy Spirit and from revelation. (We should use our intellect, but our intellect is not sufficient.) Paul was not taught the gospel by men; "it came through the revelation of Jesus Christ" (Galatians 1:12). "Our gospel did not come to you in word only, but also in power, and in the Holy Spirit and in much assurance" (1 Thessalonians 1:5). "My speech and my preaching were not with persuasive words of human wisdom, but in demonstration of the Spirit and of power, that your faith should not be in the wisdom of men but in the power of God" (1 Corinthians 2:4-5). He insisted that the man without the Holy Spirit cannot understand spiritual things, because they are spiritually discerned (1 Corinthians 2:14). (Also see 1 Corinthians 1:20-25.) Thus he prayed that God would grant believers "the spirit of wisdom and revelation in the knowledge of Him," and that "the eyes of your understanding" may be "enlightened" (Ephesians 1:17-18). He prayed "that you may be filled with the knowledge of His will in all wisdom and spiritual understanding" (Colossians 1:9).

Paul wrote that here on earth "we see in a mirror, dimly" and we "know in part" (1 Corinthians 13:12). I believe this statement applies to our understanding of Scripture and our knowledge of God. Here on earth we cannot know God fully. We cannot even understand Scripture fully. This is not because Scripture is obscure or God unknowable. Far from it. It is because our finite human minds are limited in their ability to understand. God has given us "...everything we need for life and godliness..." (2 Peter 1:3 NIV), but he does not answer all the questions we may have.

We get this same sense of mystery throughout Scripture. I have room for only a few examples. God's ways and his thoughts are immeasurably higher than our ways and thoughts (Isaiah 55:8-9). If we have the mind of Christ (1 Corinthians 2:16), we can hope to understand God's ways and thoughts somewhat better, but I think we can never achieve a complete understanding of them. Job said, "I have uttered things that I did not understand, things too wonderful for me, which I did not know" (Job 42:3). The Psalmist spoke of God's knowledge as "too wonderful for me; it is high, I cannot attain it" (Psalm 139:6).

Scripture gives us extraordinary visions of God, but they are incomplete and fragmentary. Ezekiel did his best to describe what he saw, and then confessed his inadequacy to describe it by saying, "This was the appearance of the likeness of the glory of the LORD" (Ezekiel 1:28). Scripture tells us that God knew Moses face to face (Deuteronomy 34:10). Yet it also tells us that "no one has seen God at any time" (John 1:18), and that God lives "in unapproachable light, whom no man has seen or can see" (1 Timothy 6:16). Some men have seen aspects of God, bits of God, but no human on earth has seen God in his full glory and magnificence.

God is incomparably great. "'To whom will you compare me? Or who is my equal?' says the Holy One" (Isaiah 40:25 NIV). "His greatness is unsearchable" (Psalm 145:3). He is greater than the whole earth, greater than our sun, greater than all the galaxies, greater than the millions of suns the astronomers have identified, greater than the suns they have not yet identified. His greatness is beyond our comprehension. His wisdom, his holiness, his goodness, his faithfulness, his love are all beyond our comprehension. His wrath, also, is beyond our comprehension. He is so much more than anything we can imagine that we can only stand in awe of him.

Those in Heaven, who are with God continuously, have a clearer understanding of his greatness than we do. Heavenly creatures never stop saying, "Holy, holy, holy, Lord God Almighty, Who was and is and is to come!" (Revelation 4:8). (Also see Isaiah 6:3.)

This sense of God's greatness is also expressed in the following heavenly praises, among others:

> "You are worthy, O Lord, To receive glory and honor and power; For You created all things, And by Your will they exist and were created" (Revelation 4:11).
>
> "Amen! Blessing and glory and wisdom, Thanksgiving and honor and power and might, Be to our God forever and ever. Amen" (Revelation 7:12).
>
> "Great and marvelous are Your works, Lord God Almighty! Just and true are Your ways, O King of the saints! Who shall not fear You, O Lord, and glorify Your name? For You alone are holy. For all nations shall come and worship before You, For Your judgments have been manifested" (Revelation 15:3-4).
>
> "Alleluia! For the Lord God Omnipotent reigns!" (Revelation 19:6).

All Things Belong to God (verses 35-36)

These two verses tell us that God is the source of all things, and all things belong to him. In heaven the praise goes up to God continuously, "You are worthy, our Lord and God, to receive glory and honor and power, for you created all things, and by your will they were created and have their being" (Revelation 4:11 NIV). "You alone are the LORD. You made the heavens, even the highest heavens, and all their starry host, the earth and all that is on it, the seas and all that is in them. You give life to everything…" (Nehemiah 9:6 NIV). "He commanded and they were created" (Psalm 148:5). "In the beginning you laid the foundations of the earth, and the heavens are the work of your hands. They will perish, but you remain; they will all wear out like a garment. Like clothing you will change them and they will be discarded. But you remain the same, and your years will never end" (Psalm 102:25-27 NIV). "Know that the LORD He is God. It is he who made us, and not we ourselves; we are His people and the sheep of his pasture" (Psalm 100:3). "We are the clay, and You our potter, and all we are the work of Your hand" (Isaiah 64:8). (Also see Isaiah 29:16.) "I am the LORD, who makes all things" (Isaiah 44:24). (Also see Isaiah 42:5.) God "…gives all men life and breath and everything else" (Acts 17:25 NIV).

Not only did God create all things, but he sustains all things by his powerful word (Hebrews 1:3). "…in him all things hold together" (Colossians 1:17 NIV). Nothing could continue to exist unless God were actively sustaining it and holding it together.

God has said, "…everything under heaven belongs to me" (Job 41:11 NIV). "…the world is mine, and all that is in it" (Psalm 50:12 NIV). Indeed, "…from him and through him and to him are all things…" (Romans 11:36 NIV). Whatever we may think we give to him, it is simply a matter of returning to him what is already his.

It follows also that nothing we do can put God in our debt. "Who has ever given to God that God should repay him?" (Romans 11:35 NIV). (Also see Ephesians 2:8.) God has given us so much that we could never deserve, and has blessed us so greatly, that we could have no possible basis for claiming anything from him. "How can I repay the LORD for all his goodness to me?" (Psalm 116:12 NIV). God does not owe us anything. He gives to us, generously, abundantly, but he does not owe us anything.

I think there is a broader implication to all this, which I can only briefly sketch here. "The LORD our God, the LORD is one" (Deuteronomy 6:4). He is "the only true God" (John 17:3). "I am God, and there is no other" (Isaiah 46:9). "Apart from me there is no God" (Isaiah 44:6 NIV). There is nothing, and no one, that is equal to God. There is nothing that is independent of God. Everything is subject to God. Everything is under God's control. No purpose of God can fail (Isaiah 14:24, 46:10, 11, 55:11). No plan of God can be thwarted (Job

42:2). God "works out everything in conformity with the purpose of his will" (Ephesians 1:11 NIV). (Also see Psalm 57:2.) Not only does everything belong to God, but he controls everything.

Offer Yourself As a Living Sacrifice (Romans 12:1)

Chapter 12 starts with the word "therefore." There is a causal relationship to the preceding verses. It is **because** God is so incomparably great, beyond our capacity to understand or imagine, and **because** all things belong to God and are controlled by God, that we should offer ourselves as living sacrifices. (There may also be a broader causal relationship to everything else in the letter to the Romans, but I want to focus on the relationship to the immediately preceding verses.)

God wants us to live a life that is totally surrendered to him. Note that I am here, and in the rest of this chapter, deliberately broadening Paul's language. Where Paul speaks of offering our body, *soma*, I believe what God really wants is an offering of our whole self, of everything. We can't really offer him our body without offering our mind, will, emotions and spirit. They go together. I think other passages of Scripture make this clear. (See, for example, Romans 6:13 NIV, "...offer yourselves to God...", and Psalm 51:17, "The sacrifices of God are a broken spirit, a broken and a contrite heart—These, O God, you will not despise.")

How do we do this? What does it mean to do this? I shall attempt to deal with such questions in the next part of this chapter. But I want to continue with the context in which this verse appears. There is a sequence to Romans 12:1-2 that I think is quite important to understand.

Do Not Be Conformed to the Pattern of This World (verse 2)

I have discussed this passage in chapter 13. I there point out that it comes down to something very basic. Whom will we serve? Will we serve the world and its principles? Or will we serve Almighty God and his son Jesus Christ? In this sense, it is very closely related to Romans 12:1.

Be Transformed (verse 2)

This transformation is basic to our life and growth in Christ. In a sense this transformation is part of the way we offer ourselves as a living sacrifice. Our old self passes away and we become a new creation. We die to Christ and Christ lives in us. We put off the old self, and put on a new self created in the image of God. It is only as we sacrifice the old that we can put on the new. (I have discussed this in chapter 14.)

But I think there is significance in the sequence in which Paul has expressed these truths. That sequence suggests that the process of transformation cannot fully occur unless and until we have made a decision to commit ourselves totally to Jesus Christ, and to offer ourselves to him as living sacrifices. There is an overlap, but the full transformation requires the total commitment to Jesus Christ that is involved in offering ourselves as a living sacrifice.

Test and Approve God's Perfect Will (verse 2)

Here Paul makes the sequence absolutely clear. "**Then** you will be able to test..." (Romans 12:2 NIV). He is saying that it is only after we have done three things—sacrificed ourselves to Christ, ceased conforming to this world, and been transformed by the renewing of our minds—that we can test and approve God's perfect will for our lives. Only after we have done these things can we be fully sure that we know what his perfect will is for our lives.

OFFERING OURSELVES AS A SACRIFICE

Let us now explore what it means to offer ourselves as a sacrifice, and how we can do it.

General Comments

In one sense we have nothing to offer. Everything belongs to God. We have nothing to give. We have nothing that we can call our own. This is the ultimate spiritual reality.

But in another sense, we do have something to offer. In worldly, material terms we have certain exclusive rights to various things. We can exclude other humans from them. We also have something we call ourself, which we will not allow others to invade. Apart from God, this self (shabby as it may be) is our most precious possession. So we do have to be willing to give up something that we have considered of great importance.

There is yet another sense in which what we offer is not a sacrifice, because what God gives us in return is far greater than what we have given up. Jesus used two images, of a man who found a great treasure buried in a field, and of another man who found a pearl of great price, the most wonderful jewel imaginable (Matthew 13:44-46). In each case, the man sold everything he had to acquire the treasure. Jesus said the first man did this in joy, and I think we can assume the second man did so also. We, too, can find joy in the sacrifice that Romans 12:1 calls on us to make. In some cases, however, it may seem like a sacrifice at the time, and the joy does not come until later. At any rate I shall, as Paul did, refer to it as a sacrifice.

In what follows I shall list some ways in which we can commit ourselves wholly to God, and in which some Christians have committed themselves wholly to God. I am not saying that all of us need to do all of these things. We need to be ready to do whatever God calls on us to do in our particular situation, and he puts different calls on different people. I am also not saying that I have achieved all, or even many, of these. But I think it is useful to study Scripture for the purpose of setting the goals towards which we can aim.

Literally Offering Our Bodies

Until the fourth century A.D., the Christian Church was a persecuted church. Many Christians were fed to wild beasts in the Roman arenas, or otherwise put to death for their faith, often in very painful ways. Such records as we have make it very likely that 10 of the original 12 apostles, and Paul, were martyred for their faith. (Judas Iscariot committed suicide, and John is believed to have died a natural death.) The book of Revelation speaks of many who were beheaded or otherwise martyred. Many have been martyred since. These men and women understood what it meant to offer their bodies to God as a sacrifice.

Today, in some parts of the world, Christians are put to death for their faith. We are told that there were more Christian martyrs in the 20th century than in all the previous history of the church.

Paul was whipped, beaten with rods, and stoned (2 Corinthians, chapter 11). The early apostles were whipped (Acts 5:40-41). Both Paul and Peter were imprisoned. Many others have been whipped, beaten, tortured, imprisoned and killed for their faith (Hebrews 11:32-38). Many Christians today, especially in

Communist or Muslim countries, have been imprisoned, sent to labor camps, whipped, beaten and tortured because of their faith. Many, also, have had to see their wives and children suffer because of their faith. In many parts of the world, Christianity is a "suffering church."

This suffering can be in material things also. Scripture speaks of those who "joyfully accepted the plundering of your goods" (Hebrews 10:34). Paul experienced need and hunger (Philippians 4:12; 2 Corinthians 11:27). Today, in Muslim and Communist countries, believing Christians, because of persecution, often find it difficult to get and keep jobs, and many live a life of great economic hardship. The families of those who are imprisoned or killed often suffer great economic hardship.

In today's Western world, we do not encounter this kind of persecution. However, there is no guarantee that it won't happen in the future. Are we prepared to face it if it does come? For myself, I cannot say. I hope that, with God's strength, I will be able to if I am put to the test, but I cannot be sure unless it happens.

Being a Slave of Christ

Many of the epistles begin with the apostles referring to themselves as bondservants. "Paul, a bondservant of Christ Jesus" (Romans 1:1). (Also see Philippians 1:1; Titus 1:1.) "James, a bondservant of God" (James 1:1). "Simon Peter, a bondservant and apostle of Jesus Christ" (2 Peter 1:1). "Jude, a bondservant of Jesus Christ" (Jude 1). John calls himself a servant of Jesus Christ (Revelation 1:1). Paul also calls himself "a prisoner of Christ Jesus" (Philemon 1). The Greek word translated "bondservant" (or "servant" in some translations) is *doulos.* It has a variety of meanings, but its root meaning is that of a "slave." It means "one who is in a permanent relationship of servitude to another, his will altogether consumed in the will of the other."[27]

Other Scriptures use *doulos* to describe the Christian's relationship to God or to Jesus Christ. (See, for example, Acts 20:19; Romans 12:11; 1 Thessalonians 1:9.) Jesus said, "No servant can serve two masters; for either he will hate the one and love the other, or else he will be loyal to the one and despise the other. You cannot serve God and mammon" (Luke 16:13). ("Mammon" is wealth personified, or avarice deified.)[28]

Paul writes that, as the result of Jesus Christ's atoning act of sacrifice on the Cross, we have now been freed from slavery to sin and have "become slaves [*doulos*] of God" (Romans 6:22). Peter writes, "Live as free men, but do not use your freedom as a cover-up for evil; live as servants [*doulos*] of God" (1 Peter 2:16 NIV). (Also see Galatians 5:13.)

"Do you not know that…you are not your own? For you were bought at a price. Therefore glorify God in your body and in your Spirit, which are God's" (1 Corinthians 6:19-20). The image is that of a slave, who was redeemed from his former master by the payment of a price, and who now belongs to the one who redeemed him.

This idea of our being slaves to God may be shocking and repulsive to some. In today's Western society, we value our freedom. But it is the vocabulary that Scripture uses over and over. Being a slave to a master who is all-good, all-wise, all-powerful and all-loving is a good place to be. And it is by our submission to this perfect master that we become free from slavery to anyone or anything else. It is when we are servants of God that we can live as free men (1 Peter 2:16). It is by committing ourselves to Jesus that we become free (John 8:31-32).

Not all Christians are called to be martyrs, but all of us, I believe, are called to be servants of Jesus Christ, voluntary slaves of Jesus Christ.

Serving

The function of a slave or servant is to serve. He puts his master's interests ahead of his own, his master's will ahead of his own.

Jesus taught his disciples to pray, "Your will be done on earth as it is in heaven" (Matthew 6:10). I believe this must be the essence of all prayer. Let God's will be done. One of the purposes of prayer is to find out what God's will is, so that we can pray in accordance with it. In the Garden of Gethsemane, Jesus prayed, "not as I will, but as You will" (Matthew 26:39). We know that "if we ask anything according to His will, He [God] hears us" (1 John 5:14).

Jesus spoke a parable that illustrates the kind of service we are called to. He spoke of a servant who worked all day in the field, and then had to fix his master's supper and wait on him before he could do anything for himself. Jesus said, "Does he thank the servant because he did the things that were commanded him? I think not. So likewise you, when you have done all those things that you are commanded, say, 'We are unprofitable servants. We have done what was our duty to do'" (Luke 17:9-10).

This applies to Christian leaders as well as to the rest of us. What someone may call "my ministry" is not his, but God's. The credit, the glory, the power, all belong to God. "Not to us, O LORD, not to us but to your name be the glory…" (Psalm 115:1 NIV). When the lame man was healed, Peter said, "Why look so intently at us, as though by our own power or godliness we had made this man walk?...His [Jesus'] name, through faith in His name, has made this man strong, whom you see and know" (Acts 3:12, 16). (Also see Acts 14:8-18.) Paul warns us, "Let nothing be done through selfish ambition or conceit" (Philippians 2:3). And he said he would "boast" about his own infirmities, "that the power of Christ may rest upon me" (2 Corinthians 12:9).

When God gives us strength and wisdom, it is so that we can do the work God has for us to do. When God gives us provision, it is so that we can do the work that God has for us to do. Whatever God entrusts us with is to be used for his purposes, not ours. It all belongs to him anyhow.

Obeying God

Paul described his entire ministry in these terms: "Through him [Jesus] and for his name's sake we received grace and apostleship to call people from among the Gentiles to the obedience that comes from faith" (Romans 1:5 NIV). (Also see 1 Peter 1:2.) Jesus "learned obedience by the things which He suffered" and thereby "became the author of eternal salvation to all who obey Him" (Hebrews 5:8-9). "Not everyone who says to Me, 'Lord, Lord,' shall enter the kingdom of heaven, but he who does the will of My Father in heaven" (Matthew 7:21). "They profess to know God, but in works they deny Him" (Titus 1:16). "This is the love of God, that we keep His commandments" (1 John 5:3).

Obedience is a word that many of us do not like to hear today. But I believe it is central to our faith as Christians. (See Chapter 17.)

Giving Up Our Agendas

Part of what it means to be a servant is that we give up our own agendas. According to the *Hebrew-Greek Key Word Study Bible*, it means that our will is totally consumed in the will of the one we serve.

Jesus modeled this for us. He came to do his Father's work (John 4:34, 6:38). During his earthly ministry, he did only what he saw the Father doing, and said only what the Father told him to say. (See John 5:19, 7:16-18, 8:28-29, 12:49, 14:10.) He said, "the Son can do nothing of Himself" (John 5:19). He said, "I always do those things that please Him" (John 8:29). And then he said that "He who believes in Me, the works that I do he will do also" (John 14:12). Those who have faith in Jesus should be doing the Father's work, doing what pleases the Father, just as Jesus did. Jesus had no agenda of his own. His agenda was to do the Father's will. If we are to walk as Jesus did (1 John 2:6), our agenda should be to do the Father's will.

The disciples modeled this. Jesus said, "follow me," and they left whatever they were doing and followed him. Peter, James, John and Andrew left their fishing boats and their families and followed him. Matthew, a tax collector, was sitting at his tax booth with money in it; he got up, left everything, and followed Jesus (Luke 5:28). As Peter said, "We have left all and followed You" (Mark 10:28).

Paul modeled it. Paul was a comer, what we today would call a Yuppie. He was trained by the best rabbinical teacher, and entrusted by the Sanhedrin with important tasks. He was on the way up. Listen to his own words, "...circumcised the eighth day, of the stock of Israel, of the tribe of Benjamin, a Hebrew of the Hebrews, concerning the law, a Pharisee; concerning zeal, persecuting the church; concerning the righteousness which is in the law, blameless. But what things were gain to me, these I have counted loss for Christ. Yet indeed I also count all things loss for the excellence of the knowledge of Christ Jesus my Lord, for whom I have suffered the loss of all things, and count them as rubbish that I may gain Christ and be found in Him, not having my own righteousness, which is from the law, but that which is through faith in Christ, the righteousness which is from God by faith" (Philippians 3:5-9).

Paul, with a brilliant future before him, gave up that future, gave up his own agenda completely, so that he could become a slave of Jesus Christ.

Then Paul reached another point of submission. After he had founded many churches, and was very busy, keeping track of how they were doing, and correcting them when they started to go wrong, God seemingly put an end to that ministry. God told him to go to Jerusalem. The Holy Spirit repeatedly warned him that he would face imprisonment and hardship, but he insisted on obeying the call of God. Here are his words, "And now, compelled by the Spirit, I am going to Jerusalem, not knowing what will happen to me there. I only know that in every city the Holy Spirit warns me that prison and hardships are facing me. However, I consider my life worth nothing to me, if only I may finish the race and complete the task the Lord Jesus has given me—the task of testifying to the gospel of God's grace" (Acts 20:22-24 NIV).

Paul did go to Jerusalem; he almost lost his life there; and then he was imprisoned for two years in Palestine and for several years in Rome. We are not sure what happened after that, but many scholars think he was released from prison for a time, went back to Ephesus, and then was reimprisoned and executed.

At what seemed the height of his ministry, Paul was suddenly called by God to interrupt it all and spend a good many years in jail. It did not seem to make sense, but Paul was obedient. And he wrote some of his finest letters from a Roman jail. God may interrupt our ministry.

I want to make one thing very clear. In saying that we should give up our agendas, I am **not** saying that every Christian should give up what he or she is doing and become a full-time pastor, evangelist, or missionary. God uses us in different ways. He has different callings on our lives. Those who are called to the professional ministry should answer the call. But we should not attempt to perform a function to which we are not called. Increasingly, today, we are hearing about the importance of serving God in the "marketplace." Many of us are called to live committed Christian lives as businesspeople, professionals, politicians, workers, teachers, parents, etc. In whatever capacity we function, we can serve God. Whatever we are doing, we can "Serve wholeheartedly, as if you were serving the Lord, not men" (Ephesians 6:7 NIV). We can be "an epistle of Christ...written not with ink but by the Spirit of the living God" (2 Corinthians 3:3). Whatever our occupation may be, we can so live that those who see us will have caught at least a glimpse of Jesus Christ.

Whatever our calling, whatever the occupation in which we find ourselves, we need to live lives of commitment to God. Too many Christians, today, live lives that are compartmentalized. While in church on Sunday, and during our times of devotion, Scripture reading or prayer during the week (if we have any such times), we pay attention to the things of God. But for the rest of our lives, we ignore him. This is not the kind of commitment that God wants. It is in God that we live and move and have our being (Acts 17:28), not just for a few hours a week, but all day every day.

Do Not Be Conformed to the Pattern of This World

This principle is absolutely basic to our Christian life. I discuss it in chapter 13, and refer you to that discussion. What it comes down to, I think, is the question of whom we will serve. Will we serve the world? Or will we serve Almighty God? Thus it relates directly to the issue of commitment, which I am dealing with in this chapter.

Be Transformed by the Renewing of Our Minds

The transformation which Romans 12:2 calls for is a total one. The Greek word is *metamorphoo*, which suggests a change as complete and radical as that from a caterpillar to a butterfly. (See Chapter 14.)

To make this transformation requires a sacrifice. (What we receive is far better than what we give up, but still it often seems like a sacrifice.) In order to put on the new self, we have to put off the old self. In order to become a new creation, we must allow the old creation to pass away.

Scripture puts this in vivid terms. It tells us to put to death our old nature (Colossians 3:5), to crucify it (Galatians 5:24). (Also see Romans 6:6-8, 11; Galatians 2:20.) It tells us to die to sin (1 Peter 2:24). "I have been crucified with Christ; it is no longer I who live, but Christ lives in me" (Galatians 2:20). Christ died for us "...so that we might die to sins and live for righteousness..." (1 Peter 2:24 NIV). I suggest that this is part of what Paul means when he tells us to offer our bodies as living sacrifices.

Paul tells us to crucify "the sinful nature, its passions and desires" (Galatians 5:24 NIV). He says that "our old man was crucified with Him [Christ], that the body of sin might be done away with, that we should no longer be slaves of sin. For he who has died has been freed from sin. Now if we died with Christ, we believe that we shall also live with Him...Reckon yourselves to be dead indeed to sin, but alive to God in Christ Jesus our Lord" (Romans 6:6-8, 11). "If Christ is in you, the body is dead because of sin, but the Spirit is life because of righteousness" (Romans 8:10).

Acknowledge Him in All Our Ways

"In all your ways acknowledge Him [God]" (Proverbs 3:6). "Ways" refers to a journey, a path, a way of life. It refers to our goings in and our comings out. This passage, which underlies much of the Book of Proverbs, is saying that in everything we do, we should acknowledge God. Paul said something quite similar when he said, "in Him [God] we live and move and have our being" (Acts 17:28).

We are not our own. We belong to God. Apart from God we can do nothing (John 15:5). We can prevail only in God's mighty power (Ephesians 6:10). Hence we need to get rid of everything that conflicts with God's way and his purposes.

I suggest that all this is part of what Jesus meant when he said, "He who finds his life will lose it, and he who loses his life for My sake will find it" (Matthew 10:39). If we hold on to what we think of as ours, we will lose the life that Jesus Christ wants to give us. If we surrender everything to him, he will give us an abundant life on this earth and eternal life with him in heaven. This is the sacrifice we are called on to make, and the tremendous reward we receive for making it.

Our Spiritual Act of Worship

Paul tells us that to sacrifice our body to God is "…our spiritual act of worship" (Romans 12:1 NIV). (KJV has "reasonable service.") The word translated "worship" literally means service as a hired servant. It also came to mean service to God in a religious ceremony. But in a broader sense, all worship can be seen as a declaration of God's worthiness. In heaven, the continuous worship of God declares, "You are worthy, O Lord, to receive glory and honor and power; for you created all things" (Revelation 4:11). God is worthy of all our praise. He is worthy of everything we can give him. God is worthy.

God welcomes our praise and worship in church. He inhabits the praises of his people (Psalm 22:3 KJV). But I think what he most wants is for us to give our whole lives to him, to be totally committed to him in all our ways. It is by a totally committed life that we best declare God's worthiness.

Be United With Christ

One of the goals of all this is that we become united with Christ.

Jesus prayed, on the night before he was crucified, "[I pray] also for those who will believe me through their [the disciples'] word, that **they all may be one, as you, Father, are in Me and I in You;** that they also may be **one in Us,** that the world may believe that you sent Me. And the glory which You gave Me I have given them, that **they may be one just as We are one**, I in them and you in me, that **they may be made perfect in one,** and that the world may know that you have sent Me, and have loved them as you have loved Me" (John 17:20-23). This is not an easy passage to understand in detail. We need to chew on it. But the basic prayer for unity is clear.

If we are truly committed to Jesus Christ, then Christ is in us. (See Chapter 11.) But also we are in Christ. "Reckon yourselves to be dead indeed to sin, but alive to God in Christ Jesus our Lord" (Romans 6:11). "If anyone is in Christ, he is a new creation" (2 Corinthians 5:17). We can "live godly in Christ Jesus" (2 Timothy 3:12). "Peace to you all who are in Christ Jesus" (1 Peter 5:14). Many other Scriptures speak of us as being "in Christ." Perhaps it is in this sense that we can "be partakers of the divine nature" (2 Peter 1:4).

In order to achieve this amazing unity, we must be totally committed to God. We must acknowledge him in **all** our ways, in everything we say and do. We must get rid of everything in us that is not consistent with his will for us. If we are all truly serving God and seeking his will, we will be united.

CONCLUSION

What does all this tell us? God wants us to commit ourselves **totally** to him, holding nothing back. Give him all our agendas, hopes, plans, achievements, desires, thoughts, habits, personality traits. Everything. He wants us to acknowledge that we are created and he is the Creator, that everything in the universe is his, and that without him we can do nothing of value. He wants us to acknowledge that whatever we give him is his already. He wants us to present ourselves totally to him and allow him to do his work in us. He wants us to give all of ourselves with no strings attached.

The wonderful thing about this is that when we lose ourselves in him, then we truly find our life (Matthew 10:39). It is then that he is able to give us his more abundant life (John 10:10). He is "able to do exceedingly abundantly above all that we ask or think" (Ephesians 3:20).

God wants a life that is totally yielded to him. What he does with it is up to him. How he uses us, and how much he uses us, is up to him. We give all of ourselves with no strings attached.

17

The Importance of Obedience

o o o o o o o o o o o o o o o o o o o o o o o o o o o o o o o

"Therefore submit to God."

—(James 4:7)

Obedience is not a popular word today. For generations we have been taught to avoid such words. One result has been a lack of discipline in our homes and schools, which is an important factor in the progressive decline of our students in every objective test of performance.

Scripture, however, makes it very clear that obedience is a necessary and crucially important part of our life as Christians.

I believe the key to obedience is submission to God. What matters is, not external adherence to specific rules, but a heart that is submitted to God. If our heart is submitted to God, then we will obey his specific requirements. It is the heart attitude that is crucial.

What is our motive for this obedience, or submission? At the risk of oversimplification, let me say that I see three basic motives.

Fear

We obey because we fear someone who is more powerful than we are. This does enter into our obedience. Scripture tells us to fear the Lord, and, indeed, he is a God of awesome power. He is capable of great wrath. "It is a fearful thing to fall into the hands of the living God" (Hebrews 10:31). (Also see Romans 1:18; Ephesians 5:6; Colossians 3:6; 2 Thessalonians 1:7-9; Revelation 6:16-17.) At a minimum, we obey him to avoid his wrath and punishment. But there are better motives for obedience.

Self-Interest

God told Joshua, "This Book of the Law shall not depart from your mouth, but you shall meditate in it day and night, that you may observe to do according to all that is written in it. For then you will make your way prosperous, and then you will have good success" (Joshua 1:8).

Let me use a simple analogy. When we buy an automobile, we receive an owner's manual in which the manufacturer tells us the conditions under which his product must be operated if it is to function well. If we do not follow these instructions, we are apt to have something bad happen to the automobile. I sometimes think of the Bible as an owner's manual in which our Creator has told us the conditions under which his creation, man, will function best. If we follow the instructions, we will prosper; in Biblical terms, we will be blessed. If we do not follow the instructions, bad things will happen; in Biblical terms, we will be cursed. So if we want to prosper and live fruitful lives, we will follow our Creator's instructions. It's a simple matter of self-interest.

But God does not want us to submit to him just because of the benefits we hope to get. That was the issue in the book of Job, where God allowed satan to test Job to see if he loved him only because of what God had done for him. (See Job, chapters 1 and 2.) God wants us to love him, and to obey him, for who he is, and not just for what he does for us.

Love

Our relationship with the automobile manufacturer is impersonal; we do not even know him. Our relationship with God is, or should be, highly personal. God loves us and we love him. When you love someone, you want to do what pleases him. Scripture makes it inescapably clear that we show our love by our obedience. Jesus said, "If you love me, keep My commandments" (John 14:15). "He who has my commandments and keeps them, it is he who loves Me" (John 14:21). John wrote, "This is the love of God, that we keep His commandments" (1 John 5:3). The primary motive we have for obeying God is that we love him, we want to do what pleases him, and we want to become like him in character.

While all three of these motives enter into our obedience, I suggest that, particularly since Jesus Christ has come on earth, our primary motive for obedience is and should be our love for God and for his only son Jesus Christ. One of the best ways we can show that love is by obedience.

I, personally, am a long way from the obedience that I describe in this chapter. I doubt that any one, other than Jesus Christ, can be said to have achieved perfect obedience. We are all working towards it, and are at various stages in our pursuit of it. From my study of Scripture, I think I have been able to form a fairly clear picture of where we need to be, and I hope that picture will be of value to all of us who are working on this essential aspect of our lives in Christ.

DEFINITIONS

The usual Old Testament word translated "obey" is *shama*. It literally means "to hear." Strong's *Dictionary of the Hebrew Bible* defines *shama* as "to hear intelligently, often with implication of attention, obedience, etc." Vine's *Expository Dictionary of Biblical Words* describes it as "to hear, hearken, listen, obey, publish," and says that it appears about 1,160 times in the Old Testament.

The principal New Testament word for obey is *hupakouo*, from *hupo*, "under" and *akouo*, "to hear." Strong's *Dictionary of the Greek Bible* defines it as "to listen attentively, by implication, to heed or conform to a command or authority." Many other New Testament words for "obey" have the idea of hearing.

In both the Old and New Testaments, the central idea of "obey" is "to hear, to listen attentively." I think this is significant. It suggests that, when we speak of obedience to God, we are speaking of more than just observing and following the words written in Scripture, important as they are. We are also speaking of seeking and obeying the specific guidance of God in our daily lives, and following out the calling he has placed on our lives. Paul speaks of living a life controlled by the Holy Spirit (Romans 8:6-14) and of having the mind of Christ (1 Corinthians 2:16). Jesus speaks of doing the will of God (Matthew 7:21, 12:50). I believe this includes responding to the promptings of the Holy Spirit, as well as obeying God's general will expressed in Scripture.

OBEDIENCE IN THE OLD TESTAMENT

The people of Israel were a covenant people; they had a covenant relationship with their God. That relationship was stated in various terms at various times, but its essence is expressed thus, "Obey my voice and I will be your God, and you shall be My people" (Jeremiah 7:23). If the people of Israel wanted God to guide them, protect them, provide for them, bless them, and cause them to prosper, they had to obey God's voice and be his people. God "...keeps his covenant of love with all who love him and obey his commands" (Daniel 9:4 NIV).

I think it can be said that the history of the nation of Israel, as recorded in the Old Testament, revolves around the issue of obedience to God's commands. Repeatedly God told them to obey, repeatedly they disobeyed, repeatedly God warned them that their disobedience would bring disaster, repeatedly they ignored the warning, and finally their disobedience caused the destruction of both Israel and Judah.

God warned his people of the consequences of disobedience, but they refused to listen. "When I called, you did not answer; when I spoke, you did not hear" (Isaiah 65:12). (Also see 66:4.) "The LORD warned Israel and Judah through all his prophets and seers: 'Turn from your evil ways. Observe my commands and decrees, in accordance with the entire Law that I commanded your fathers to obey and that I delivered to you through my servants the prophets.' But they would not listen and were as stiff-necked as their fathers, who did not trust in the LORD their God. They rejected his decrees and the covenants he had made with their fathers and the warnings he had given them..." (2 Kings 17:13-15 NIV).

I want to note one thing about this Old Testament record. The emphasis in most of the texts is on keeping God's commands and laws. Do not do what God has told you not to do. But there are quite a few times when it is clear that the obedience called for is to do the affirmative things God has called on you to do. God told Noah to build an ark, and "Noah did according to all that the LORD commanded him" (Genesis 7:5). God told Abraham to take his family and household on a long and difficult journey to a country he did not know, and Abraham obeyed (Genesis 12:1-5). God told Abraham to sacrifice his only son, Isaac, in whom all God's promises rested; Abraham raised the knife, and then God spared his son. God said that "because you have obeyed My voice" (Genesis 22:18), all nations would be blessed through Abraham's offspring. God called Moses, Joshua, the judges and others to specific tasks, and they obeyed him.

Two of the most serious acts of disobedience in the Old Testament consisted of refusing or failing to do what God told someone to do. God told the Israelites to take the land of Canaan and promised that they would succeed. They refused (Numbers, chapters 13-14), and had to wander in the wilderness for forty years. This refusal is referred to in Scripture as an act of unbelief, disobedience, rebellion, and contempt for God (Hebrews 3:12-19, 4:6; Numbers 14:11, 23). God told King Saul to destroy the Amalekites totally, but Saul did not fully obey him. Samuel told him, "You have rejected the word of the LORD, and the LORD has rejected you as king over Israel" (1 Samuel 15:26). Obedience, even in the Old Testament, is more than just obeying rules. It is doing what God tells you to do.

OBEDIENCE IN THE NEW TESTAMENT

The central importance of obedience in the New Testament is dramatically shown by Romans 5:19, "For as by one man's disobedience many were made sinners, so also by one Man's obedience many will be made righteous." Through Adam's disobedience, sin came into the world. With it came sickness and death. By it man's dominion over the world was handed over to satan, and satan became the god of this age (2 Corinthians 4:4). Then through the obedience of Jesus, the Kingdom of God came into the world, man was freed from the burden of sin, and satan's authority was overthrown. Through the obedience of Jesus, God established a "new covenant" (Matthew 26:28) with his people that is based on our obedience to Jesus. It was disobedience that caused the Fall; it was obedience that undid its effects.

Jesus' victory at the Cross was based on his obedience. He said, "...I do exactly what my Father has commanded me..." (John 14:31 NIV). Before the Crucifixion, he prayed three times to his Father, "Not as I will, but as You will" (Matthew 26:39). Paul tells us that Jesus "humbled Himself and became obedient to the point of death, even the death of the cross. Therefore God has highly exalted Him and given Him the name which is above every name" (Philippians 2:8-9). Hebrews says that Jesus "learned obedience by the things which He suffered. And having been perfected, He became the source of eternal salvation to all who obey Him" (Hebrews 5:8-9). It was by his obedience that he was able to become the source of eternal salvation for those who obey him. The whole "new covenant" (or "new testament" KJV) is based on Jesus' perfect obedience to his Father. And it calls on us to obey. If we are to be imitators of the Lord (1 Thessalonians 1:6), and walk as Jesus did (1 John 2:6), we need to be obedient.

Jesus Is Lord

"...If you confess with your mouth 'Jesus is Lord,' and believe in your heart that God raised him from the dead, you will be saved" (Romans 10:9 NIV). Jesus is not just our Savior, wonderful as that is. He is our Lord. Unless we make him Lord of our lives, our salvation is not complete.

Jesus is above everything. All authority in heaven and on earth has been given to him. He has the supremacy in everything. Every knee will bow to him and every tongue confess that he is Lord. When Thomas saw the resurrected Jesus, he said, "My Lord and my God!" (John 20:28). When John saw Jesus in his glory, he "fell at His feet as dead" (Revelation 1:17). I am sure that will be the reaction of all believers when we see him as he truly is. (See Chapter 6.)

Jesus Expects Us to Obey Him

Jesus told his disciples, and hence us, "If you love Me, keep My commandments" (John 14:15). "He who has My commandments and keeps them, it is he who loves Me" (John 14:21). "...If anyone loves me he will obey my teaching..." (John 14:23 NIV). "If you keep My commandments, you will abide in My love, just as I have kept my Father's commandments and abide in His love" (John 15:10). He said, "Why do you call Me, 'Lord, Lord' and do not do the things which I say?" (Luke 6:46). He said that when the storms come (when difficulties come), everyone who hears his words and puts them into practice will remain standing, while everyone who hears his words and does not put them into practice will fall with a great crash (Matthew 7:24-29). He wrote the church at Sardis, "Remember, therefore, what you have received and heard; obey it, and repent..." (Revelation 3:3 NIV). Revelation speaks of "...patient endurance on the part of the saints who obey God's commandments and remain faithful to Jesus" (Revelation 14:12 NIV). "Those who obey his commands live in him [Jesus], and he in them" (1 John 3:24 NIV).

Paul defined his ministry as that of calling "...people from among all the Gentiles to the obedience that comes from faith" (Romans 1:5 NIV). (Also see Romans 15:18, 16:26.) Peter tells believers that they have been "...chosen according to the foreknowledge of God...for obedience to Jesus Christ..." (1 Peter 1:2 NIV).

The Principle of Authority

Authority is a basic principle in God's Kingdom. Jesus was obedient to God, and thus became the source of salvation to those who obey him (Hebrews 5:8-9). Jesus said to his disciples, "...All authority in heaven and on earth has been given to me. Therefore go and make disciples of all nations...teaching them to obey everything I have commanded you" (Matthew 28:18-20 NIV). A disciple (*mathetes*) is a pupil. He is one under discipline, or at least in New Testament days he was. "*Mathetes* means more in the New Testament than a mere pupil or learner. It means an adherent who accepts the instruction given to him and makes it his rule of conduct."[29] It was because Jesus had been given all authority that he could authorize and commission his disciples to raise up other disciples who would raise up still others, etc.

It is the power of God working in us that enables us to be effective (Ephesians 1:19, 6:10). Paul said, "I can do all things through Christ who strengthens Me" (Philippians 4:13). How do we get this power? Paul had it because he was a servant (or slave) of Jesus Christ. We receive power when the Holy Spirit comes upon us (Acts 1:8), and the Holy Spirit is given to those who obey God (Acts 5:32). (Also see John 14:15-16.) God empowers those who obey him.

The centurion understood authority. He said, "I also am a man under authority, having soldiers under me" (Matthew 8:9). (See verses 5-10.) Because he understood authority, he believed that Jesus could heal his servant by a word. Jesus praised him, saying, "I have not found such great faith, not even in Israel" (Matthew 8:10).

The New Life

Jesus has given us a new life as the result of our salvation. Let us look at the part that obedience plays in this process of transformation. I shall do this briefly, because much of this has been dealt with in other chapters.

SALVATION—Hebrews 5:9 says that Jesus "became the author of eternal salvation to all who obey Him." You may say, "Wait a minute, I thought we were saved by faith and only by faith." We are saved by faith. That is what Ephesians 2:8-9 and many other Scriptures say. But Scripture does not contradict itself. As I shall develop more fully in chapter 18, faith, or belief, as used in Scripture, implies obedience.

RECEIVING THE HOLY SPIRIT—A crucial part of the new life is that we receive the Holy Spirit and allow him to take up residence inside us. The Holy Spirit comes only to those who obey God (Acts 5:32). Jesus told his disciples, "If you love Me, keep My commandments. And I will pray the Father and he will give you another Helper [the Holy Spirit], that He may abide with you forever" (John 14:15-16). God gives the Holy Spirit to those who keep Jesus' commandments, to those who obey God. If we want the Holy Spirit to live within us, guide us, teach us, and empower us, we need to obey God. As John said, "Those who obey his [God's] commands live in him, and he in them. And this is how we know that he lives in us: We know it by the Spirit he gave us" (1 John 3:24 NIV).

LIVING BY THE SPIRIT—The key to the new life that we have been promised, is that we should live by the Holy Spirit. (See Chapter 15.) To live by the spirit is to be controlled by the spirit, to submit your soul and body to the control of the Holy Spirit. The new life is a life that is lived in submission to the Holy Spirit who is within us.

Note that what Paul is talking about is not an obedience that is imposed on us by force. It arises because we have chosen to offer ourselves to God and to obey him. It is a willing obedience.

KNOWING GOD—Knowing God is essential to our new life. But we cannot know him unless we obey him. "By this we know that we know Him, if we keep His commandments. He who says, 'I know him,' and does not keep His commandments, is a liar, and the truth is not in him. But whoever keeps his word, truly the love of God is perfected in him. By this we know that we are in Him. He who says he abides in Him ought himself also to walk just as He walked" (1 John 2:3-6). Paul spoke of those who "profess to know God, but in works they deny Him" (Titus 1:16).

FREEDOM—Jesus told his disciples, "If you abide in My word, you are My disciples indeed. And you shall know the truth, and the truth shall make you free" (John 8:31-32). As we continue to dwell in Jesus' word, and hold fast to his teachings, we become his disciples, his *mathetes,* his followers, who are taught to "obey everything I have commanded you" (Matthew 28:29). And it is this commitment to his word, this obedience to his word, that sets us free. Obedience to Jesus, far from being a burden, is something that frees us.

Colossians 1:13 says, "He has delivered us from the power of darkness and conveyed us into the kingdom of the Son of His love." We have been freed from satan's power by accepting the greater power and authority of Jesus Christ. (Also see Romans 6:15-19.)

PRAYER—Jesus taught us to pray, "Your will be done on earth as it is in heaven" (Matthew 6:10). He gave us the example in Gethsemane, when he asked that he not have to endure the Crucifixion, but then, in agony, prayed, "not as I will, but as You will" (Matthew 26:39). I believe this is at the heart of all true prayer. In prayer, we seek to know God's will, and then unite ourselves to his will to pray that his will shall be done. "Whatever we ask we receive from Him [God], because we keep His commandments and do those things that are pleasing in His sight" (1 John 3:22). "Now this is the confidence we have in Him, that if we ask anything according to His will, He hears us. And if we know that he hears us, whatever we ask, we know that we have the petitions that we have asked of Him" (1 John 5:14-15).

WORSHIP—An essential part of the new life is to worship God. We worship him in spirit and in truth (John 4:23-24). To worship (*proskuneo*) is to prostrate oneself before in homage, to do reverence to, to adore. It is, among other things, an act of submission.

Our worship is not just an act we do at certain specified times and places. It is, or should be, a continuous state of submission. As Samuel told King Saul, "To obey is better than sacrifice" (1 Samuel 15:22). True worship is giving God the priority in our life. It is seeking first God's kingdom and his righteousness (Matthew 6:33). It is fixing our eyes on Jesus, the author and finisher of our faith (Hebrews 12:2), and setting our hearts and minds "on those things which are above, where Christ is, sitting at the right hand of God" (Colossians 3:1-2). (Also see 2 Corinthians 4:18.)

Paul defines worship in these terms, "Therefore, I urge you, brothers, in view of God's mercy, to offer your bodies as living sacrifices, holy and pleasing to God—this is your spiritual act of worship" (Romans 12:1 NIV). To worship is to surrender our lives totally to God. It is to die to self and live for God. (See Chapter 16.)

DOING THE WILL OF GOD

"The primary concern in Christian living is doing the will of God."[30] This was Jesus' purpose. "My food is to do the will of Him who sent me, and to finish His work" (John 4:34). "I do not seek My own will but the will of the Father who sent me" (John 5:30). "I have come down from heaven, not to do My own will, but the will of Him who sent Me" (John 6:38). In the Garden of Gethsemane, he prayed, "not as I will, but as You will" (Matthew 26:39). (Also see Matthew 26:42, 44.)

If we are to be imitators of Jesus, if we are to do the things he was doing, should we not seek to do the will of God in everything? That is exactly what Scripture says. Jesus taught us to pray, "Your will be done, on earth as it is in heaven" (Matthew 6:10). He said, "Who is My mother and who are My brothers?...Whoever does the will of My Father in heaven is My brother and sister and mother" (Matthew 12:48, 50). He said, "Not every one who says to Me, 'Lord, Lord,' shall enter the kingdom of heaven, but he who does the will of My Father in heaven" (Matthew 7:21). Paul prayed that "you may be filled with the knowledge of His will in all wisdom and spiritual understanding, that you may have a walk worthy of the Lord, fully pleasing Him" (Colossians 1:9-10). (Also see Ephesians 6:6.) The author of Hebrews prayed that God would "make you complete in every good work to do His will, working in you what is well pleasing in His sight" (Hebrews 13:21). John wrote, "The world and its desires pass away, but the man who does the will of God lives forever" (1 John 2:17 NIV).

Doing the will of God is much more than obeying a set of external rules. God has a purpose for the life of each one of us. "We are His [God's] workmanship, created in Christ Jesus for good works, which God prepared beforehand that we should walk in them" (Ephesians 2:10). "'For I know the plans I have for you' declares the LORD 'plans to prosper you and not to harm you, plans to give you hope and a future'" (Jeremiah 29:11 NIV). He wants to be able to say to each one of us, "Well done, good and faithful servant" (Matthew 25:21). To say "yes" to the things God is calling you to do may often be more important than to say "no" to the things God has told you not to do.

There are three things that try to keep us from doing the will of God: the world, the flesh and the devil.

THE WORLD—If we would know what God's will is for us, we must not conform to the pattern of this world. (See Chapter 13.) This means that we should seek to please God and not people. Jesus even warned, "Woe to you when all men speak well of you, for so did their fathers to the false prophets" (Luke 6:26). I believe one of the greatest blocks in this nation, today, to our doing the will of God is our desire to please all people, and our fear of their disapproval or ridicule.

A major weakness in the body of Christ today is that we are too much conformed to the pattern of this world. Many who profess to believe in Christ live lives that are almost indistinguishable from those of non-believers. Many churches have conformed in great measure to the pattern of this world. Some have adopted theologies that are not based on the word of God, and even deny much that Scripture teaches; some have gotten into New Age philosophy and practices. Many have adopted for themselves worldly standards of emphasis on material success and pursuit of human agendas. We need to stop conforming to the pattern of this world.

THE FLESH—If we would be controlled by the Spirit, we need to put to death the desires of the flesh. (See Chapter 15.) We need, as I have said earlier, to die to self and live for God. Today I'm afraid there are quite a few who call themselves Christians but who are basically self-centered rather than God-centered. Self-centeredness is a problem for most of us, and it is encouraged by our modern culture.

THE DEVIL—The devil and his evil spirits come to steal and kill and destroy (John 10: 10). (See Chapter 12.) He tries to exalt himself against the knowledge of God (2 Corinthians 10:5). Whenever we give in to the world or the flesh, whenever we focus on ourselves rather than on God, we invite the devil to attack us. We need to avoid giving him a foothold. We need, at every turn, to submit ourselves to God and resist the devil.

HOW IS IT THAT WE SHOULD OBEY?

In this section I can only sketch out what I believe to be the basic approach that is called for in this matter of obedience.

Under the Old Testament, the emphasis tended to be on outward obedience to a prescribed set of detailed rules—the many laws and commands which God gave through Moses, as recorded in Exodus, Leviticus, Numbers and Deuteronomy, and the words God gave the writing prophets. There are exceptions to this. But the primary emphasis is on outward observance. "If you fully obey the LORD your God and carefully follow all his commands…" you will be blessed (Deuteronomy 28:1 NIV). (Also see Deuteronomy 28:15.) "Observe to do according to all the law which Moses My servant commanded you; do not turn from it to the right hand or to the left" (Joshua 1:7). This got to the point that the apostle James could say, "Whoever shall keep the whole law, and yet stumble in one point, he is guilty of all" (James 2:10).

Jesus changed this emphasis. Twice in the Sermon on the Mount he took a command that related to outward actions and extended it to a condition of the heart. "You shall not murder" (Matthew 5:21) became "Do not be angry." "You shall not commit adultery" (Matthew 5:27) became "Do not look at a woman lustfully." (See Matthew 5:21-30.) When the Pharisees spoke to him about outward ceremony, Jesus said that it is the things that come from the heart that make a man unclean, and not outward observances (Matthew 15:16-21). He told the teachers and legalists of his time, "Woe to you, scribes and Pharisees, hypocrites! For you pay tithe of mint and anise and cumin [herbs], and have rejected the weightier matters of the law: justice and mercy and faith" (Matthew 23:23). In

New Testament obedience, the primary emphasis is on a totally submitted heart, rather than on detailed adherence to a mass of regulations.

Paul made it clear that the Mosaic law was powerless to free us from sin because no one could obey it completely. "For what the law was powerless to do in that it was weakened by the sinful nature, God did by sending his own Son in the likeness of sinful man to be a sin offering…" (Romans 8:3 NIV). We are not justified by observing the law, but by belief in Jesus Christ. We are no longer under bondage to the law (Galatians chapters 1-5). We have an obligation, but it is to be led and controlled by the Holy Spirit (Galatians 5:13-26; Romans 8:4-17).

Paul also made it very clear that in the moral realm believers are not free to do as they choose. "…do not use your freedom to indulge the sinful nature" (Galatians 5:13 NIV). (Also see Romans 6:1, 15.) Scripture commands us to "be holy in all your conduct" (1 Peter 1:15). Without holiness, no one will see the Lord (Hebrews 12:14).

Jesus has given some specific commands in the Sermon on the Mount and elsewhere in the Gospels. Paul has listed acts of the sinful nature which we must avoid (Galatians 5:19-21; Ephesians 4:29-31, 5:3-7; Colossians 3:5-9). The epistles contain other specific indications of God's will for us. But over and above these specifics are the general commands. We are to be imitators of Christ, be like Christ, have the mind of Christ. We are to fix our eyes on Christ, fix our minds on things above. We are to live by the Holy Spirit, be led and controlled by the Holy Spirit. This means, I believe, that we need to be receptive to what the Holy Spirit shows us, and to follow whatever guidance he gives us.

If we are Biblically obedient, then we will seek to know God's will in each situation we are in, and we will do our best to act according to his will. Such obedience leads us to listen to the inner promptings of the Holy Spirit, and to follow those promptings. This may start out as something we do self-consciously from time to time, but it should grow beyond that to habitual obedience that is so normal that we hardly notice it. It is in God that we live and move and have our being (Acts 17:28). The ideal of obedience would be to achieve what Jesus had achieved when he told us that he did only what he saw the Father doing and said only what the Father told him to say. As we are transformed into God's image, we can hope to come closer to this ideal.

As I see it, New Testament obedience is primarily a matter of attitude, of desiring to please God, to be like Jesus Christ, to be controlled by the Holy Spirit. Following specific rules is less important than growing to maturity and carrying out the calling that God has placed on your life. Where there are specific rules, we follow them as the clearest evidence of what God would have us do. But in all things we need to have an attitude of submission to his will. Perhaps the clearest expression of this is the following:

> "For through the law I died to the law so that I might live for God. I have been crucified with Christ and I no longer live, but Christ lives in me. The life that I live in the body, I live by faith in the Son of God, who loved me and gave himself for me" (Galatians 2:19-20 NIV).

Where the Old Testament called for obedience to a host of specific requirements, the New Testament calls for such total submission to God that Paul could say, "It is no longer I who live, but Christ lives in me" (Galatians 2:20).

HINDRANCES TO OBEDIENCE

Some of the things that hinder us from obeying God are obvious: pride, rebellion, self-centeredness. But I think the greatest thing that keeps people from obeying him is that we just don't take seriously the need to obey.

We live in a permissive society where many have not been taught to obey parents, teachers, or others in authority. We live in a society where many do not understand the laws of cause and effect. Many of us have not been taught to understand that our actions or inactions have consequences, and that we are responsible for what we do and do not do. And so we tend too easily to think that it does not matter whether we obey God or not, or that we can obey him in some things and not others, or that "a little" disobedience now and then is all right.

That is why I have thought it important to emphasize the many Scriptures that talk about obedience. If we will read them, and take them seriously, I think we will see that obedience is an essential part of our Christian life. Our God is an awesome God. He is a mighty, and a powerful God. When he tells us to obey him, we had better take him very seriously. When he tells us that those who do not obey him cannot know him, we had better believe him. Scripture tells us that the fear of the Lord is the beginning of wisdom. Part of that fear means that we don't fool around with God, we don't presume on God, we pay close attention when he says something in his Scripture. We need to take this issue of obedience very seriously.

CONCLUSION

Some years ago, Aleksandr Solzhenitsyn, that extraordinary Russian dissenter from Communism, in a speech at Harvard University, said that in the Soviet Union they had rejected God, and in the West we had forgotten God. Of the two, he thought what the West had done was the more dangerous.

There are many things in our nation today that are spiritually wrong. One could mention abortion, the "sexual revolution," the high divorce rate, the high rate of children born out of wedlock, high crime rates, drug addiction and the drug traffic, pornography, and the like. One could mention business and government corruption. More basic, I believe, are such things as a preoccupation with material concerns, a basic selfishness ("What's in it for me?"), a prevalent philosophy that there are no objective moral laws and no such thing as objective truth, an objection to every form of discipline, and a constant blame-shifting that denies one's personal responsibility. There is a prevalent pride that says, "Look at all we have accomplished by our own abilities," and fails to give thanks to God. Underlying all of this is the fact that for many (perhaps most) Americans, God and God's will are simply not seen as significant elements in our decisions and actions.

There has been considerable outright rejection of God. But I believe Solzhenitsyn was right that the major problem has been that we have forgotten God.

God has said, "Blessed is the nation whose God is the LORD" (Psalm 33:12). Do we want that blessing for our nation, or do we not?

I believe that our nation, like Israel, has been favored by God for several centuries, but that we are now close to a point where God may judge us. And I believe that he will first judge his church, especially those who profess to believe in him but have gotten to the point where he no longer has much, if any, importance in their lives.

God still wants to give us an opportunity to come back to him. I believe he is saying to us, as he did to the people of Israel almost 3,000 years ago, "If My people who are called by My name will humble themselves, and pray and seek My face, and turn from their wicked ways, then I will hear from heaven and will forgive their sin and heal their land" (2 Chronicles 7:14). (Also see Jeremiah 18:7-10.) This humbling process must start with "my people," those who profess to believe in him. Then it can extend to the rest of the nation.

God still wants to be able to say that we are his people and he is our God. For him to do this, we must submit ourselves to him, individually, as the body of Christ, and then as a nation. I believe that a fuller understanding of what it means to obey God, to submit to him, can help bring us to the point where we can indeed return to God and serve him, and he can heal our land.

18

Faith

o o o o o o o o o o o o o o o o o o o o o o o o o o o o o o

"Contend earnestly for the faith."

—*(Jude 3)*

The theme of this book is standing firm in the faith. So we need to understand what faith is. In our Western world, faith, or belief, is often thought of as intellectual assent. To the New Testament writers, it meant very much more than that. It meant total trust, total obedience, and total commitment. Faith is what we live by.

Faith means much more than intellectual assent. (The Greek word for faith is *pistis*, and the related verb is *pisteuo*.) We believe in our heart and not just our mind (Romans 10:9-10). Few, if any, people have been saved by mere intellectual assent. Intellectual assent, without more, can hardly give us the courage and perseverance to stand firm against obstacles and disapproval. There has to be a faith that is rooted firmly in our heart, in our guts.

Strong's *Dictionary of the Greek Bible* defines faith as "persuasion, i.e. credence, moral conviction…especially reliance on Christ for salvation." He says that the related verb *pisteuo* means "to entrust (especially one's spiritual well-being to Christ)." Vine's *Expository Dictionary of Biblical Words* says that *pisteuo* signifies "reliance upon, not mere credence." Biblical faith is not just believing in a set of doctrines or principles; it is believing, and putting one's trust, in the person of Jesus Christ. "Whoever believes **in Him**" is saved (John 3:16). Paul wrote, "I know **whom** I have believed" (2 Timothy 1:12). "Whom" (a person) rather than "what" (a set of doctrines).

J.I. Packer says, "True faith is an exclusive, wholehearted trust, a complete going out of oneself to put one's entire confidence in God's mercy."[31] Donald G. Bloesch defines faith as "a radical commitment of the whole man to the living

Christ, a commitment that entails knowledge, trust and obedience."[32] I believe Bloesch has it exactly right. Paul puts it this way, "The life which I now live in the flesh, I live by faith in the Son of God, who loved me and gave Himself for me" (Galatians 2:20). Faith is a matter of our whole being, our whole life.

Actually, all of us live by faith. We all trust our lives, our health, our physical safety, our finances, and much else, to others. The question is, where will we put our primary faith?

We drive into traffic having faith in our vehicle, our driving skill, and the reasonableness of most drivers. We step into an airplane having faith in the competence and physical condition of the pilot, the thoroughness of the plane's maintenance, and the expertness of the airport controllers. We entrust our life to a surgeon. We entrust our finances to an economic system, and to various financial institutions. Etc. Etc.

The real question is, will we place all of our faith in ourselves and other humans, who are fallible and sometimes deceitful? Or will we place our primary faith in God, our Creator, who is all-powerful, all-wise and all-good?

The religion of humanism, which is so prevalent today, says that we should place all of our faith and trust in man's knowledge, wisdom, ability, and goodness. Scripture says the opposite. Paul desired that our "faith should not be in the wisdom of men but in the power of God" (1 Corinthians 2:5). Proverbs tells us, "Trust in the LORD with all your heart, and lean not on your own understanding; In all your ways acknowledge Him, and He shall direct your paths. Do not be wise in your own eyes; fear the LORD and depart from evil" (Proverbs 3:5-7). When we trust in man's ability and wisdom, we are leaning on our own understanding and being wise in our own eyes. Scripture tells us to trust in the Lord.

Jeremiah puts it plainly. "Cursed is the man who trusts in man, and makes flesh his strength, whose heart departs from the LORD…Blessed is the man who trusts in the LORD, and whose hope is in the LORD" (Jeremiah 17:5, 7). (Also see Psalms 118:8-9; 146:1-3.) He goes on to explain why this is so. "The heart [of man] is deceitful above all things, and desperately wicked" (Jeremiah 17:9). Only God is worthy of complete trust. Humanism—putting your faith and trust solely (or even primarily) in man—leads to curses and failure. I think we are beginning to see the practical results of that today.

I want to look at some aspects of this faith in God. The faith I am talking about is not just what is called "saving faith," important though that is. Faith is more than just a matter of deciding to come to Jesus. It is a matter of believing Scripture, of believing all the promises of the Bible, of believing that God is watching over us and guiding us, and much more.

THE SIGNIFICANCE OF FAITH

Faith Is Central

As Paul says, we live by faith (Galatians 2:20; 2 Corinthians 5:7). "The just shall live by faith" (Romans 1:17). (Also see Habakkuk 2:4.) As Christians, every aspect of our life is based on faith in God. "In Him [God] we live and move and have our being" (Acts 17:28). "Without faith it is impossible to please Him [God]" (Hebrews 11:6).

Faith Is a Decision

Faith is not just intellectual assent. It is a decision that has very important consequences for our lives.

A story is told of a high wire performer, who stretched a wire across Niagara Falls and planned to push a wheelbarrow on the wire from one side to the other. He asked a bystander, "Do you believe I can do it?" "Oh yes," said the man. "Fine," said the performer, "Get in the wheelbarrow." That's what faith is. It's not just assenting intellectually to something. It's getting in the wheelbarrow. It's making a decision and committing your entire life to it. Intellectual acceptance is not enough. It takes commitment.

Faith Shows Itself in Our Actions

When we come to Jesus Christ, and accept him as our Savior and Lord, it should result in a changed life. Jesus began his preaching by saying, "...Repent and believe the good news" (Mark 1:15 NIV). To repent, *metanoeo,* is to change directions, to turn around. "If anyone is in Christ, he is a new creation; old things have passed away; behold, all things have become new" (2 Corinthians 5:17). We are transformed (Romans 12:2). If we do not see this kind of transformed life, we are entitled to question whether a person's faith is genuine.

Scripture speaks over and over of the fact that our faith, to be genuine, must show itself in our actions. Jesus said, "...anyone who has faith in me will do what I have been doing. He will do even greater things than these..." (John 14:12 NIV). Genuine faith results in action. Jesus said, "Why do you call me 'Lord, Lord,' and not do the things which I say?" (Luke 6:46). He said, "Not everyone who says to Me, 'Lord, Lord,' shall enter the kingdom of heaven, but he who does the will of My Father in heaven" (Matthew 7:21). He spoke, critically, of those who honor God with their lips, but their heart is far from him (Matthew 15:8, quoting Isaiah 29:13).

James wrote, "…faith by itself, if it is not accompanied by action, is dead" (James 2:17 NIV). Paul would not disagree. He spoke of those who "…claim to know God, but by their actions they deny him…" (Titus 1:16 NIV). He described the purpose of his entire ministry as "…to call people from among all the Gentiles to the obedience that comes from faith" (Romans 1:5 NIV). He preached to Jews and Gentiles alike that "they should repent, turn to God, and do works befitting repentance" (Acts 26:20). He admonished believers to "…live a life worthy of the calling you have received…" (Ephesians 4:1 NIV), to live a life controlled by the Holy Spirit of God (Galatians 5:16, Romans 8:13), and to have "an abundance for every good work" (2 Corinthians 9:8). (Also see Titus 3:8.) He emphasized that the Bible is useful "that the man of God may be complete, thoroughly equipped for every good work" (2 Timothy 3:16). The author of Hebrews prayed, "Now may the God of peace…make you complete in every good work to do his will, working in you what is well pleasing in his sight, through Jesus Christ, to whom be glory forever and ever. Amen" (Hebrews 13:20-21). In Hebrews, chapter 11, we see over and over how faith is shown by action, and results in action.

When Jesus commended people for their faith, or criticized them for their lack of faith, it was usually in the context of their actions. The centurion told Jesus that he did not need to come to his house; saying, "only speak a word, and my servant will be healed" (Matthew 8:8). Jesus responded, "I have not found such great faith, not even in Israel" (Matthew 8:10). The centurion showed his faith by his action. When the friends of the paralytic took the extraordinary step of lowering him through the roof, "Jesus saw their faith" (Matthew 9:2) and healed their friend. When the woman with an issue of blood pressed through the crowd to touch his garment, Jesus said, "your faith has made you well" (Matthew 9:22). When the Canaanite woman persisted in asking that Jesus heal her demonized daughter, Jesus said, "O woman, great is your faith! Let it be to you as you desire" (Matthew 15:28). When blind Bartimaeus persisted in calling out, despite every effort of the disciples to silence him, Jesus said, "Your faith has made you well" (Mark 10:52). (See Chapter 21.) In each case, it was their action, their persistence, their pressing in, that showed their faith.

When the disciples feared that they would drown in a storm, Jesus said, "Why are you fearful, O you of little faith?" (Matthew 8:26). Peter walked on the water for a while, and then became afraid and began to sink. Jesus said to him, "O you of little faith, why did you doubt?" (Matthew 14:31). When the disciples could not heal a demonized boy, Jesus said it was "Because of your unbelief" (Matthew 17:20). In each case, their actions showed their lack of faith.

I want to make one thing very clear. We are saved by faith, and only by faith. "Not of works, lest anyone should boast" (Ephesians 2:9). (Also see Titus 3:5.) But if our faith does not affect our actions, if it does not lead to action, if it is not demonstrated by our actions, then it may be doubted whether it is genuine faith. Our actions cannot save us, but they are evidence of the faith that saves us.

Faith Implies Trust

Jesus said to his disciples, "Do not let your hearts be troubled. Trust in God; trust also in me" (John 14:1 NIV). Paul wrote, "May the God of hope fill you with all joy and peace as you trust in him, so that you may overflow with hope by the power of the Holy Spirit" (Romans 15:13 NIV). "I will wait on the LORD…I will hope in Him" (Isaiah 8:17 NIV). "Behold, God is my salvation, I will trust and not be afraid" (Isaiah 12:2). "Commit your way to the Lord; trust also in him" (Psalm 37:5). (Also see Psalms 25:2, 37:3, 62:8, 115:11; Isaiah 26:4; Jeremiah 39:18.)

Because God is all-powerful, all-wise and all-good, we can put our trust in him and we need not fear anything. "God is our refuge and strength, a very present help in trouble. Therefore we will not fear" (Psalm 46:1-2). "Whenever I am afraid, I will trust in you…In God I have put my trust; I will not fear. What can flesh do to me?" (Psalm 56:3-4).

It is by faith that we overcome fear. When Jairus heard that his daughter was dead, Jesus told him, "Do not be afraid; only believe" (Mark 5:36). When the disciples feared the storm on Lake Galilee, Jesus said, "Why are you fearful, O you of little faith?" (Matthew 8:26).

When Joshua was about to invade Canaan, God told him, "Be strong and of good courage; do not be afraid, nor be dismayed, for the LORD your God is with you wherever you go" (Joshua 1:9). When God is with us, we have no reason to fear.

When a vast army attacked Judah, King Jehoshaphat prayed to God, "…we have no power to face this vast army that is attacking us. We do not know what to do, but our eyes are upon you." Then a prophet declared, "…Do not be afraid or discouraged because of this vast army. For the battle is not yours but God's." The King declared to his people, "…Have faith in the LORD your God and you will be upheld; have faith in his prophets and you will be successful" (2 Chronicles 20:12, 15, 20 NIV). The next morning they went out to battle and God gave them the victory. It was their faith that enabled them to trust in God and in the prophetic word he had given, and to have the courage to go out against a greatly superior force.

Paul writes, "Be anxious for nothing, but in everything, by prayer and supplication, with thanksgiving, let your requests be made known to God; and the peace of God, which surpasses all understanding, will guard your hearts and minds through Christ Jesus" (Philippians 4:6-7). The key to overcoming worry and anxiety is to trust in God, and to put our problems in his hands, confident that he will work them out.

I am not saying that we should sit back, do nothing, and just say, "Let God take care of it." That is never God's way. He expects us to do all that we can. But when we have done all that we can, then we can call on him for help, knowing that ultimately "the battle is the Lord's." This is made clear in Ephesians 6:10-18. Paul tells us to "...be strong in the Lord and in his mighty power" (Ephesians 6:10 NIV). Then he tells us to "...stand your ground, and **after you have done everything**, to stand" (Ephesians 6:13 NIV). We stand in God's mighty power. But we also need to do everything we can.

Faith Implies Obedience

"By faith Abraham **obeyed** when he was called to go out to the place which he would receive as an inheritance. And he went out, not knowing where he was going" (Hebrews 11:8). Because of his faith in God, Abraham, at age 75, took his wife, and other relatives, associates and servants, on a journey of over 400 miles through difficult county, to a land he knew nothing about and where he had no acquaintances. "By faith Abraham, when he was tested, offered up Isaac" as a sacrifice (Hebrews 11:17), in obedience to God's command.

"By faith Noah, being divinely warned of things not yet seen, moved with godly fear, prepared an ark for the saving of his household" (Hebrews 11:7). Scripture tells us of Noah's total obedience. "Noah did according to all that the LORD commanded him" (Genesis 7:5). (Also see 6:22.) This involved building a boat 450 feet long, 75 feet wide and 45 feet high out of cypress wood (no small task for a man 600 years old and his three sons), in order to find safety from an event which had never before occurred on earth. Until the flood, there had been no rain.

We see the other side of this. "See to it, brothers, that none of you has a sinful, unbelieving heart that turns away from the living God" (Hebrews 3:12 NIV). The reference is to the time when the Israelites, responding to ten of the twelve spies, refused to go into Canaan even though God, by prophetic words given through Moses, had promised that they would conquer it. Scripture refers to this unbelief (lack of faith, *apistia*, from *a*, without, and *pistis*, faith) as rebellion and disobedience (Hebrews 3:16, 4:6, 11), and contempt for God (Numbers 14:11).

Faith Implies Total Commitment

"Commit your way to the LORD; trust also in Him" (Psalm 37:5).

Paul wrote to believers, "I beseech you therefore, brethren, by the mercies of God, that you present your bodies a living sacrifice, holy, acceptable to God, which is your reasonable service" (Romans 12:1). Paul lived this total commitment. He gave up a great opportunity for worldly success and approval in return for a life of extraordinary hardship and suffering. (See Chapter 16.)

Paul expressed this total commitment in another way in the following passage, "I have been crucified with Christ; it is no longer I who live, but Christ lives in me; and the life which I now live in the flesh I live by faith in the Son of God, who loved me and gave Himself for me" (Galatians 2:20). Paul's faith led to a total surrender and commitment to Jesus Christ.

I am not saying that every Christian is expected to live the same life of total commitment that Paul did. But faith implies that we need to be prepared to commit ourselves to Jesus Christ in whatever way, and to whatever degree, he calls on us to do.

Faith Means Trusting God Rather Than the Apparent Circumstances

Faith is based on the unseen, eternal things rather than the visible, immediate circumstances. Jesus said to Thomas, "Because you have seen Me, you have believed. Blessed are those who have not seen and yet have believed" (John 20:29). Hebrews tells us, "...faith is being sure of what we hope for, and certain of what we do not see" (Hebrews 11:1 NIV). Paul tells us, "We walk by faith, not by sight" (2 Corinthians 5:7). "We do not look at the things which are seen, but at the things which are not seen. For the things which are seen are temporary, but the things which are not seen are eternal" (2 Corinthians 4:18).

This is not easy to do for those of us who live in our Western materialistic world. Most of our training is to focus on the "facts," the things that we see, feel or hear around us. My father grew up in this tradition, and all my early training was based on it. The only things my father considered real, almost the only things he was able to deal with, were material facts, such as what could be measured or detected by scientific instruments, and the "facts" of business and commerce. I think many of us in the United States have grown up in that tradition. But Paul says that all these "facts"—"the things which are seen"—are only temporary, and that the real truth, the only permanent truth, is to be found in "the things which are not seen."

Scripture gives us a number of examples of this principle. I shall mention three.

God promised to Abraham that he would bear a child who would bear innumerable progeny. Abraham "believed in the LORD, and he accounted it to him for righteousness" (Genesis 15:6). (At the time, Abraham was over 75 years old, and his wife, Sarah, had been barren all her life.) At first, Abraham tried to do this by human means. This was a mistake. He had a son, Ishmael, by his maidservant, of whom God's angel said, "He shall be a wild man; his hand shall be against every man, and every man's hand against him" (Genesis 16:12). This was not the son God wanted. Later God renewed the promise, saying specifically that Sarah would have a child (Genesis 18:10). And so it was; Abraham and Sarah had a son, Isaac, when Abraham was 100 years old and Sarah about 90 (Genesis 21:1-5).

Scripture says of this, "Against all hope, Abraham in hope believed and so became the father of many nations, just as it had been said to him, 'So shall your offspring be.' Without weakening in his faith, he faced the fact that his body was as good as dead—since he was about a hundred years old—and that Sarah's womb was also dead. Yet he did not waver through unbelief concerning the promise of God, but was strengthened in his faith and gave glory to God, being fully persuaded that God had power to do what he had promised" (Romans 4:18-21 NIV). Hebrews puts it thus, "By faith Abraham, even though he was past age—and Sarah herself was barren—was enabled to become a father because he considered him faithful who had made the promise" (Hebrews 11:11 NIV).

According to all the worldly circumstances, it was impossible for Abraham and Sarah to have a child. But Abraham put his trust, not in the worldly circumstances, not in the "things which are seen," but in the promise of God, and in God's power and faithfulness to carry out the promise. He looked to the "things which are unseen." And it came about as God had promised.

Another example is that of Jehoshaphat, to which I have already referred. By every worldly evidence, it was impossible for Jehoshaphat to stand against a greatly superior force. Again, Jehoshaphat put his focus on the promise of God, given through a prophet. He told the people of Judah to trust in the Lord and in his prophets, he went out to meet the enemy, and God gave him the victory. In the face of what seemed insuperable odds, the power of God prevailed because of men's faith.

The Psalmist tells us, "Some trust in chariots and some in horses, but we trust in the name of the LORD our God" (Psalm 20:7 NIV). Some trust in the things that are seen, but we trust in an unseen God. I believe that is where we need to be today. I rejoice in our excellent military forces, in their weaponry, in their skill and training, and in their commitment. We need them. But our primary trust should be in God. With God to protect and sustain us, we can prevail even against superior forces. Without his protection, we cannot prevail.

My third example is that of Jesus. Jesus went to his Crucifixion knowing that he would be resurrected. He prophesied it many times. When he was hanging, in agony, nailed to the Cross, the outward circumstances did not look like a victory. The disciples certainly did not see it as one. But Jesus looked beyond the outward circumstances to the promise of God.

Let me express a word of caution here. We do not want to commit our lives to something unless we are sure that it is God's will. In the examples I have given, God's will was clearly expressed. When the devil tempted Jesus, the devil told him to throw himself down from the Temple, saying that Psalm 91:11-12 promised that God's angels would protect him from harm. Jesus refused to do as the devil told him. If God had told him to throw himself down from the Temple, Jesus would have done it. He always obeyed his Father. But he would not put God to the test by calling on God to protect him from the consequences of something God had not told him to do. Our faith should be in God, not in our own desires or whims.

In my present situation, I get medical reports of blood tests, CT scans and the like, and it is easy to think of these as being the real truth about my condition. Basically they tell me that the cancer is not going away and is starting again to increase. Over against this, I have the fact that nothing is too difficult for God, that God can heal any medical condition, and that I believe he is healing and will heal my cancer completely. Which will I believe? Whose report will I believe? I have chosen to believe the eternal truths of God. I do everything the doctor tells me to, but I put my faith in God. I find that I have to keep reaffirming that choice, to keep reminding myself that, whatever the medical data may seem to say, God is greater than the medical data.

It may be that God will not give me the complete healing I expect. That's OK too, as I have said earlier. God is sovereign and he is good, and whatever he does is for the good. But my faith, my reliance, is not just on the medical data, the "things which are seen," but is primarily on the God who is unseen, and permanent, and greater than the medical data.

Faith Results in Thankfulness

If we truly believe that God has acted in our lives, and that he is acting and will act in our lives, we will feel a tremendous gratitude to God for all that he has done, is doing and will do. If we do not feel that gratitude, that thankfulness, that desire to praise him, are we not saying that we don't really believe he has done anything for us?

David wrote, "Bless the LORD, O my soul, and forget not all His benefits" (Psalm 103:2). We tend much too easily to forget God's benefits, to forget, or not notice, the things God has done in our lives. We need to keep reminding ourselves of all he has done for us. When we do this, it builds our faith.

God Responds to Our Faith

"The eyes of the LORD run to and fro throughout the whole earth, to show Himself strong on behalf of those whose heart is loyal to Him" (2 Chronicles 16:9). "The people that do know their God shall be strong, and carry out great exploits" (Daniel 11:32). Jesus said, "...anyone who has faith in me will do the things I have been doing. He will do even greater things..." (John 14:12 NIV). "All things are possible to him who believes" (Mark 9:23). (Also see Mark 11:23-24.) Paul speaks of "the exceeding greatness of His [God's] power toward us who believe" (Ephesians 1:19). (Also see Ephesians 3:20; Philippians 2:13.) Paul tells us to "be strong in the Lord and in the power of His might" (Ephesians 6:10). Faith is essential.

James tells us that those who doubt will not receive anything from God (James 1:6-8). It was because David was absolutely convinced that "the battle is the LORD's, and He will give you into our hands" (1 Samuel 17:47) that he was able to confront and defeat the Philistine giant, Goliath.

HOW DO WE GET FAITH?

There is no simple formula for getting faith. Let's consider first, faith for salvation. We are saved by grace through faith (Ephesians 2:8-9). The faith that saves us is the gift of God. Jesus said, "No one can come to Me unless the Father who sent Me draws him" (John 6:44). Salvation, including getting the faith for salvation, is the work of God. We cannot create, or call up in ourselves, the faith that saves us.

As with any free gift, however, there are things we can do to put ourselves in a position to receive the gift. The most important of these, I believe, is to seek it. God said, "You will seek Me and find Me when you search for Me with all your heart" (Jeremiah 29:13). "He who comes to God must believe that He is, and that He is a rewarder of those who diligently seek him" (Hebrews 11:6). "Whoever calls on the name of the Lord shall be saved" (Romans 10:13). "Ask, and it will be given to you; seek, and you will find; knock, and it will be opened to you. For everyone who asks receives, he who seeks finds, and to him who knocks it will be opened." (Matthew 7:7-8). "Keep on asking," "keep on seeking," "keep on knocking."

Also important is an openness, a willingness to receive.

There are those who are drawn to saving faith by hearing the gospel, the "good news," spoken by others (Romans 10:17). There are those who are drawn by seeing godly people and wishing to be like them. We are Jesus' witnesses (Acts 8:8) at least as much by what we are as by what we say. There are those who are drawn by becoming convicted that their worldly way of living is not working for them.

Perhaps an analogy will be helpful. What is it that leads a man and a woman to decide to commit themselves to each other in marriage? Sometimes it is just physical attraction, but more often there is a drawing together that is hard to define or explain. I think it is a little like that with saving faith. There is a drawing that is hard to explain or define. This is the work of the Holy Spirit. What we need to do is to keep ourselves open to it (1 Thessalonians 5:19).

One thing seems clear. This drawing to saving faith is not primarily by the intellect. The intellect may be part of it, but it is basically something deeper and stronger. It is a felt need for something more.

Once we have received saving faith, and have accepted Jesus Christ as our Lord and savior, then we need to grow in faith. The disciples said to Jesus, "Increase our faith" (Luke 17:5). A father prayed, "I do believe; help me overcome my unbelief" (Mark 9:24 NIV). Jude tells us to be "building yourselves up in your most holy faith" (Jude 20). I find that, time after time, there are points at which I find doubt and unbelief creeping in. Each time this happens, I need to reject the doubt and refuse to entertain it. And I need to pray, "Help me to overcome my unbelief." It is a continuing struggle. In the garden of Eden, satan tried to sow doubt (Genesis 3:1, 4), and he has continued to do so ever since. We must keep resisting him.

I believe growing in our faith is also a gift from God. We cannot achieve it by our own efforts. But it does require of us a decision, a seeking, and constant effort. It may require a willingness to step out in faith. Jesus is "…the author and perfecter of our faith…" (Hebrews 12:2 NIV). God gives us our initial, saving faith, and then he increases and perfects our faith.

CONCLUSION

Faith is a big subject. I have given only some thoughts about it, that I hope will be useful. Faith is something we need to keep studying, and working on, and living by, throughout our Christian life. It is central to that life. We all need to keep praying, "Lord, increase our faith." It is as we step out in faith that God increases our faith.

At times we may feel that our faith is not sufficient for something we have undertaken or some situation we find ourselves in. I think one of the keys is in what God told Gideon, when he doubted his strength to do what God was calling him to do. "Go in the strength you have…Am I not sending you?" (Judges 6:14 NIV). If we go in the faith we have, however inadequate it may seem, God will supply the additional faith that we need. But we have to take the first step. We have to use what we have, and then God will add to it.

19

Dealing With Pain and Suffering

o o o o o o o o o o o o o o o o o o o o o o o o o o o o o o

"In the world you will have tribulation; but be of good cheer, I have overcome the world."

—*(John 16:33)*

One of the problems we all have to deal with is that of pain and suffering. Some even find that the existence of pain and suffering, to the degree that we see it in this world, causes them to doubt their faith in God. They say, "If God is both all-powerful and loving, how can he allow so much pain and suffering?" Some conclude either that God is not all powerful (which means that he is not God), or that he is not loving (which is a denial of Scripture). Implicit in this kind of question is the assumption: "God, if I were in charge I would not do it your way." This is an assumption we are not entitled to make.

Most people can handle a good deal of pain if they can see a reason for it. Athletes, mountain climbers and others who place great demands on their physical bodies willingly subject themselves to a great deal of pain. Soldiers accept suffering, hardship and death in the service of their country. Most women are able to accept the pain of childbirth, because they see something wonderful coming out of it. Many will work very hard if they see their work as bringing a reward. But when suffering seems meaningless, it is hard to accept.

Pain and suffering is a large subject. Much has been written about it.[33] I can only point to a few basic guidelines that Scripture clearly gives us, and that I hope will be useful in enabling us to understand and deal with it.

PAIN AND SUFFERING ARE PART OF LIFE

I start with what may seem an obvious proposition. In this imperfect world, pain and suffering are a part of life. No one is immune from them. No one can claim any right to be free of them. Some suffer more than others, and that may be thought to raise a question of fairness, which I shall address later. But no one is exempt.

When we accept Jesus Christ as our Lord and Savior, our sins are forgiven, we enter into eternal life, and we can look forward to spending eternity in heaven with God. We have the Holy Spirit living within us, we become adopted sons of God, and we are enabled to start a remarkable process of transformation in our lives. These are tremendous gifts, which we do not deserve, and for which we should be very thankful. We receive them by the grace of God, and part of the definition of grace is "unmerited favor." But I do not see anything in Scripture that says that we are exempt from pain and suffering. Scripture says that we can expect difficulties, testing and suffering. One difference is that we are much better able to deal with them because of the power of God working in us, because of the hope that God always gives us, and because of the support and love of our fellow-believers.

God has many blessings for us. He is "able to do immeasurably more than all we ask or think, according to his power that is at work within us" (Ephesians 3:20 NIV). But blessings are gifts. No one is entitled to them. When we get them we give thanks, but if we do not get all that we hoped for, we have no right to complain. God does not owe us anything (Romans 11:35; Job 41:11). In the light of the tremendous blessing of forgiveness of sins and eternal salvation, everything else becomes relatively unimportant. (See 2 Corinthians 4:17.)

We Live in an Imperfect World

When God created the earth, put plants and animals on it, and created man, he looked at everything he had made and saw that it was very good (Genesis 1:31). There was no sin and no death. I believe there was no pain or suffering. Eventually, there will be a world in which there is no sin, no death, no pain and no suffering. But for the present, pain and suffering are a part of our life. How did this come about?

THE FALL IN EDEN—At the Creation, God put Adam and Eve in the Garden of Eden. He gave them everything they needed. They had food, shelter, and dominion over the earth. They walked with God every afternoon. He put only one restriction on them. He told them not to eat the fruit of one tree. He did not want them to know (experience) evil. They disobeyed and were driven out of Eden. Adam and Eve, who knew God intimately, chose to believe the serpent (satan) rather than God. They chose to do things their way rather than God's way.

The result was that sin and death came into the world for the first time. "Through one man sin entered the world, and death through sin" (Romans 5:12). (Also see 1 Corinthians 15:21.) Pain is mentioned for the first time. God told Eve, "in pain you shall bring forth children"; he told Adam that he would "toil" and would have to struggle against "thorns and thistles" (Genesis 3:16-18). Pain and suffering came into the world as a result of the wrong decision Adam and Eve made.

Since the Fall in Eden, the earth has been under a curse. "The whole creation groans and labors with birth pangs until now" (Romans 8:22).

Why did God allow this to happen? Because he wanted men and women to have free will, to have genuine freedom of choice. He wanted them to serve him and love him by their own free choice, and not because they were incapable of doing anything else. Having free will means that you can choose wrongly. The price for giving man free will was that man, in the persons of Adam and Eve, made a terrible mistake, which had profound consequences.

Some might question God's decision to give man free will. But God is God, and we cannot change him, nor should we want to. "O man, who are you to reply against God? Will the thing formed say to him who formed it, 'Why have you made me like this?'" (Romans 9:20). God said to Job, "Would you indeed annul My judgment? Would you condemn Me that you may be justified?" (Job 40:8). We have to accept God as he is, and give thanks that he is such a wonderful God.

If we want to blame someone for our suffering, we should not blame God. If anyone is to blame, it is Adam and Eve.

THERE WILL BE A WORLD WITHOUT PAIN AND SUFFERING—At some time in the future, there will be a world without pain and suffering for those who are righteous and follow God. "And God shall wipe away every tear from their eyes; there shall be no more death nor sorrow, nor crying. There shall be no more pain, for the former things have passed away" (Revelation 21:4). "The voice of weeping shall no longer be heard in her, nor the voice of crying" (Isaiah 65:19). There will be "everlasting joy" and "they shall obtain joy and gladness, and sorrow and sighing shall flee away" (Isaiah 35:10). (Also see Isaiah 51:11.) "They shall not hurt or destroy in all My holy mountain" (Isaiah 11:9; 65:25). "There shall be no more curse" (Revelation 22:3). Our bodies now are perishable, dishonorable and weak; but we shall eventually have bodies that are imperishable, glorious, and powerful (1 Corinthians 15:42-44). Even animals will no longer eat each other (Isaiah 11:6-9, 65:25). The present world is not the way God finally wants it. But for the present, we have to deal with the world as it now is.

In This Imperfect World, Pain and Suffering Serve a Useful Function

In the present imperfect world, pain and suffering serve a useful, and even necessary, function. Let me illustrate this in several ways:

THE PHYSICAL BODY—For our physical bodies, pain serves as a necessary warning system. We put our hand on a hot burner and instantly snatch it away. We cut or scratch ourselves and react instantly to get away from whatever is causing the injury and to deal with the injured tissue. We feel an internal pain which gets us to the doctor, who tells us that our appendix is inflamed, we have kidney stones, or whatever else is wrong, and we get it attended to. Pain is like the warning lights on a car, which alert us to things that need attention. Our pain system is carefully designed and adapted to our bodies' needs. For instance, the pain sensors are much more strongly concentrated in some areas than in others; some areas are very sensitive to pressure but less so to pricks or scratches; etc. The system is carefully and specifically designed. Interestingly, the same nerves that transmit pain, also transmit pleasurable sensations.

There are some who are unable to feel pain, such as lepers, advanced diabetics, and some others. They can injure themselves and not know it. Their life is full of hazards and very difficult. They would give much to be able to feel pain.

Study with these people, including unsuccessful attempts to create a workable man-made warning system, has made it clear that any warning system must give a strong enough signal so that we cannot ignore it. Physical pain cannot be turned off, and it is so insistent that we cannot ignore it. It's a good thing that the signal is strong and unpleasant.

Does pain also serve a function in our spiritual life? I think it does.

RESPONSIBILITY FOR OUR CHOICES—There are many "natural laws." Ignoring them often results in pain. If we try to walk off a rooftop, we will fall and hurt ourselves. Foolish, dare-devil actions can produce painful consequences. If we touch a hot thing, we will get burned. If we smoke heavily, we have a greater likelihood of getting cancer or respiratory illness. Drinking heavily, overeating, and using "recreational" drugs can all have painful consequences. If we were to be relieved from all pain and suffering, we would never have to face the consequences of our actions.

The same is true with spiritual laws. There is a spiritual principle called sowing and reaping. "Do not be deceived, God is not mocked; for whatever a man sows, that will he also reap" (Galatians 6:7). If we sow anger, hatred, hostility, bitterness, unforgiveness, ingratitude, selfishness and the like, we shall receive the same from others. If we choose to cause harm to others, we can expect to receive harm. By the same principle, if we are giving, loving, considerate, thoughtful, and unselfish towards others, we shall receive many blessings. "Give, and it will be given to you: good measure, pressed down, shaken together, and running over will be put into your bosom. For with the same measure that you use, it will be measured back to you" (Luke 6:38).

This principle does not work perfectly. Nothing does in this imperfect world. But it still is true, in my experience and that of many others, that those who choose to be giving and loving usually receive love and generosity, while those who choose to give anger and hatred receive anger and hatred. If there were no painful consequences to our negative actions, would we ever learn to give them up? Would we perceive them as harmful and spiritually dangerous if we did not have a pain mechanism to warn us? If there were no unpleasant consequences from violating them, could these even be said to be laws?

The principle applies more broadly. God has given us certain commandments and laws. For them to be meaningful, there need to be consequences from following them or violating them. In many places, Scripture sets forth blessings and curses. God says, behave in this way and you will be blessed; behave in that way and you will be cursed. In Deuteronomy, chapter 28, for example, God set forth a series of blessings and curses. If his people obey his law and commands, they will be blessed with prosperity, military success, and honor and recognition. If they disobey, God will send on them plagues, wasting diseases, military defeats, oppression, madness, blindness, confusion of mind, and much more. Then in Deuteronomy 30:19 he says, "I have set before you life and death, blessing and cursing; therefore choose life, that both you and your descendants may live." God is using the possibility of intense suffering as a way of bringing his people into obedience.

In the New Testament, Paul contrasts two ways of life: living by the flesh and living by the Holy Spirit. Living by the flesh results in sexual impurity, idolatry, hatred, discord, jealousy, dissensions, drunkenness, and the like. "Those who practice such things will not inherit the kingdom of God" (Galatians 5:21). "Because of these things the wrath of God comes upon the sons of disobedience" (Ephesians 5:6). In contrast, those who live by the Spirit receive the "fruit of the Spirit," which is "love, joy, peace, longsuffering, kindness, goodness, faithfulness, gentleness, self-control" (Galatians 5:22-23). One group is miserable and suffers; the other group is blessed. Paul expresses the difference as that between life and death (Romans 8:5-17). (See Chapter 15.)

God has declared that those who believe in Jesus Christ will have eternal life, while those who do not believe in him are condemned already (John 3:16, 18). He has established a judgment in which the righteous go to "eternal life" and the unrighteous to "everlasting punishment" (Matthew 25:46). The righteous "will shine forth as the sun in the kingdom of their Father," while the wicked will be thrown into a "furnace of fire" (Matthew 13:42-43, 50). (Also see John 5:29.)

In all of these, we see the use of pain and suffering as a means of enforcing the laws God has established, and as a consequence of violating those laws.

GOD USES SUFFERING AS A WAY TO TRAIN AND STRENGTHEN US—God's priorities are not our priorities. We tend to want physical health, freedom from physical and emotional pain, and enough material possessions to live comfortably. We may feel deprived and unjustly treated if we do not have these. I believe God wants us to have "good" things. But his primary concern is not with our physical circumstances. I believe his primary concerns are: (1) our eternal salvation, (2) our growth into Christian maturity and character, and (3) our usefulness, "fruitfulness," in the kingdom of God.

The early Christians endured a great deal of suffering. They were a persecuted church. What was their reaction to hardship and suffering? The record of Scripture is absolutely amazing! They did not complain about it, or say that it was more than they could bear. They welcomed it as something that taught them and strengthened them! Look at what they said about it:

> "Consider it pure joy, my brothers, whenever you face trials of many kinds, because you know that the testing of your faith develops perseverance. Perseverance must finish its work so that you may be mature and complete, not lacking anything" (James 1:2-4 NIV).

> "...we also rejoice in our sufferings, because we know that suffering produces perseverance; perseverance, character; and character, hope. And hope does not disappoint us, because God has poured out his love into our hearts by the Holy Spirit, whom he has given us" (Romans 5:3-5 NIV).

> "...now for a little while you may have had to suffer grief in all kinds of trials. These have come so that your faith—of greater worth than gold, which perishes even though refined by fire—may be proved genuine..." (1 Peter 1:6-7 NIV).

> "...God disciplines us for our good, that we may share in his holiness. No discipline seems pleasant at the time, but painful. Later on, however, it produces a harvest of righteousness and peace for those who have been trained by it. Therefore, strengthen your feeble arms and weak knees" (Hebrews 12:10-12 NIV).

The unanimous voice of the New Testament writers is that pain and suffering teach us and strengthen us and help us to become mature. These were writers who had, themselves, experienced considerable suffering.

There is a principle in athletic training that says, "No pain, no gain." I suggest that the same principle applies to our growth into spiritual maturity. Quite often it seems that we grow only in the presence of discomfort or pain that makes us feel the need for change, and forces us to cry out to God.

I want to make one thing clear. These New Testament writers did not seek out pain. They did not deliberately inflict it on themselves. But when it came, they welcomed it as an opportunity to grow and to learn. There have been, and still are, some people who deliberately inflict pain on themselves as a way of showing devotion to God or attempting to achieve holiness. I find no support for such a view in Scripture. This kind of self-inflicted pain is not what I am talking about in this chapter.

GOD USES HARDSHIP AND SUFFERING TO GET US TO DEPEND ON HIM—God can also use hardship, pain and suffering to get us to depend on him rather than ourselves. Paul refers to the great pressure he was under in the province of Asia, which was so great that he despaired of life, and then says, "...But this happened that we might not rely on ourselves but on God, who raises the dead" (2 Corinthians 1:9 NIV). Again, Paul asked God to take away his "thorn in the flesh" and God replied, "My grace is sufficient for you, for My strength is made perfect in weakness" (2 Corinthians 12:7, 9). Paul added, "That is why, for Christ's sake, I delight in weaknesses, in insults, in hardships, in persecutions, in difficulties. For when I am weak, then I am strong" (2 Corinthians 12:10 NIV). Paul's weakness made him strong in the sense that it caused him to rely to a greater degree on God's incomparably great strength. God used this "thorn in the flesh" (which evidently bothered Paul quite a bit, whatever it was), to cause Paul to depend on God at a deeper level.

This is an important principle. We see it illustrated in a number of ways. For example, Jesus said that it is hard for a rich man to enter into the kingdom of heaven (Matthew 19:23-24). The reason is, I believe, that a rich person tends to rely on his own riches rather than on God. More generally, those who are comfortably off, and successful by this world's standards, often feel that they do not need God. Those who are in very difficult situations, and do not see how they can get through them, may be much readier to turn to God for help. When things are going well, we can easily believe that we are self-sufficient. In the face of hardship and suffering, the myth of self-sufficiency loses credibility.

We see this in another way. In the relatively affluent West, the Christian church has tended to be weak. Not only are its numbers declining, but many individuals and churches seem to be lacking in strong commitment to God. In other parts of the world, such as Africa, where many people face hardships, the Christian church is growing and strong. It is striking that in China, where the independent Christian church faces severe persecution, the church has been growing rapidly. The rate of growth has been far greater under Communist persecution than it ever was before.

I have seen this operate in my own life. The experience of having to deal with advanced cancer has not been easy. But I can see that it has done several things for me. It has increased my faith. I have been put in a position where I had only God to depend on, and I have become willing to depend on God. I have identified and gotten rid of a number of things that had been weakening my faith. I have been praying more consistently and more effectively. I have gained a greater appreciation and thankfulness for the many blessings God has given me. I believe that it has helped me to get my knowledge and understanding of God beyond the intellectual, head level, to a level that reaches the heart. My wife and I were commenting the other day that, on the whole, this has been a good experience.

GOD WANTS US TO LOVE HIM FOR WHO HE IS AND NOT FOR WHAT HE DOES FOR US—This is the issue in the Book of Job. Job was a wealthy man, with a large family; "the greatest of all the people of the east" (Job 1:3). Satan said to God, "Does Job fear God for nothing?...Stretch out Your hand and touch all that he has, and he will surely curse You to Your face" (Job 1:9,11). Then he said, "Stretch out Your hand now and touch his bone and his flesh, and he will surely curse You to Your face" (Job 2:5). Job's wife told him to "curse God and die" (Job 2:9). But Job replied, "You speak as one of the foolish women speaks. Shall we indeed accept good from God, and shall we not accept adversity?" (Job 2:10). Job complained to God, he demanded explanations, he showed anger at God, but he never turned away from God. At the end, when God gave him no explanations, he was content with the fact that "now my eye sees you" (Job 42:5). He remained faithful to God for who God was, even though God had allowed satan to take away his family and wealth, and to inflict on him a painful disease. He served God for who he was and not for what he had bestowed on Job.

David wrote, "Delight yourself also in the LORD, and He shall give you the desires of your heart. Commit your way to the LORD, trust also in Him, and He shall bring it to pass" (Psalm 37:4-5). Often, before God is ready to give us the desires of our heart, he may test us to see whether we have truly committed our ways to him and are willing to trust him. It is when things are going "badly" that we have to trust in God because we have nowhere else to turn. Just as he did with Job, God may test us with troubles so that he, and we, can know whether we are really committed to him and trust in him.

When the three young Hebrews refused to worship Nebuchadnezzar's statue, he threatened to throw them into a very hot furnace. They replied, "Our God whom we serve is able to deliver us from the burning fiery furnace, and He will deliver us from your hand, O king. But if not, let it be known to you, O king, that we do not serve your gods, nor will we worship the gold image you have set up" (Daniel 3:17-18). They believed that God would save them from suffering. But even if he did not, they would serve him. Their serving God did not depend on what he did or did not do for them, but on who he is.

If God always blessed us with good things, and rescued us from suffering, then we would be tempted to love and serve him just for what he does for us. Our faith in him would be based on greed and self-advantage. God does not want that kind of faith. He wants us to believe in him, and to love and serve him, for who he is, and not for what he does for us.

THE ISSUE OF FAIRNESS

When we encounter suffering we often ask, "Why me? What have I done to deserve this?" Our sense is that it is unfair for us to have to suffer. When "good" things happen, we seldom ask, "Why me? What have I done to deserve this?" Perhaps we should. But let's look at this issue of "fairness" in a little more depth.

Scripture speaks much about God's grace, the unmerited favor he bestows on us. Would we want to receive only what we deserve and never receive God's grace, his unmerited favor? Would we want to deny ourselves the "exceeding riches of His [God's] grace" (Ephesians 2:7) by insisting that we receive only what we deserve? Scripture says, "See to it that no one misses the grace of God..." (Hebrews 12:15 NIV). Would we want to miss the grace of God by insisting on a principle that we receive only what we deserve?

If we received only what we deserved, none of us could be saved! We are saved by grace, by God's unmerited favor (Ephesians 2:8). Whatever may happen to us in this life is minor compared to the suffering of spending eternity in hell separated from God. If we complain about suffering here on earth, are we not a little bit in the position of someone who receives an unmerited gift of $1,000 and complains because it is in $20 bills rather than $100 bills? So long as we have the unmerited gift of eternal salvation, should we complain to God because our life on this earth is relatively more or less difficult? This idea of asking God only to let us have what we deserve cuts two ways, and I suggest we should not want to have him establish such a principle.

C.S. Lewis deals with this in a delightful way in *The Great Divorce*. A visitor to heaven complains, "I'm asking for nothing but my rights." To which his heavenly guide answers, "Oh no. It's not so bad as that." He adds, "I haven't got my rights, or I should not be here. You will not get yours either. You'll get something far better. Never fear."[34]

We can truly be thankful that "it's not so bad as all that." God "...does not treat us as our sins deserve, or repay us according to our iniquities" (Psalm 103:10 NIV). So let us not complain that sometimes we may have to undergo suffering that we think we do not deserve.

People also say, "Why is this happening to me and not to this other person?" Would we want to have God make things "fair" by making the other person suffer as much as we suffer? "Fairness" really has nothing to do with it.

Jesus predicted to Peter how Peter would die. When Peter saw John he asked, "Lord, what about him?' and Jesus answered, "If I will that he remain till I come, what is that to you? You follow Me" (John 21:22). It is none of our concern how God treats somebody else. We need to focus on **our** relationship with him.

Jesus told a parable about workers in a vineyard. Some came to work in the beginning of the day, and agreed to receive one denarius as a wage. Others started work at the third, the sixth, the ninth and the eleventh hour. He paid each of them the same wage. Those who had worked the longest complained that this was not fair, and the master (God) replied, "…I am not being unfair to you. Didn't you agree to work for a denarius? Take your pay and go. I want to give the man who was hired last the same as I gave you. Don't I have the right to do what I want with my own money? Or are you envious because I am generous?" (Matthew 20:13-15 NIV).

Scripture tells us not to compare ourselves with others (Galatians 6:4). One reason this principle is applicable here is that we cannot know fully what the other person may be going through. Often others, who seem outwardly to be doing well, may be struggling with difficulties we know nothing of. Or they may have come through periods of severe pain in the past. And how are we to measure pain? How do we compare the pain of arthritis or cancer with the pain of a marriage that is breaking up, or a rebellious child? It is better to stay with Jesus' "What is that to you?" (John 21:22).

EXAMPLES OF DEALING WITH SUFFERING

Scripture gives a number of examples of those who dealt with suffering. Above all, there is Jesus, "who for the joy that was set before Him endured the cross, despising the shame" (Hebrews 12:2). Whenever we feel overwhelmed by the pain we have to endure, we can consider the agony that Jesus voluntarily suffered for us. Whenever we complain about what we consider the unfairness of our suffering, we can consider the injustice that Jesus suffered.

There is also Joseph, who was sold into slavery by his brothers, unjustly accused by his master's wife and thrown into jail, and forgotten by those who promised to help him. So far as Scripture records, he never complained. Eventually he became one of the rulers of Egypt and was able to save his family from starvation. He told his brothers, "You meant evil against me; but God meant it for good" (Genesis 50:20).

There is David, who for years was running for his life, just a step away from death. His Psalms are full of words of pain and agony, physical and spiritual. (See, for example, Psalms 6:1-3, 13:1-3, 38:68, 55:4-5, 69:1-3.) Yet David always sensed that God was with him. David said, "Though I walk in the midst of trouble, You will revive me" (Psalm 138:7). "Yea, though I walk through the valley of the shadow of death, I will fear no evil, for You are with me, Your rod and Your staff they comfort me" (Psalm 23:4). One of the noteworthy things about the psalms is that, while they often start in despair, they usually end in affirmation, as David turns his eyes from his own suffering to the greatness of God. "Why are you cast down, O my soul? And why are you disquieted within me? Hope in God, for I shall yet praise Him, for the help of His countenance" (Psalm 42:5, 11).

But I want to talk about Paul. When Paul accepted Jesus as his Lord and Savior, God said, "I will show him how many things he must suffer for My name's sake" (Acts 9:16). Paul later said, "We must through many tribulations enter the kingdom of God" (Acts 14:22). And suffer he did. Read this recital and think what each phrase of it must have meant:

> "In labors more abundant, in stripes [whippings] above measure, in prisons more frequently, in deaths often. From the Jews five times I received forty stripes minus one. Three times I was beaten with rods; once I was stoned; three times I was shipwrecked; a night and a day I have been in the deep; in journeys often, in perils of waters, in perils of robbers, in perils of my own countrymen, in perils of the Gentiles, in perils in the city, in perils in the wilderness, in perils in the sea, in perils among false brethren; in weariness and toil, in sleeplessness often, in hunger and thirst, in fastings often, in cold and nakedness—besides the other things, what comes upon me daily: my deep concern for all the churches" (2 Corinthians 11:23-28).

Even this list may not be complete, for elsewhere he speaks of fighting wild beasts (1 Corinthians 15:32), and of encountering such hardships in the province of Asia (part of modern Turkey) that he despaired of his life (2 Corinthians 1:8).

What would five whippings, three beatings with rods, and a stoning do to a man's back? I expect that Paul was in almost constant pain. This may be why he said, "I keep under my body, and bring it into subjection" (1 Corinthians 9:27 KJV). (The Greek word translated "keep under" can mean to "subdue.")

Yet Paul, writing from a Roman jail, could say, "Rejoice in the Lord always. Again I will say, rejoice!" (Philippians 4:4). He wrote, "Rejoice always, pray without ceasing, in everything give thanks" (1 Thessalonians 5:16-18). He could say, "I have learned in whatever state I am, to be content" (Philippians 4:11).

How did Paul achieve this? I think we can see some keys.

- Paul took his eyes off of the circumstances and focussed them on eternal things (2 Corinthians 4:18). This is what David did. He took his eyes off his problems and put them on God. We generally cannot control our circumstances. If we see ourselves as "victims" of circumstances we cannot control, then we feel helpless and abused. If we focus on God, on his almighty power, and the security of our relationship with him, then we can see ourselves as overcomers.

- He looked to see what he could learn from difficult experiences. "…we also rejoice in our sufferings, because we know that suffering produces perseverance; perseverance, character; and character, hope" (Romans 5:3 NIV).
- He understood that he did not have to deal with difficulties, danger and suffering in his own strength. He could call upon God's great power (Ephesians 1:19, 6:10). "I can do all things through Christ who strengthens me" (Philippians 4:13). He even rejoiced in his own weakness, because in it God's power was made greater (2 Corinthians 12:9-10).

I want also to mention one fairly contemporary example, from among a great many. The terrible suffering of the Nazi Holocaust has been hard for many to accept and understand. Yet there are those who overcame it. One such was Corrie ten Boom. During the Nazi occupation of Holland, her family hid a number of Jews in their home and enabled many of them to get out of Holland, knowing the great risks of doing so. They were betrayed, and imprisoned by the Nazis. Corrie's father died in prison. Corrie and her sister Betsy were sent to one of the Nazi death camps, Ravensbruck. Betsy died there. Corrie, by what may have been a clerical error, was released just before she was scheduled to be gassed. She spent the rest of her life ministering to others, telling them of God's greatness, his love, his tender mercy, his goodness. She was even able to forgive one of the Nazi guards who had mistreated her and her sister, and to bring to Christ the man who had betrayed her family. She lived a life of joy and gave great joy to many. Despite the terrible things she endured, Corrie was an overcomer. I believe that she, too, kept her eyes on the greatness of God, rather than the terrible circumstances in which she had found herself.

HOW CAN WE DEAL WITH PAIN AND SUFFERING?

There are no easy answers, no formulas. Everyone has to work it out for themselves. Dealing with suffering can be extremely difficult, but with God's help, it is possible.

We need to be wary of the pat answers that are sometimes given. They usually do not work. Job's "comforters" gave him pat answers, and God said of them, "You have not spoken of me what is right" (Job 42:8).

One pat answer is that suffering is always the result of sin, so the way to deal with it is to discover and get rid of the sin. It is well to examine ourselves and see if there is sin that needs to be dealt with. I have heard of people suffering from painful arthritis who finally brought themselves to forgive someone and found that the arthritis had gone. But suffering is not always caused by sin. Jesus was sinless; yet he suffered terribly. Paul suffered much; can we say that this was because of sin he had not dealt with? Christians have been persecuted and martyred from the First Century until today. Would anyone suggest that this is because of sin?

Another pat answer is that, if our prayer to be relieved of suffering is not answered, it must be because of lack of faith. We do need to pray, believing (James 1:6). There have been times in my present illness when I realized that I lacked faith, and was able to do something about it. But lack of faith is not the only reason why men endure suffering. The prophets who suffered in terrible ways were commended for their faith (Hebrews 11:32-40). When God refused to heal Paul's "thorn in the flesh," he said nothing about a lack of faith; he said, "My grace is sufficient for you, for My strength is made perfect in weakness" (2 Corinthians 12:9). God did not answer Jesus' prayer that he not have to endure the Crucifixion (Matthew 26:36-42). Would anyone suggest that it was because of a lack of faith?

Let me suggest a few Scriptural principles that may be helpful.

Have the Right Attitude

Underlying everything else is the attitude with which we deal with pain, suffering and difficulties when they come, as they will to most of us. I can identify three general kinds of attitudes.

(1) When suffering, difficulties, or hardships come, we say, "Why me?" We dwell on the seeming injustice and unfairness of it. This easily leads to self-pity, to feeling sorry for ourselves, which is one of the devil's most effective schemes for making a Christian ineffective. From there it can go on to blaming God for allowing the suffering, and to anger and bitterness at God. Ultimately, this can in some cases lead to a total turning away from God, a total rejection of God.

This approach can be very damaging, very destructive. It does nothing to relieve the suffering or make it easier to bear.

Many of us go through the early stages of this approach for a while when suffering or difficulties come. But if we stay there, and do not move on, the result can be very destructive to us.

(2) We can decide to take a constructive attitude. We can say, "God, this suffering, this difficulty, is here. I don't like it but I need to accept it. What are you

trying to teach me by it? How can I use it to grow? How can I bring good out of it?"

With this approach, we can turn the suffering, the difficulty, to our good. We can use it to increase in maturity and strength. We get our mind off our suffering and onto God and what he is doing in our lives. And I think we will find that, if we can see some good purpose in the suffering, it becomes easier to handle.

(3) There is a third approach which builds on the second and is even better. Paul asked that he might "know Him [Jesus] and the power of his resurrection, and the fellowship of his sufferings" (Philippians 3:10). What does this mean? I am not sure. I am not there and have not experienced what Paul is talking about. But I suggest that Paul is saying that, when suffering comes, we can see it as a means of drawing closer to Jesus. As we suffer, we can begin to understand better what Jesus voluntarily suffered for us, and appreciate more fully what he did for us. As we are unjustly treated, we can begin to understand more fully the rejection, injustice and false accusations that Jesus continually suffered. We can become more like Jesus, which is the goal of our transformation. (See Chapter 14.)

A related concept is found in 2 Corinthians 1:4-5, where Paul says that God "comforts us in all our tribulation, that we may be able to comfort those who are in any trouble with the comfort with which we ourselves are comforted by God. For as the sufferings of Christ abound in us, so our consolation also abounds through Christ."

Those who have lost a spouse can understand what others are going through who have lost a spouse; they can speak to them in a way that others cannot. Those who have been physically or sexually abused can understand what others are going through who have suffered abuse. Those who have endured physical pain can understand what others are going through who have to deal with physical pain. Etc. Our own suffering enables us to minister more effectively to others who are suffering. Thus our suffering helps to bring us together more closely as the body of Christ and it helps us "…encourage one another and build each other up…" (1 Thessalonians 5:11 NIV).

Once we have taken care of our attitude, there are some other specific things we can do.

Accept Suffering

Pain and suffering occur. They are part of this world. No one is immune or exempt from them. There is no guarantee that they will not occur. When they come in our life, we need to be able to accept them. As Peter wrote, "Dear friends, do not be surprised at the painful trial you are suffering, as though something strange were happening to you" (1 Peter 4:12 NIV). This is not easy, but it is essential.

Scripture tells us to go further, and to consider it pure joy when trials come. I confess that I am not yet at this point! But if we can see pain and suffering as experiences from which we can learn and grow, then perhaps we can begin to see them as things that God is using for our good, and be able to rejoice in them.

Decide to Overcome

Scripture says that, in God's power, we can be overcomers. We need to come to a decision to believe those Scriptures. We need to make a conscious decision that, with God's help, we can and will overcome the pain and suffering. We need to decide that we will not allow it to undermine our faith in God, our joy, our peace, or our ability to function.

Do What You Can

Paul wrote, "Therefore put on the full armor of God, so that when the evil day comes, you may be able to stand your ground, and **after you have done everything**, to stand" (Ephesians 6:13 NIV). He was talking about facing the devil, but I think the principle applies to every kind of adversity. God wants us to do everything we can.

In the case of pain and suffering, this means to get all the help you can. Medical science knows quite a lot about pain management. What they have to offer does not always work, does not always work fully, and sometimes has side effects we prefer to avoid, but we might as well use it when we can. If the pain is emotional or psychological, there are various counseling resources; some of them can be helpful if they are based on Christian principles. Most churches offer ministry of one kind or another; some have small groups, which can be very supportive. There are other support groups. Having a prayer partner, or a close friend in whom you can confide, can be very helpful. Prayer is always valuable. My point is, avail yourself of anything that will be genuinely helpful in relieving your pain. There is no virtue in unnecessary suffering.

There are, however, some techniques of pain relief that Christians should avoid. Two examples are hypnosis (which involves allowing someone else to manipulate your mind while you are not aware of what he is doing) and New Age forms of meditation (which originate in pagan religions). Anything that derives from, or involves, a pagan religion should be avoided by Christians. There is little sense in relieving physical pain at the cost of spiritual harm to yourself!

Pray

One of the things we can always do, and one of the first things we should do, is to pray. "Is any among you suffering? Let him pray" (James 5:13). Prayer brings us in touch with the almighty power of God. God does not always take us out of difficult circumstances. But he is with us in them. He is "a very present help **in** trouble" (Psalm 46:1). "Yea though I walk through the valley of the shadow of death, I will fear no evil for you are with me. Your rod and your staff they comfort me" (Psalm 23:4). Prayer also takes our mind off of our circumstances and puts it on God.

Focus on God, and Not Your Circumstances

Paul, who went through a remarkable amount of suffering, wrote that in all circumstances we should give thanks (1 Thessalonians 5:18). Our thanks do not depend on the circumstances. Our thanks depend on who God is, on the salvation he has so freely given us, and on the relationship we have with him. As Paul wrote, "Our light affliction, which is but for a moment, is working for us a far more exceeding and eternal weight of glory, while we do not look at the things which are seen, but at the things which are not seen. For the things which are seen are temporary, but the things which are not seen are eternal" (2 Corinthians 4:17-18).

To Paul, five whippings, three beatings with rods, stoning, and many other hardships were a "light affliction," which was just for a moment! This seems amazing. But when we compare all that Paul suffered during some 60 years on earth to the joy of spending eternity in heaven with God, it becomes quite minor.

Because our thanksgiving does not depend on the circumstances, we are not at the mercy of the circumstances. I think this is what Paul was talking about when he said that he had learned how to be content in every situation (Philippians 4:12). You don't look at the situation, you look at God. It is by this, also, that we can achieve "the peace of God, which surpasses all understanding" (Philippians 4:7).

Our faith and hope also need to rise above our circumstances. Abraham "in hope believed" (Romans 4:18). All the circumstances gave Abraham reason to believe that he and Sarah could not have a child. But against that expectation based on the circumstances, Abraham set his hope, his confident expectation, based on God's promise to him. He went past all the natural circumstances to believe God's promise. Whatever the circumstances, we need to believe that God is bigger than the circumstances, he will enable us to bear them, and he will bring us through them. Whatever the circumstances, we need to believe that God will strengthen us with all power according to his glorious might, so that we may have great endurance and patience (Colossians 1:11).

In painful situations, many have found that it helps to focus on God. Jesus endured the Cross "for the joy that was set before him" (Hebrews 12:2). He looked at God's power and his promise rather than at his own physical agony. Stephen, while being stoned, had a vision of heaven with Jesus standing at the right hand of God (Acts 7:55-56). After Paul and Silas were beaten with rods and put in stocks in the inner prison, they prayed and sang hymns to God, and God moved mightily (Acts 16:25). The Christian martyrs in the Roman arena, we are told, sang hymns as they faced the wild beasts who were about to eat them. Many other martyrs have faced their martyrdom with praise to God.

Let God Bring Good out of the Situation

There is a further reason to focus on God rather than the circumstances. God works for good in all things, even in the most unlikely situations (Romans 8:28).Use praise, prayer, Scripture reading, meditation on Scripture, whatever works for you, to draw closer to God and see things more from his perspective. Turn your situation over to him in prayer. Ask him to deal with you and to show you anything he wants to show you about it. "Draw near to God and He will draw near to you" (James 4:8).

Be honest with God. He can handle anger, frustration, and even discouragement and despair. Job complained and got angry at God. And God spoke to him at length, revealed himself to him, and said that Job had "spoken of Me what is right" (Job 42:8). David often complained and poured out his heart to God, and God called him "a man after my heart." God does not mind hearing the distress and even anger of one who is genuinely seeking after him.

Remain Faithful to God

"Shall we indeed accept good from God, and shall we not accept adversity?" (Job 2:10). When suffering comes, that is always the question. Do we love God for what he gives us, or for who he is? Can we love him and serve him even in suffering, even when he seems to have deserted us, even when he seems not to answer our prayers?

In his great end-time prophecy, Jesus told the disciples that they would be persecuted and put to death, that many would turn away from the faith, and the love of many would grow cold, but that "he who endures to the end will be saved" (Matthew 24:13). (Also see Matthew 24:3-14.) In each of the letters to the churches in the Book of Revelation, there is a promise of blessings to the one who overcomes. God has promised that we can be more than conquerors (Romans 8:37). "Whatever is born of God overcomes the world" (1 John 5:4). God has made it possible to overcome pain and suffering, no matter how severe and prolonged.

20

The Vigorous Christian Life

o o o o o o o o o o o o o o o o o o o o o o o o o o o o o o o o o o o

"...let us run with perseverance the race set before us..."

—(Hebrews 12:2 NIV)

Much of our Christian life calls for a balance between extremes. One area where this is needed is the balance between striving and allowing God to act in our lives. In most of our Christian life, we work and God works. There are times when we can strive too hard. Sometimes we need simply to get out of the way and let God do what he wants to do. And we should never try to do in our own strength what only God can do in his strength.

But there are also times when we need to put forth effort, sometimes quite strenuous effort, in order to achieve and receive the best that God has for us. In this and the next chapter, I want to emphasize that side of the issue. We American Christians, living relatively comfortable lives, need to be reminded of the importance of struggling against apathy and self-satisfaction. As always, I am speaking as much to myself as to anyone else.

There are a large number of energetic verbs in the New Testament, which speak of the effort we may need to put forth. They speak of very strenuous effort; putting forth all the energy we are capable of. Most are in a tense that speaks of continuing effort. We are exhorted to keep on making every effort, working, straining, struggling, pursuing, running with diligence the race set before us, fighting the good fight, waging war, persisting, resisting, standing, taking hold, guarding, and enduring to the end. These passages are not talking in terms of an "easy" Christianity!

One of the themes of this book is that, to a great degree, the Christian church has sat passively by while other forces have eroded the religious and godly basis on which our nation was founded. Evil has prevailed because, to a large degree, good people have done very little. In part, I believe, this is the result of some misconceptions some of us have had about our function as members of the body of Christ. In this chapter, I want to deal with some of those misconceptions, which have tended to encourage some to be passive. In the next chapter, I shall give some examples of what it means to press in vigorously to God.

PROFESSIONALISM

In many parts of the Christian church, there has been, for centuries, a sharp distinction between clergy and laity. When we speak of "ministry," many, today, think of professionally trained, ordained clergy, and perhaps also of lay "elders" who have been officially designated for a ministry function. This can lead to two attitudes.

- There is a tendency to sit back and say, "Let the professionals do it. That's what we pay them for. They are trained. They are the experts."
- There is a tendency to view church as an activity in which the professionals—clergy, musicians, etc.—perform, and the rest of the congregation sit as an audience to be amused, entertained or instructed. Both attitudes tend to produce congregations who view their functions as primarily those of pew-sitters, payers of financial contributions, and, perhaps, critics.

This is not Scriptural. Peter referred to **all** believers as "a holy priesthood," a "royal priesthood" (1 Peter 2:5, 9). Paul tells us that **all** believers are God's "workmanship, created in Christ Jesus for good works, which God prepared beforehand that we should walk in them" (Ephesians 2:10). He says that Scripture is useful "that the man of God may be complete, thoroughly equipped for every good work" (2 Timothy 3:17). **Every** believer is expected to be thoroughly equipped to do good works.

Paul makes this very clear in Ephesians 4. I have quoted this passage before, but let us look at it again in this context, and in the New King James translation:

> "He Himself [Jesus] gave some to be apostles, some prophets, some evangelists, and some pastors and teachers, **for the equipping of the saints for the work of ministry**, for the edifying of the body of Christ, till we all come to the unity of the faith and of the knowledge of the Son of God, to be a perfect man, to the measure of the stature of the fullness of Christ; that we...speaking the truth in love, may grow up in all things into him who is the

head—Christ—from whom the whole body, joined and knit together **by what every joint supplies**, according to the effective working by which **every part does its share**, causes growth to the body for the edifying of itself in love" (Ephesians 4:11-16).

Two things are very clear from this text.

- The primary function of the professional clergy is to equip believers "for the work of ministry." (In the New Testament, "saints" is always used to mean the body of believers, all who truly believe in Jesus Christ. See, for example, Ephesians 1:1; Philippians 1:1; 2 Corinthians 1:1; Romans 1:7; Jude 3.) So the entire body of believers is called to the work of ministry, and the primary job of the professional leaders is to equip and train them for that call.
- All believers are part of the body of Christ, and each one is expected to do his share. **Each** believer has a function, and only as each one fulfills his function will the body grow and develop as it is supposed to.

We see this second thought repeated elsewhere. In 1 Corinthians 12:12-31, Paul compares the body of believers to the human body. Like the human body, the body of Christ has many parts, and each part, each believer, has a necessary function to play. Again, in Romans 12:3-8, Paul says that "we being many, are one body in Christ, and individually members of one another. Having then gifts differing according to the grace given us, let us use them" (verses 5-6). Each member should use the gifts he has been given for the benefit of the whole body. In 1 Corinthians 12:4-11, Paul says that the Holy Spirit has given each of us different gifts for the common good. Peter says, "Each one should use whatever gift he has received to serve others, faithfully administering God's grace in its various forms" (1 Peter 4:10 NIV). Each believer can administer God's grace to serve others. Christ "died for all, that those who live should live no longer for themselves, but for Him who died for them and rose again" (2 Corinthians 5:15).

We need to expand our concept of "ministry." Ministry is not just something that goes on inside the walls of our church buildings. There is a good deal of talk these days about the "ministry of the marketplace." It's a good phrase. The point is that every Christian, in whatever his occupation or activity, is called to ministry. Those who are in business, government, teaching, and the like are called to live daily by Christian principles, to embody those principles in all that they do, to be models and examples of those principles. Quite a few do so, but it is important to be conscious that this is a form of ministry that may be at least as valuable as anything that a pastor does behind his pulpit. I have a friend who is a former pastor, and now manages a group of retail stores. I believe that what he is doing now in managing these stores according to Christian principles, and modeling those principles for his customers and employees, is a ministry that is every bit as important as what he used to do as a pastor.

All of us can minister to those we come in contact with in terms of showing kindness and interest, giving a helping hand, spending some of our time and energy on their behalf. We can, as seems appropriate, pray for others, openly or silently. We can, as seems appropriate, speak to others about the gospel of Jesus Christ, always remembering that the witness of our actions and lives may speak much more powerfully than the witness of our words. The professionals are called on to minister in certain ways. But the whole body of Christ needs to minister in whatever way God is calling on them to minister.

FAITH AND WORKS

We are saved by faith and only by faith. It is the gift of God. No one can earn it or deserve it. Ephesians 2:8-9 and many other Scriptures make this abundantly clear.

But this does not mean that, once we have made a profession of faith, we can just sit back and relax. It does not mean that our actions, our works, have no importance. We are called on to press in vigorously to the kingdom of God. (See Chapter 21.) We are called on to grow and change. We are called on to do godly actions. Indeed, in the very next verse in Ephesians, Paul says, "For we are God's workmanship, created in Christ Jesus to do good works, which God prepared in advance for us to do" (Ephesians 2:10 NIV). If we were created in Christ Jesus to do good works, then should we not be very active in doing what we were created for?

Other Scriptures confirm this. "Do not merely listen to the word, and so deceive yourselves. Do what it says" (James 1:22 NIV). "Faith by itself, if it does not have works, is dead" (James 2:17). James develops this thought in many ways in James 2:14-26. Jesus said much the same. He never accepted mere lip service; he asked for faith that showed itself in actions. "Why do you call Me 'Lord, Lord,' and not do the things which I say" (Luke 6:46). Then he went on to tell a parable of two men. One put Jesus' words into practice, and the structure he erected stood against every storm. The other did not put Jesus' words into practice, and the structure he erected was quickly destroyed by the storms. Is it not clear that, if we would stand firm against difficulties and obstacles, we need to be like the man who built his house on a rock? We need to put our faith into action; to demonstrate it by our actions. This means that we live an active Christian life, not a passive one.

Again, Jesus said, "Not everyone who says to Me, 'Lord, Lord,' shall enter the kingdom of heaven, but he who does the will of My Father in heaven" (Matthew 7:21). Paul said, "They claim to know God, but by their actions they deny him…" (Titus 1:16 NIV). Our actions are the test of our faith.

Jesus expects us to bear fruit (Matthew 7:15-19; Luke 8:11-15; Matthew 25:14-30; John 15:1-6). "Every tree that does not bear good fruit is cut down and thrown into the fire" (Matthew 7:19). (Also see John 15:6.)

Why are our actions, our works, important? I think there are several basic reasons.

- Our faith is not genuine unless it is reflected in our actions. Our works do not save us, but they are the evidence that our faith is genuine.
- We are called on to grow to Christian maturity. (See Chapter 10.) Growing requires a lot of activity on our part, to pursue the good and to cast off the evil.
- Scripture tells us that we are created in Christ Jesus to do good works. We need to fulfill the purpose for which we were created.
- We cannot know God, or love him, unless we obey his commands (1 John 2:3-6, 5:2-3). As I have pointed out elsewhere, obedience is not just observing all the "don'ts". (See Chapter 17.) It is even more important that we fulfill the purpose and calling that God has placed on our lives.

In our zeal to insist that we are saved by faith and not by works, let us not neglect the many Scriptures which tell us that, once we have been saved by faith, we are expected to do godly works.

SECURITY OF SALVATION

The security of our position as saved Christians is an important principle. I don't intend to discuss it here. But one misuse of that principle has relevance to what I am saying here. Some have tended to act as if they felt that, once they have prayed for salvation, they are free to do or not do whatever they please, and are therefore under no obligation to put forth any further effort in their Christian life. This is not Scriptural. Paul tells us not to follow the desires of the flesh. (See Chapter 15.) And everything in this book emphasizes that our coming to salvation is only the beginning of a life of activity, growth and work in Christ. If all that our salvation means to us is our own eternal life in heaven, then our faith is very self-centered.

Jesus used the image of a gate and a path, or road (Matthew 7:13:14). We enter the narrow gate, and then proceed along the narrow path or road. Both are important. Both are necessary. Entering the gate (initial salvation) is only the starting point. It makes it possible for us to begin to grow to maturity, to be transformed, to learn to live by the Holy Spirit, to do the good actions we were created to do, and to do our part in the body of Christ. Our salvation should not be an excuse for inaction.

THE RAPTURE

There are those who say that Jesus is coming soon, that when he comes he will take us out of the world (rapture), and that therefore we don't need to worry about all the problems of the world around us. We can just sit back and wait to be taken up out of this world.

I have several problems with this idea:

- We do not know when Jesus will come again. "No one knows about that day or hour, not even the angels in heaven, nor the Son, but only the Father" (Matthew 24:36 NIV). Many have predicted specific dates for it, only to be proved false. As I read Matthew, chapter 24, we should not even be trying to predict it.
- Matthew 24:45-51 makes it pretty clear in this context, that until Jesus returns, he expects us to keep busy with whatever he has made us responsible for. The servant who is carrying on with his assigned functions and is taking proper care of the other servants is praised; the one who neglects his duties and abuses the other servants is condemned. In another parable, in which a master went away for an indeterminate time, he told his servants, "Occupy till I come" (Luke 19:13 KJV). According to Strong's *Dictionary of the Greek Bible*, the word "occupy" means "to busy oneself." Paul condemned idleness and urged all Christians to be busy (1 Thessalonians 5:14; 2 Thessalonians 3:6-15). I see nothing in Scripture that supports the idea that we should just sit back, relax, and wait for the Second Coming. I believe that, until he comes, we should "occupy," keep busy, with everything the Lord is calling on us to do, so that he will call us good and faithful servants.

- As I understand it, Jesus is coming down to earth to rule for a thousand years, and some of us are to rule with him. If this is true, then we may be called to a life here on earth of intense activity. I suggest that the best way to prepare for that intense activity is to be active now in doing everything that God is calling us to do, and in developing our character and skills to prepare for our future work with Jesus.
- Matthew 24:4-13 says that many will turn away from the faith, and the love of many will grow cold, but he who stands firm to the end will be saved. It is not until verses 30-31 that Jesus speaks of the Second Coming and the rapture. Is not this saying that we need to be able to stand firm for some time **before** the rapture? Whether or not the rapture comes before or after the "great tribulation," I think we can expect difficult times now and in the future. We need to be able to "stand firm" during those difficult times, and this means working hard to develop our Christian maturity and to do all the other things I have spoken of in this book. The fact that times are growing more difficult is an argument for greater, rather than less, activity.
- We all want to hear Jesus say, "Well done, good and faithful servant" (Matthew 25:21, 23). Can we expect him to say it if we have not been actively doing the things he has called on us to do?
- There are many things that we can accomplish only while we are here on earth. Should we not be making the most of our opportunity to accomplish them for as long as we remain on earth? It seems to me that the possibility of the rapture should spur us on to greater activity, because we should want to accomplish as much as we can while we have the opportunity to do so. Scripture tells us, "Be very careful, then, how you live—not as unwise but as wise, making the most of every opportunity…" (Ephesians 5:15-16 NIV).

William Tyndale was sentenced to be burned at the stake for translating the Bible into English. He spent the last days of his life working on translations and commentaries on the Bible, right up until the moment he was taken out to be burned. Is not that an example for us to follow? Should not we also be making the most of whatever time we have here on earth?

21

Pressing in to God

o o o o o o o o o o o o o o o o o o o o o o o o o o o o o o

"I press toward the mark for the prize of the high calling of God in Christ Jesus."

—(Philippians 3:14 KJV)

In Matthew 11:12 (NIV), Jesus declared, "From the days of John the Baptist until now, the kingdom of heaven has been forcefully advancing, and forceful men lay hold of it." Luke 16:16 is similar. What does this passage mean?

In what sense could it be said that the Kingdom of God was advancing forcefully? The statement must have surprised the disciples. They were expecting a kingly Messiah who would advance by military force to drive out the Roman occupiers, and restore the kingdom of Israel to the glory it had in the days of King David. They were puzzled and confused by a Messiah who showed no sign of doing any such thing. (See Acts 1:6.)

But in the spiritual sense, I think we can see that Jesus' coming to earth was a frontal assault on the kingdom of satan.

With the Fall of Adam, satan had become "the ruler of this world" (John 12:31, 14:30), the "god of this age" (2 Corinthians 4:4). (Also see Ephesians 2:2; 1 John 5:19.) When, in the wilderness, satan offered to give Jesus "all the kingdoms of the world and their glory" if Jesus would "worship" him (Matthew 4:8-9), satan had the authority to make the offer.

One reason Jesus came to earth was to "destroy the works of the devil" (1 John 3:8), to "destroy him who had the power of death, that is, the devil" (Hebrews 2:14). When Jesus brought God's kingdom to earth, there were now two kingdoms, existing side by side: the kingdom of darkness and the kingdom of God. (See Colossians 1:13.) There are "children of God" and "children of the devil" (1 John 3:10). (Also see John 8:42-47.)

Satan sensed this attack. He tempted Jesus. He tried many times to have him killed. Wherever Jesus went, the demons manifested. They sensed the threat, for they cried out, "Did You come to destroy us?" (Mark 1:24), "Have you come here to torment us before the time?" (Matthew 8:29).

Shortly before his Crucifixion, Jesus declared, "Now the ruler of this world will be cast out" (John 12:31). Paul says of Jesus, "having disarmed principalities and powers, He made a public spectacle of them, triumphing over them in it" (Colossians 2:15).

The victory is not yet complete, but it is clear that, in the spiritual world, the kingdom of God has advanced forcefully with the coming of Jesus on earth.

What does it mean to say that "forceful men lay hold of it"? A look at some examples in which people have pressed in vigorously to the kingdom of God may be helpful.

EXAMPLES OF PRESSING IN TO THE KINGDOM OF GOD

The Bible gives us a number of examples of pressing in, arising in many areas of Christian life. When we add them all together, they show that God wants us to pursue him, his gifts and his promises, with an intense passion.

Healing

BLIND BARTIMAEUS—As Jesus was passing by, a blind beggar named Bartimaeus was sitting by the roadside. "When he heard that it was Jesus of Nazareth, he began to cry out and say, 'Jesus, Son of David, have mercy on me!' Then many warned him to be quiet; but he cried out all the more, 'Son of David, have mercy on me!' So Jesus stood still and commanded him to be called." And he received his sight. Then Jesus commended him, saying, "Your faith has made you well" (Mark 10:47-49, 52). (The verb is *sozo*, which can mean "heal" but is more often used in the sense of "save.")

Bartimaeus wanted one thing with all his heart. He wanted to see. He let nothing stop him. Many told him to be quiet, but he kept on crying out. We don't know how long this went on; it could have been for some time. He would not be kept from the healing he sought. When Jesus commended his faith, I believe Jesus was saying that he had shown his faith by his persistence in the face of obstacles. Our faith is demonstrated by action, and this blind beggar demonstrated his by strong, persistent action against obstacles. He pressed in.

THE WOMAN WITH THE ISSUE OF BLOOD—On another occasion, as Jesus was walking, "A great multitude followed Him and thronged him." They crowded around him. A woman, who had "had a flow of blood for twelve years," pressed in, touched his cloak, and was healed. Jesus asked who had touched him, and she fell at his feet, "fearing and trembling." Then Jesus said, "Your faith has made you well" (Mark 5:25, 33, 34). (Again, the verb is *sozo,* to save.) This woman persisted in the face of a number of obstacles:

- Women were not supposed to push in through a crowd of men.
- She was ceremonially unclean, and it was unlawful for her to touch anyone who was clean.
- She was probably weak after a twelve-year illness involving loss of blood.
- She was afraid.

Her urgent need motivated her to overcome all these obstacles and receive the healing she desired. Again I believe that it was because she pressed in, in spite of heavy obstacles, that Jesus praised her faith.

THE CANAANITE WOMAN—When Jesus was in the region of Tyre and Sidon, a Canaanite woman came "and cried out to Him, saying, 'Have mercy on me, O Lord, Son of David! My daughter is severely demon-possessed.' But He answered her not a word. And His disciples came and urged Him, saying, 'Send her away, for she cries out after us.' But He answered and said, 'I was not sent except to the lost sheep of the house of Israel.' Then she came and worshiped Him, saying, 'Lord, help me!' But He answered and said, 'It is not good to take the children's bread and throw it to the little dogs.' And she said, 'Yes, Lord, yet even the little dogs eat the crumbs which fall from their masters' table.' Then Jesus answered and said to her, 'O woman, great is your faith! Let it be to you as you desire.' And her daughter was healed from that very hour." (Matthew 15:22-28).

Again, we can see great persistence in spite of seeming rejection. And again, Jesus saw her persistence, her pressing in, as evidence of "great faith."

THE PARALYTIC—Once there was a great crowd in the house where Jesus was. Some men came bringing a paralytic on a mat or bed. They could not get him to Jesus because of the crowd; so they made an opening in the roof and lowered the paralyzed man on his mat down to Jesus. "When Jesus saw their faith,

He said to the paralytic, 'Son, your sins are forgiven you.'" Then "He said to the paralytic, 'Arise, take up your bed, and go to your house.' Immediately he arose, took up the bed, and went out in the presence of them all" (Mark 2:5, 11-12).

The paralytic's friends pressed in. It seemed impossible to get their friend to Jesus, but they found a way. They had to lift him up onto the roof (while on his mat), make a hole in the roof, and then lower him down into the dense crowd—an operation which must have involved both difficulty and danger. They must have risked the anger of the owner of the house at this damage to his dwelling. Jesus was impressed with their persistence in the face of seemingly insuperable obstacles. "When he saw their faith" he healed their friend.

THE LEPER—A leper came to Jesus and knelt before him, saying, "If You are willing, You can make me clean." He must have come quite close, because Jesus "put out His hand and touched him, and said to him, 'I am willing; be cleansed'" (Mark 1:40-41). He was healed immediately. Luke says that the man was "full of leprosy" (Luke 5:12). He was doubtless grotesque and repulsive in appearance. Lepers in those days were not allowed to get within 6 feet of anyone. They were not supposed to speak to anyone. The Jewish teaching was that leprosy was a punishment for sin. Pharisees and others would have nothing to do with them. So the leper would appear to have violated several rules, and taken a great risk of rejection or punishment. Because his need was so great, he pressed in, in spite of the obstacles, and Jesus healed him.

Prayer

"Then Jesus told his disciples a parable to show them that they should always pray and not give up" (Luke 18:1 NIV). The parable was that of the widow who kept insisting that an unjust judge give her justice. Jesus ended, "And will not God bring about justice for his chosen ones, who cry out to him day and night?..." (Luke 18:7 NIV).

Earlier he had told another parable about a man who needed bread to give a visitor. He knocked at his neighbor's door at midnight to try to borrow bread. The neighbor at first refused, saying he was in bed, but eventually yielded. Jesus said, "Because of his persistence he will rise and give him as many as he needs" (Luke 11:8). (KJV has "importunity." The word can mean recklessness or shamelessness.)

Then Jesus went on, "So I say to you, ask, and it will be given to you; seek, and you will find; knock, and it will be opened to you. For everyone who asks receives; he who seeks finds, and to him who knocks it will be opened" (Luke 11:9-10). The Greek verbs mean, "continue to ask," "continue to seek," "continue to knock." It seems clear in context that Jesus is saying that if we keep on asking, seeking, and knocking with the same persistence as was shown by the man in the parable, we will receive.

It is those who seek God "with all your heart" who will surely find him (Jeremiah 29:13). God rewards "those who diligently seek Him" (Hebrews 11:6). It is the "fervent" prayer of a righteous man that accomplishes much (James 5:16). Paul says that "the Spirit Himself makes intercession for us with groanings that cannot be uttered" (Romans 8:26). Jesus says that it is right, and sometimes necessary, to "cry out" to God, day and night. All of these passages say that there needs to be an intensity and fervency in our prayers. There needs to be passion, and also persistence.

Worship

When Jesus was having dinner at the home of a Pharisee, a woman who had led a sinful life came in, wet his feet with her tears, dried them with her hair, kissed them, and poured perfume on them. The Pharisee said to himself, "This man, if he were a prophet, would know who and what manner of woman this is who is touching Him, for she is a sinner." But Jesus received her worship and told her, "Your sins are forgiven" (Luke 7:39, 48).

Not only did this woman come into the house uninvited, but she must have sensed the scorn and rejection in the face of the Pharisee and probably many of his guests. Pharisees would have nothing to do with "sinners," particularly with immoral women. Yet she persisted in her act of worship and service, and received a great blessing.

Blessing

"Blessed are those who hunger and thirst for righteousness, for they shall be filled" (Matthew 5:6). "Hunger" and "thirst" are words of desiring. They can mean a very intense desire. Strong's *Dictionary of the Greek Bible* says that the Greek word for "hunger" means "famish," from a related word meaning "starving." The form, in the Greek, is "the hungering ones," that is, those who keep hungering. "Thirst," in the arid Near East, can often be an intense thirst. I believe this Beatitude speaks of an intense, continuing desire for God's righteousness that may be filled at one level only to break out again at another level, and is completely satisfied only in heaven.

We see the same image in one of the Psalms. "As the deer pants for the water brooks, so pants my soul for You, O God. My soul thirsts for God, for the living God" (Psalm 42:1-2). The image is that of a deer who desperately needs water for survival. Men and animals need water. They will die if they do not get water.

Jacob wrestled with God all night. (The passage speaks of wrestling with a man but later says he saw God face to face.) God lamed his hip but Jacob would not let go. Jacob said, "I will not let You go unless You bless me" (Genesis 32:24-30). Jacob persisted until he got his blessing.

Salvation

We usually think of salvation as a free gift from God. All we have to do is to be willing to accept it. That is the way many of the Scriptures relating to salvation speak. But there is another thread in Scripture, which is often not noticed, and which seems to call for a vigorous effort on our part. We need to follow the whole counsel of Scripture. We cannot win salvation, or earn it, by our effort, but there are Scriptures that suggest that sometimes we receive it only after a good deal of effort. We may have to press in to receive it. The devil resists our being saved.

I believe Matthew 11:12 is talking about salvation. What does laying hold of the kingdom of God mean, if it does not include laying hold of the promise of salvation—a victorious life here on earth and eternal life in heaven? And Jesus says that it is forceful (or violent) men who lay hold of this salvation. But there is more.

ENTER THE NARROW DOOR—"Someone asked him, 'Lord, are only a few people going to be saved?' He said to them, '**Make every effort** to enter through the narrow door, because many, I tell you, will try to enter and will not be able to'" (Luke 13:23-24 NIV). (We know from Matthew 7:13-14 that the narrow gate or door leads to eternal life and the wide gate leads to destruction.) The verb "make every effort" (KJV "strive") is *agonizomai*, closely related to our word "agony." It means to struggle, to compete, to contend with an adversary, to contend for victory. It is in a continuing tense, "keep on striving." It speaks of an intense struggle.

WORK OUT YOUR SALVATION—"...continue to work out your salvation with fear and trembling, for it is God who works in you to will and to act according to his good purpose" (Philippians 2:12 NIV). The word "salvation" is *soteria*, the usual word for spiritual salvation. The verb "work out," *katergazomai*, is from *ergazomai*, to toil, labor, work (the root of our words "energy" and "erg"—a measure of work) and the prefix *kata* which, according to Strong's *Dictionary of the Greek Bible*, "frequently denotes opposition…or intensity." The verb form involves continuous or repeated action. So we must continue to toil or labor against opposition to complete our salvation. It is an intense effort. We do it "with fear and trembling."

THE PEARL OF GREAT PRICE—A different kind of intensity is expressed in one of Jesus' kingdom parables. "The kingdom of heaven is like a merchant seeking beautiful pearls, who, when he had found one pearl of great price, went away and sold all that he had and bought it" (Matthew 13:45-46). The picture is of a man who has devoted his life to an intense search. When he finally finds what he is seeking, he sacrifices everything he has in order to get it. He is happy to make the sacrifice for his joy in what he is to receive, but it is still a sacrifice. (Compare this with verse 44.) We see this in Paul's life. Paul, who was a "comer" with a very promising future before him as a Pharisee, gave it all up "for the excellency of the knowledge of Christ Jesus my Lord; for whom I have suffered the loss of all things, and do count them but dung, that I may win Christ" (Philippians 3:8 KJV).

Scripture talks a good deal about the cost of following Jesus. Most of the early disciples faced persecution and many were martyred. Many Christians today, in Muslim and Communist countries, face severe persecution, economic hardship, and intense rejection by their families and friends. Some face martyrdom. Why are they willing to do so? Because they have such an intense desire for the kingdom of God!

Sanctification and Growing to Maturity

Once we are saved, we start the process of growing to Christian maturity. This process has a number of aspects. Each of them, at times, calls for us to put forth significant effort.

BE HOLY—"As He who called you is holy, you also be holy in all your conduct, because it is written, 'Be holy, for I am holy'" (1 Peter 1:15). "For God did not call us to be impure, but to live a holy life. Therefore he who rejects this instruction does not reject man but God, who gives you his Holy Spirit" (1 Thessalonians 4:7-8 NIV).

Being holy, or sanctification, is a necessary part of our Christian growth. Many Scriptures speak of this as something God does. (See, for example, John 17:17; 1 Peter 1:2.) But these verses speak of it as something we must decide to do and then do. "**Make every effort** to live in peace with all men and to be holy; without holiness no one will see the Lord" (Hebrews 12:14 NIV). Even though God does it, we also must "make every effort" to be holy.

LIVE BY THE SPIRIT—The way to become holy is to live by the Holy Spirit, to live a life controlled by the Holy Spirit. Scripture makes it clear that this is a choice we must make, and that it requires constant application on our part. There is continuous conflict, warfare, between our sinful nature and the Holy Spirit within us. (See Chapter 15.)

We may have to take very strenuous measures to achieve victory in this warfare between the sinful nature and the Holy Spirit. "**Put to death**, therefore, whatever belongs to your earthly nature: sexual immorality, impurity, lust, evil desires and greed, which is idolatry. Because of these the wrath of God is coming" (Colossians 3:5-6 NIV). (Also see 1 Corinthians 15:31; Galatians 2:20; 1 Peter 2:24.)

Jesus put it vividly. "If your hand causes you to sin, cut it off. It is better for you to enter life maimed, rather than having two hands, to go to hell, into the fire that shall never be quenched—where 'Their worm does not die and the fire is not quenched.' And if your foot causes you to sin, cut it off. It is better for you to enter life lame, rather than having two feet, to be cast into hell, into the fire that shall never be quenched—where 'Their worm does not die and the fire is not quenched.' And if your eye causes you to sin, pluck it out. It is better for you to enter the kingdom of God with one eye, rather than having two eyes, to be cast into hell fire—where 'Their worm does not die and the fire is not quenched'" (Mark 9:43-48). Jesus is using vivid imagery, but the point is clear. Whatever you have to do to get rid of the sinful nature, do it. For example, this could involve breaking off a relationship which has been very important to you but is not godly.

BE TRANSFORMED—Scripture tells us to offer ourselves as living sacrifices to God, and to be transformed by the renewing of our minds (Romans 12:1-3). (See Chapters 16 and 14.) Offering our bodies as living sacrifices requires decision and vigorous action on our part. So, at times, does the transformation—the metamorphosis—called for by this passage.

How do we achieve this transformation? In part it is by deliberately feeding our inner man with scripture, worship music, prayer, and sound teaching and preaching. By becoming filled with God's word and allowing it to work in us (1 Thessalonians 2:13). By allowing the word of God to be "engrafted" in us (James 1:21 KJV). This takes a conscious decision and constant application.

In part it is by recognizing every false belief, attitude, and action, and by confronting it with the truth of God's word, and deciding to live by God's truth. This is part of the daily, even hourly or minute-by-minute, process of "bringing every thought into captivity to the obedience of Christ" (2 Corinthians 10:5). It is part of the process of throwing off everything that hinders us (Hebrews 12:1). It takes watchfulness, determination and effort on our part.

PUT ON THE NEW SELF—Scripture refers to this transformation as putting off the old self and putting on the new self, which is "…created to be like God in true righteousness and holiness" (Ephesians 4:24 NIV). (Also see Colossians 3:9-10.) This is a gradual process. It requires repeated decisions. "Which self am I being in this matter? Which self do I want to be?" It requires action.

HOLD FIRMLY TO THE WORD—"By this gospel you are saved, **if you hold firmly** to the word I preached to you. Otherwise, you have believed in vain" (1 Corinthians 15:2 NIV). We are reconciled to God by Christ's death "**if you continue** in your faith, established and firm, not moved from the hope held out in the gospel…" (Colossians 1:23 NIV). (Also see Colossians 2:6.) "…**stand firm and hold to the teachings** we passed on to you…" (2 Thessalonians 2:15 NIV). "**Guard the good deposit** that was entrusted to you…" (2 Timothy 1:14 NIV). "…**be on your guard** so that you may not be carried away by the error of lawless men and fall from your secure position" (2 Peter 3:17 NIV). (Also see 2 John 8.) These call for vigilance, diligence and determination.

Jesus warned against deception (Matthew 24:4), false teaching (Matthew 16:12) and false prophets (Matthew 7:15). Paul warned that in later times "some will depart from the faith, giving heed to deceiving spirits and doctrines of demons" (1 Timothy 4:1). He warned against being "tossed to and fro and carried about with every wind of doctrine, by the trickery of men, in the cunning craftiness of deceitful plotting" (Ephesians 4:14). He speaks of those who have "…wandered from the faith…" (1 Timothy 6:21 NIV). (Also see 2 Timothy 2:18.) Peter warns against "false teachers" who will "secretly bring in destructive heresies" and whom many will follow (2 Peter 2:1). John wrote, "...do not let anyone lead you astray..." (1 John 3:7 NIV). Jude warns of false teachers and then tells us to be "building yourselves up in your most holy faith, praying in the Holy Spirit" (Jude 20).

Hebrews is full of warnings about falling away from true faith. "We must pay more careful attention, therefore, to what we have heard, so that we do not drift away" (Hebrews 2:1 NIV). "See to it, brothers, that none of you has a sinful, unbelieving heart that turns away from the living God" (Hebrews 3:12 NIV). "We want each of you to show this same diligence to the very end, in order to make your hope sure. We do not want you to become lazy, but to imitate those who through faith and patience inherit what has been promised" (Hebrews 6:11-12 NIV). "...let us hold unswervingly to the hope we profess..." (Hebrews 10:23 NIV). "So do not throw away your confidence; it will be richly rewarded. You need to persevere, so that when you have done the will of God, you will receive what he has promised" (Hebrews 10:35-36 NIV). Do not "...grow weary and lose heart" (Hebrews 12:3 NIV). "Therefore strengthen your feeble arms and weak knees" (Hebrews 12:12 NIV). "See to it that no one misses the grace of God..." (Hebrews 12:15 NIV). "See to it that you do not refuse him who speaks..." (Hebrews 12:25 NIV). "Do not be carried away by all kinds of strange teachings..." (Hebrews 13:9 NIV).

Our protection from falling away or being carried away lies in three things, all of which take continuing effort.

WE MUST BE ALERT—"...watch out..." (Romans 16:17 NIV). "...pay more careful attention..." (Hebrews 2:1 NIV). "Be on your guard..." (1 Corinthians 16:13 NIV). "Beware" (Colossians 2:8).

WE MUST CONSCIOUSLY FILL OURSELVES WITH TRUE TEACHING—"building yourselves up on your most holy faith" (Jude 20).

WE MUST HOLD TO THE TRUTH—"...hold firmly..." (1 Corinthians 15:2 NIV; Titus 1:9 NIV). "...hold unswervingly..." (Hebrews 10:23 NIV). "...continue in the faith" (Colossians 1:23). The image is that of someone who holds on with all his strength to something that others are trying to take away from him.

Throwing Off the Things That Hinder

In order to become mature Christians, we must make a determined effort to get rid of those things that hinder our growth to maturity. Scripture tells us, "…let us throw off everything that hinders and the sin that so easily entangles…" (Hebrews 12:1 NIV). This passage lists two things—things that hinder, and sin. We need to get rid of sin, because it gives the devil a foothold. But there may be things that hinder us which are not sins. If they hinder us, we need to get rid of them. Note also the energy of the verb. We don't just discard these things, or let them drop. We throw them off. We hurl them as far away as we can. We make a conscious and vigorous effort to get rid of them. This may take a strenuous effort. My experience is that we have to keep fighting these hindrances. Part of this is because we have a spiritual enemy (the devil) who wants to use them to keep us from being effective and fruitful.

God has given us spiritual weapons with divine power to demolish strongholds (2 Corinthians 10:5). He has given us everything we need for the life he wants us to lead (2 Peter 1:3). It is up to us to use what he has given us and to throw off every hindrance. This takes decision, determination and persistence on our part. It is a necessary part of growing to maturity.

A hindrance is anything that gets in the way. It may be an addiction, a habit, an ingrained pattern of behavior, a built-in mindset, a preconception, a blind spot, or anything else that gets in the way of our growth. My sense is that each person has his own set of hindrances, and that part of our job is to find out what they are. But I think there are some kinds of hindrances that tend to be major problems for almost everybody. I want to identify some of these in what follows. But first, here is another poem by my wife.

THE FIG TREE

Praise to the Son of Man
Who withered the fruitless fig tree,
giving by example
a new found liberty.

Now we can stand and declare
to each fruitless tree in our heart

taking up space on our land
from the mists of time long past:

"Be gone from this place!
Be pruned and away—
Your barrenness glares as offense;
Your presence invites me to stray.

"We look to new roots
new leaves and new shoots
springing from richness of soil
prepared for fruit that matures."

Praise to His Word that lasts!

UNFORGIVENESS—Jesus told us to pray, "Forgive us our debts, as we forgive our debtors" (Matthew 6:12). He went on to say, "For if you forgive men when they sin against you, your Heavenly Father will also forgive you. But if you do not forgive men their sins, your Father will not forgive your sins" (Matthew 6:14-15 NIV).

In Matthew, chapter 18, Jesus returned to this theme. He told Peter that we need to keep forgiving over and over (Matthew 18:21-22). Then he told a parable of a servant whose master forgave him a tremendous debt, so large that it was impossible to pay off. The servant then refused to forgive a small debt owed him by a fellow servant. The master "...turned him over to the jailers to be tortured, until he should pay back all he owed" (Matthew 18:34 NIV). Since his debt was so large that it was impossible for him to pay it, this means eternal torment. Jesus added, "This is how my heavenly Father will treat each of you unless you forgive your brother from your heart" (Matthew 18:35 NIV).

The application is clear. God has forgiven each of us a tremendous debt, a debt we could never pay off, when he brought us to salvation and forgave our sins. But if we do not forgive the relatively small things that other people owe us or have done to us, God will turn us over to eternal torment.

Unforgiveness is a very serious matter. Consider this. We can enter into eternal life in heaven because God has forgiven our sins. They are forgiven and he no longer sees them. Otherwise we could not enter heaven, because no sin can be permitted in heaven. But if we do not forgive our fellow men, then our sins are not forgiven. How can we then enter eternal life in heaven? I say this, not to raise a theological issue, but simply to emphasize the extreme seriousness of unforgiveness.

At times, to forgive may be very difficult. It requires decision. It requires "going against the grain." It may come only after a struggle. It may take pressing in.

BITTERNESS—"See to it that no one misses the grace of God and that no bitter root grows up to cause trouble and defile many" (Hebrews 12:15 NIV). Bitterness causes trouble and defiles many. Bitterness eats up the one who is bitter. It makes it almost impossible for that person to give thanks to God, or even to recognize the ways in which God has been blessing him. It makes it almost impossible for him to find the peace or the joy that God has for him. Bitterness towards others can lead to bitterness towards God. Bitterness is very destructive. It does far more damage to the bitter person than it does to the one he is bitter against. Whenever we find it in ourselves, we must decide to get rid of it, and then do whatever we must to get rid of it. This is often difficult and takes effort, but it is necessary.

VICTIM MENTALITY—One of satan's deadliest devices is what we may call a victim mentality. One who has a victim mentality sees himself as constantly acted on by forces beyond his control. He sees himself as helpless and defeated. He sees himself as unjustly treated. He sees himself as doomed to constant failure. Such a person has lost sight of the fact that God is in charge, and God is greater than any circumstances or problems he may face.

The person with a victim mentality is at the mercy of the circumstances around him. God does not want us to be at the mercy of the circumstances. He wants us to rise above the circumstances, and to say, "Whatever the circumstances, I can, in God's power, overcome the circumstances. I am not a victim. I am an overcomer." There is a story about a pastor who asked a man how he was doing. "Pretty well, under the circumstances," was the reply. "I am sorry to hear it," said the pastor. "We should never be **under** the circumstances."

FEAR—God does not want us to live in fear. "For God has not given us a spirit of fear, but of power and of love and of a sound mind" (2 Timothy 1:7). "God is our refuge and strength, an ever present help in trouble. Therefore we will not fear" (Psalm 46:1-2 KJV).

Fear is the opposite of faith. When the disciples were afraid because of the storm on Lake Galilee, Jesus said, "You of little faith, why are you so afraid?"

(Matthew 8:26 NIV). When Jairus learned that his daughter had died, Jesus said to him, "Do not be afraid; only believe" (Mark 5:36). We fear because our faith is weak, our trust in God is weak.

I am not talking about occasional moments of fear. Many of us have those, and sometimes they are what lead us to call on the Lord for help. Many soldiers go into battle in spite of being afraid. But those who are fearful much of the time, or who have long stretches of fear, need to recognize the problem and deal with it. This kind of fear can shut you down and make you ineffective. All of us have to deal with fear from time to time. We need to catch it whenever it begins to appear, and make a conscious decision to replace it with faith.

DOUBT—Closely related to fear is doubt. Doubt also is the opposite of faith. When Peter, after walking on the water for a while, began to sink, Jesus said to him, "O you of little faith, why did you doubt?" (Matthew 14:31). Doubt, like fear, can shut us down. James says that, when a person prays to God for something, "...he must believe and not doubt, because he who doubts is like a wave of the sea, blown and tossed by the wind. That man should not think he will receive anything from the Lord; he is a double-minded man, unstable in all he does" (James 1:6-8 NIV).

What I find often happens is that I believe one thing in my mind, but in my heart I do not yet believe it. I think I believe something, and then I find myself thinking or saying things contrary to that belief. I need to make a conscious effort to stop saying or thinking things contrary to what Scripture says, and to make a conscious decision that I will follow the words of Scripture. This is part of taking thoughts captive to the obedience of Christ (2 Corinthians 10:5).

DISCOURAGEMENT—One of the devil's greatest attacks on us is discouragement. If he can take away our hope and our courage, if he can get us to feel that nothing is working out right, that we have no prospects and no future, he will have done a lot to keep us from functioning effectively. We need constantly to fight against discouragement. We need to keep reminding ourselves of our position in Christ, and the incomparably great power which God has made available to us. We need to remind ourselves that we can do all things through Christ's strength (Philippians 4:13), and that God works out all things for good for those who love him (Romans 8:28). We must make a conscious effort not to give in to discouragement.

We also need to encourage others. (See, for example, 1 Thessalonians 5:11.) As we sow encouragement, we shall reap encouragement.

WHY DO WE NEED TO STRIVE?

Why do we need to strive, to be forceful? Let me suggest a few reasons:

Are We Serious About God?

Sometimes God wants to be sure that we are serious, that we mean business with him. Jesus had many followers. Only a few of them became disciples, and it was to the disciples that he devoted most of his training effort. Do we seek salvation just as an insurance policy against eternal damnation, or do we genuinely seek to accept the Lordship of Jesus Christ and serve him?

Character Development

God is primarily interested in developing our character. Often the best way to develop character is to have to struggle against obstacles. (See Chapter 19.)

The Flesh Fights Against the Spirit

When we accept Jesus Christ as our Lord and Savior, and allow the Holy Spirit to enter into us, there inevitably begins a struggle, a warfare, between the old self and the new self, between the desires of the flesh and the Holy Spirit. That struggle is not resolved until the Holy Spirit has won complete control over our soul and body. (See Chapter 15.)

The Devil's Opposition

The devil seeks to kill, steal and destroy. If he cannot prevent us from being saved, he will seek to lead us into falsehood so that we will do his work. If he cannot do that, he will seek to shut us down and make us ineffective. We need constantly to struggle against the devil. (See Chapter 12.)

CONCLUSION

God does not want lukewarm Christians (Revelation 3:16). He wants men and women who will love him "with **all** your heart, with **all** your soul, with **all** your mind, and with **all** your strength" (Mark 12:30). It is those who seek him "with **all** your heart" who find him (Jeremiah 29:13). He wants **total** commitment.

We cannot serve two masters (Matthew 6:24). We must not be "double minded" (literally, "two-souled") (James 1:8). We cannot conform to the pattern of this world, and at the same time expect to be transformed by the renewing of our minds (Romans 12:2). There are things in us that we have to put to death if we would live by the Spirit.

In these difficult days, I believe God wants to raise up Christians to a new level of intensity. In order for this to occur, we may have to cry out for it, seek it with everything in us, hunger and thirst for it.

But we need to remember that in our striving we strive with **his** mighty power, not our power. "Be strong in the Lord and in the power of His might" (Ephesians 6:10). We need to know "the exceeding greatness of His power toward us who believe" (Ephesians 1:19). When we rely on his mighty power, we can, indeed, be "more than conquerors" (Romans 8:37). We can overcome every adversity through Christ who strengthens us (Philippians 4:12-13).

PART V
STANDING FIRM

22

Standing Firm

o o o o o o o o o o o o o o o o o o o o o o o o o o o o o o o

"...he who stands firm to the end will be saved."

—(Matthew 24:13 NIV)

Let us now look in more detail at part of Jesus' end-time prophecy in Matthew chapter 24. (I encourage you to read that whole chapter carefully.) I believe it tells us a good deal about the times we now live in, and what we need to do to stand firm in such challenging times.

The disciples asked Jesus when the end times would come.

Matthew 24:4-13 (NIV)

24:4 Jesus answered: "Watch out that no one deceives you.

5 For many will come in my name, claiming, 'I am the Christ,' and will deceive many.

6 You will hear of wars and rumors of wars, but see to it that you are not alarmed. Such things must happen, but the end is still to come.

7 Nation will rise against nation, and kingdom against kingdom. There will be famines and earthquakes in various places.

8 All these are the beginning of birth pains.

9 Then you will be handed over to be persecuted and put to death, and you will be hated by all nations because of me.

10 At that time many will turn away from the faith and will betray and hate each other,

11 and many false prophets will appear and deceive many people.

12 Because of the increase of wickedness, the love of most will grow cold,

13 but he who stands firm to the end will be saved.

Let us look at some of the themes raised by this remarkable passage.

Deception (Matthew 24:4)

By starting his answer in this way, Jesus is telling us that deception is a major characteristic of the end times. It is increasingly a characteristic of the times we live in. Others seek to deceive us, and we often deceive ourselves. The best safeguard against deception is to be very sure of what you believe, and to stand firmly on that belief. A mature Christian, who knows what he believes, will not be "tossed to and fro and carried about with every wind of doctrine, by the trickery of men, in the cunningness of deceitful plotting" (Ephesians 4:14).

I can speak to this from personal experience. During the years that my wife and I were members of a New Age organization, we thought its teachings were "spiritual" and geared to improving lives. But they were not grounded in Scripture and in many ways were contrary to Scripture. At the time we joined this organization, we were not well-grounded in Scripture, and hence did not perceive the falsity of these teachings. I believe that most people who accept false teachings do so because they are not well-grounded in God's truth. Thanks to the prayers of many, God brought us out of the error, and I think our faith now may well be stronger as the result of this experience. God can use everything for his purposes. But on the whole I think it better not to fall into error in the first place.

One of the characteristics of our time is a kind of "doublespeak." We use so many pat slogans and euphemisms to describe things, that we lose sight of what we are really talking about. We, as Christians, need increasingly to speak God's truth into every situation, rather than falling into "politically correct" jargon that obscures the truth. God's word is truth, and his truth sanctifies us (John 17:17). It is the truth that sets us free (John 8:32). Jesus Christ is "the truth" (John 14:6). We, as Christians, need to proclaim God's truth and believe that it will prevail.

Let me give a few examples of doublespeak. Many more will doubtless occur to you. Suicide bombers are murderers, not martyrs. Euthanasia is suicide or murder or both. People who are in a coma are human beings, not vegetables. A human fetus is a baby. Let us not be afraid to call things what they are.

False Christs (verse 5)

In difficult times, people often look to some persuasive individual as a "savior." (When Hitler came into power, some saw him as the savior of Europe.) Jesus is our Savior. We should not look to anyone else to save us from our difficulties and confusion. Jesus is the only way, the only truth and the only light. No matter how attractive and persuasive this or that person may be, he does not have the answers we need. This applies even to popular religious leaders. We need to be careful not to idolize them, or to put more faith in them than in the God of the Bible. This can be subtle. One good test of where our primary faith lies is to ask ourselves, "Do I use Scripture to test the teachings of this religious leader? Or do I avoid or water down Scriptures that don't seem to fit something that he teaches?"

People also look to various ideas or concepts to save them or improve their lives. As Chuck Colson points out, we have, in recent years, looked to the following, among others, to make our lives better: science and technology, "sexual liberation," New Age philosophy, and Communism. None of them work, because none deal with the basic problem of sin. In a sense, these are all false Christs.[35] Scripture tells us that salvation is only in Jesus Christ. "There is no other name under heaven given among men by which we must be saved" (Acts 4:12).

Many people have false ideas of who Jesus Christ is. Some of these I have mentioned in Chapter 6. These can become false Christs.

Don't Be Alarmed (verses 6 and 7)

Don't be surprised, or alarmed, or thrown off course, by wars, racial conflicts, famines, earthquakes, hurricanes, floods and the like. Jesus has told us ahead of time to expect them. They do not represent chaos or lack of control on God's part. God is in charge and things are happening as he has said they would. It's OK.

Birth Pains (verse 8)

A woman can endure birth pains because she knows they have a purpose. Something wonderful is coming out of them. When it seems that everything is falling apart, believe that good is coming out of it. Pearl Harbor was a disaster, but I believe it birthed something in our nation that contributed in a major way to the ultimate defeat of the axis of evil consisting of Germany, Italy and Japan.

The terrorist attack on this nation on September 11, 2001 was a tragedy, but I hope something is being birthed in our nation as a result that will cause major changes for the good. God is able to bring good out of evil. I think we can say, to those who cause events like these, "You meant evil against me; but God meant it for good" (Genesis 50:20).

Persecution (verse 9)

Christians were persecuted in the days of Peter and Paul. Christians are persecuted today in many parts of the world. We, in the Western world, cannot assume that we are immune. Jesus tells us that we can expect persecution for his sake. "Blessed are those who are persecuted for righteousness' sake, for theirs is the kingdom of heaven" (Matthew 5:10). "If they persecuted Me, they will also persecute you" (John 15:20). Paul wrote, "all who desire to live godly in Christ Jesus will suffer persecution" (2 Timothy 3:12). Jesus showed us the key to dealing with persecution. In explaining the parable of the sower, he spoke of the one "...who hears the word and at once receives it with joy. But since he has no root, he lasts only a short time. When trouble or persecution comes because of the word, he quickly falls away" (Matthew 13:20-21 NIV). If we are to handle persecution without falling away, our faith must be deeply rooted and unshakable. This is the kind of faith we see so strikingly in those parts of the world where persecution is occurring today.

Turning Away (verse 10)

The Greek verb here is *skandalizo*, which usually means "take offense." King James and New King James translate the phrase, "many will be offended." But, according to Strong's *Dictionary of the Greek Bible*, *skandalizo* can also refer to apostasy, that is, turning away from the faith. Indeed, a common result of taking offense is that the person rejects God and turns away from God.

In context, it seems to me that both meanings have validity. When "bad" things occur, or when God fails to answer our prayers in the way that we had expected and hoped he would, or when things do not happen according to our theology and expectations, it is easy to become offended and angry. Jesus has told us, "Blessed is he who is not offended because of Me" (Matthew 11:6).

So there is offense, which can lead to anger and bitterness towards one another. This offense can also result in anger and bitterness towards God and a turning away from God—what some have called "the great apostasy."

We can also become directly offended at God if our prayers are not answered in the way we had desired, or if God allows pain and suffering in our life, or if events do not turn out in accordance with the theology we have been taught.

Jesus tells us to expect all this. He also tells us not to be among those who are offended and turn away. The key is that our faith must be deeply rooted and sure. Our faith must be in God and his Scripture, and not in fallible human teachings. Our faith must be in the love, faithfulness and goodness of God the Father and God the Son, and not in what they do or do not do for us.

False Prophets (verse 11)

Jesus is warning us that in the end times, we can expect to see an increasing number of people who claim to have the truth, who claim to have a solution for the world's many problems, who claim to have a revelation from God, but who are false. What they have is not from God. It is not consistent with God's word recorded in Scripture. This is part of the end time deception that he referred to earlier. We need to be on guard against this falsity and deception.

Love Grows Cold (verse 12)

"Because of the increase of wickedness, the love of most will grow cold" (Matthew 24:12 NIV). There are two important statements in this brief verse.

First, wickedness will increase. We see this happening in our nation today. Things are being said, and done, and shown that would not even have been imagined a few decades ago. I think we can expect this to grow worse. But as Jesus said, we should not be alarmed. We should resist the wickedness, and stand up for godly conduct, but we should not be alarmed. Jesus has warned us that it would happen. God is still in control.

Second, the love of most will grow cold. Jesus warns about this also in Revelation. He commends the church at Ephesus for many things, but he says, "You have left your first love" (Revelation 2:4). If they did not repent he would remove their lampstand, which I interpret as meaning put an end to their authority as a church. God wants our love. He wants all of our love. If we do not love him, we will not really serve him.

Note that Jesus says that the love of **most** will grow cold. Apparently there will be a large-scale falling away from God. Only a relatively few will remain. I think we need to do everything we can to make sure that we are among those few.

Stand Firm to the End (verse 13)

Scripture speaks often of the importance of standing firm. Peter warns us that the devil is like a man-eating lion, and exhorts us to "Resist him, standing firm in the faith…" (1 Peter 5:9 NIV). Paul tells us to "…put on the full armor of God so that when the day of evil comes, you may be able to stand your ground, and after you have done everything, to stand. Stand firm then…" (Ephesians 6:13-14 NIV). He exhorts us to "…stand firm in all the will of God, mature and fully assured" (Colossians 4:12 NIV). In each of the letters to the churches in Revelation, chapters 2 and 3, there is a wonderful promise to the one who overcomes.

A great Scriptural example of standing firm is given by Paul: "We are hard-pressed on every side, but not crushed; perplexed, but not in despair; persecuted, but not abandoned; struck down, but not destroyed" (2 Corinthians 4:8-9 NIV). I believe God is increasingly calling on us to say, "Whatever the circumstances, however difficult and discouraging things may appear, I believe in a God who is greater than the circumstances, and I will stand firm."

The greatest need to stand firm, and the greatest test of our ability to stand firm, will come at the end times. When **many** have turned from the faith, and the love of **most** has grown cold, will we be strong enough in our faith to be able to stand firm? The more difficult things get, the more important it is to be able to stand firm. Let us see the difficulties of our present time as challenges, but also as opportunities to grow in strength, commitment and determination.

23

Conclusion

o o o o o o o o o o o o o o o o o o o o o o o o o o o o o o o o o

God "is able to do exceedingly abundantly above all that we ask or think."

—*(Ephesians 3:20)*

In the challenging and confusing world we live in, we Christians very much need certainty and assurance. We need to know that God is great, that he is in charge, and that his purposes cannot be thwarted. We need to be able to say, with David (a man who lived through great difficulties and hardships and often was a step away from death),

> "My soul finds rest in God alone; my salvation comes from him. He alone is my rock and my salvation; he is my fortress, I will never be shaken" (Psalm 62:1-2 NIV).

Because God is our fortress and our rock, and is always there, we need not fear no matter what happens. (See Psalm 46:1-3.) And we will not be shaken.

We need the assurance of knowing that Scripture is the revealed word of God, and that all of it is true. In a challenging and confusing world, it is a great blessing to know that there is something that is true for all eternity. When all around us seems like quicksand, it is a great blessing to have a solid place on which to stand.

We need the strength and conviction that come from continually growing in Christian maturity and doing what that implies.

I believe that our nation is at a dangerous point. Many Americans, including some with political power or influence, and quite a few judges, are rejecting (or ignoring) the Christian principles on which our nation was founded. I think we are in danger of losing the protection and favor of God that have made possible our remarkable success thus far. Without that protection and favor, our nation, and the principles of liberty for which it stands, can decline and disappear as so many great civilizations in the past have done. I believe that if mature, committed Christians are willing to take a firm stand for what we believe, we can stop and even reverse this tendency. To do so, we need to be very sure of what we believe. That is why I have written to "stir you up by reminding you" (2 Peter 1:13) of what the truth of Scripture tells us.

As I have said earlier, the committed Christian life is not easy. It calls for vigilance, decision, action and perseverance. At times it involves a struggle, which can be very intense. But its rewards are very great.

With God there is always hope. With God there is confidence and assurance. With God we can find peace, joy and love, regardless of the circumstances around us. With God all things are possible. With God there is always more.

> "Eye has not seen, nor ear heard, nor have entered into the heart of man the things which God has prepared for those who love Him" (1 Corinthians 2:9).

I join the Apostle Paul in praying for all of us,

> "I keep asking that the God of our Lord Jesus Christ, the glorious Father, may give you the Spirit of wisdom and revelation, so that you may know him better. I pray also that the eyes of your heart may be enlightened in order that you may know the hope to which he has called you, the riches of his glorious inheritance in the saints, and his incomparably great power for us who believe. That power is like the working of his mighty strength, which he exerted in Christ when he raised him from the dead and seated him at his right hand in the heavenly realms, far above all rule and authority, power and dominion, and every title that can be given, not only in the present age but also in the one to come" (Ephesians 1:17-21 NIV).

May God bless you!

Afterword

For nearly twenty years I have been fortunate enough to know James Morrisson. He is a man of impeccable legal credentials, great integrity, and careful scholarship. Jim cares about America and its future, about all of our futures. America will not have a good future unless its Christian citizens stand firm in their faith, both individually and corporately.

Jim believes, and I heartily agree, that as Christians we need to take a stand for what is right and godly. His main concern is that in order to take such a stand, we need to be very sure of what we believe and why we believe it. And so he has chosen to concentrate his emphasis on showing clearly what the Bible says about some of the foundational issues of our faith.

One of the main reasons for the weakness of the Christian church has been that many do not really know what they believe, nor do they understand the spiritual authority that Christ has given them. We need Christians who are mature and deeply committed, and who understand their position in Christ. Such Christians can accomplish much. Lukewarm Christians will accomplish nothing. Jim's book is a needed wake-up call.

The stakes are very serious. Our nation is in grave danger of losing the Christian basis on which it was founded and which has been a major reason for the greatness we have achieved.

How do we preserve the historical soul of America?

The historical facts of America's founding are clear and unambiguous, not obscured in political correctness. The nation's legal and moral underpinnings, guiding principles and political philosophy, are Christian. Those who say otherwise deliberately choose to ignore true historical facts. No Moslems, Buddhists, or Confucians waded ashore in Virginia in 1607 and immediately celebrated the Christian Eucharist, as history tells us the first settlers did.

It is because America's roots are Christian that those of other religions are welcomed to our shores and permitted to worship freely. If the Christian philosophy underlying this nation's founding is ever abrogated, freedom for other religions will vanish, as will America's other personal and political freedoms and liberties.

Today there is a war for the soul and for the existence of America as described in the Declaration of Independence and the Constitution. Some call it a "culture war" but its roots are spiritual. Many people are trying to remove every vestige of America's Christian history, heritage, and founding principles. Such a conflict is to be expected; the Bible speaks of it.

What is not to be expected, is the seeming indifference and passivity of the Christian Church. In the war between good and evil (which has been going on since Adam and Eve), there is nothing holy about being a conscientious objector.

Every time there is an effort to chip away a piece of America's Christian foundation, shouldn't Christians rise up to oppose that effort? Across this great nation, City officials and State and County governments should be aware that, when they try to erode our Christian foundations, there is a large body of Christian voters who will object strongly and vocally, and who will, as is their right as citizens, express their objections in the ballot box.

May the Lord help us all stand firm in the faith in these challenging times.

Jerry Ralph Curry, D.Min.
Major General, U.S. Army (retired)

NOTE: In addition to a distinguished military career as a warrior, General Curry has a doctorate in Ministry and is a scholar and teacher. I have had the privilege of hearing him speak. He reminds me of the centurion whom Jesus commended because of his great faith.

About the Author

James Lord Morrisson was born in Chicago in 1917. He graduated from Harvard University with high honors; attended Columbia University Law School, was editor-in-chief of the *Columbia Law Review*, and graduated with honors.

He then was law clerk to Chief Justice Stone of the U.S. Supreme Court. Justice Stone recommended him for the Operations Analysis Section of the Office of Strategic Services; and he served in the OSS in High Wycombe, England during World War II under the Eighth Air Force. While overseas he got to know some of the local people and played string quartets with them on a borrowed cello.

After the war he served in the U.S. Office of the Solicitor General. He argued a number of cases in the United States Supreme Court and dealt with issues of major constitutional significance. As a Government attorney, he served in several other capacities, including working directly with U.S. Attorney General Robert Kennedy.

He took early retirement from the U.S. Government and taught a college course in government.

From his university years and on, he also pursued interests in music. As a baritone, he sang in operas, oratorios and song recitals in five languages; he also directed a choir and taught singing. As a cellist, he played string quartets informally with three other attorneys for many years and also played in a community symphony orchestra for two years.

But in his sixties he became a Christian and earned an M.A. in Biblical Studies. Scripture then became his focus and essence.

He lived in Richmond, Virginia with his wife Frances, and died in April 2005 at age 88, shortly before their 64th anniversary. They have three children (Maria, Robert and Douglas); two grandsons (Matthew and Michael); and three great grandchildren.

PART VI

APPENDIX AND END NOTES

Appendix

Tools for Studying Scripture

With today's resources, it is not difficult for the average layman to do some fairly in-depth Scripture studies, and to become quite well-informed as to what it says. Scripture was written for laymen to understand. There are a great number of resources available today. I would advise most laymen to proceed slowly in building up your study resources. You can spend a lot of money on books that you end up not using much. The following are some basic tools that I think most people will find helpful:

Study Bibles

A good annotated Bible. There are many of these available, with annotations for different purposes. Consult your pastor, or other mature Christians, as to which they think would be most useful for you. For those fairly new to the study of Scripture, the *Life Application Bible* (available for various translations), can be useful in suggesting the relevance of Scripture to today's problems and concerns. I like to use a Bible with wide enough margins so that I can make my own annotations.

Taking Notes

Some take notes on sermons and teachings that they hear, seminars and workshops they attend, things that occur to them as they read their Bible, etc. Some keep these in a notebook or journal. I tend to use scraps of paper which I then mislay—not a recommended procedure!

Concordances and Bible Dictionaries

For more detailed study you will want an exhaustive concordance, such as Strong's, and a good Bible Dictionary. There are also exhaustive, multi-volume theological dictionaries of both the Old and the New Testament. These can be valuable to scholars, but I suggest that they are too expensive and too technical for most average laymen. There are also numerous commentaries on each book of the Bible. Some are technical, delving into the meaning of many of the words used. Some are practical, suggesting the application of the Scripture text to daily problems and concerns. Some can be called inspirational. Commentaries can become expensive. I suggest that you explore the different commentaries available rather carefully before deciding to buy a commentary.

What is a concordance and why is it valuable? An exhaustive concordance lists every Scripture verse that contains a particular English word. It has two main uses: (1) to enable you to find a Scripture verse if you can quote even one word of it accurately, and (2) to enable you to look at all the Scripture verses that use a particular word, and thus get a feeling for the scope and implications of that word. This is what we call doing word studies, and I find them very useful. Many Bibles have partial concordances, but they are not as useful as an exhaustive one.

Bible Study Software

If you have a computer, a good Scripture computer program can be invaluable, and is probably the least expensive and most convenient way of gathering together the research tools that you will want. If you have them in the computer program, you will not need to buy the books. There are a number of such programs available. They are not cheap, so you will want to look into alternatives carefully. A good program should contain:

- The English text of the Bible in the translation you use, keyed to definitions of each word used in the original text.
- English texts of several translations of the Bible, so that you can compare different translations of the same passage.
- An exhaustive concordance with a versatile, user-friendly search capability.
- A good Bible Dictionary. Strong's has such a dictionary. I like to use Vine's also.

- A good Bible Encyclopedia.
- A good print-out capability. This is sometimes done by storing the information you need (on a clipboard, notepad or some such name), transferring it to your word processing program, and then printing it out from that program.

For those with computer access, there are also a great number of websites on the Internet dealing with particular areas and issues.

Greek and Hebrew

I do not read either Greek or Hebrew. For real Scripture scholarship, a reading knowledge of both is indispensable. But for the ordinary layman, it is quite possible, by using the resources mentioned above, to get a pretty good feel for the meaning, and even some of the nuances, of some of the original Hebrew and Greek words of the Bible.

Study Resources

Following are some good study resources.

- **Strong**—James Strong, *Dictionary of the Hebrew Bible* and *Dictionary of the Greek Bible.* These are part of Strong's *Exhaustive Concordance* (Nashville, Tennessee: Abingdon Press, 1894).
- **Vine**—W.E. Vine, Merrill F. Unger & William White, Jr., *An Expository Dictionary of Biblical Words* (Nashville, Tennessee: Thomas Nelson, 1984).
- **Zodhiates**—Spiros Zodhiates, Ed. *Hebrew-Greek Key Word Study Bible, King James Version* (Chattanooga, Tennessee: AMG Publishers, 1991).

End Notes

1. See William J. Federer, *America's God and Country, Encyclopedia of Quotations* (St. Louis, Missouri: Amerisearch, Inc., 2000) (referred to herein as "Federer"), pp. 643, 652, 655. Federer's notes give numerous sources and printed references for the quotations he gives.

2. First Inaugural Address, Federer, p. 652.

3. Federer, p. 11.

4. Federer, p. 589.

5. *Zorach v. Clauson*, 343 US 306 (1952), 313 (opinion of the Court by Justice William O. Douglas).

6. See, for example, John W. Chalfant, *America, a Call to Greatness* (self published, 2003); Charles Crismier, *Renewing the Soul of America, One Person at a Time Beginning With You* (Elijah Books, 2002); and Tom Minnery, *Why You Can't Stay Silent: A Biblical Mandate to Shape Our Culture* (Carol Stream, Illinois: Tyndale House Publishers, 2002). For more information on America's Christian heritage, see David Barton, *Original Intent: The Courts, the Constitution, and Religion*, 3rd edition (Aledo, Texas: WallBuilder Press, 2004). Also see Barton's books and videos at the Wall Builders website.
   www.wallbuilders.com

7. Some have already seen the beginnings of persecution of Christians in America. See David Limbaugh, *Persecution: How Liberals Are Waging War Against Christianity* (Washington, D.C.: Regnery Publishing, 2003).

8. See Josh McDowell, *The New Evidence That Demands a Verdict* (Nashville, Tennessee: Thomas Nelson Publishers, 1999) (herein referred to as *Evidence*), pp 3-16. McDowell's book contains a good deal that is relevant to what I discuss in Chapters 2-4.

9. See, for example, *Evidence*, 33-119, 331-583; F.F. Bruce, *The New Testament Documents: Are They Reliable?* (Downers' Grove, Illinois: InterVarsity Press, 1964).

10. See *Evidence*, pp. 33-68, especially pp. 33-44.

11. See *Evidence*, pp. 69-118.

12. See *Evidence*, pp. 61-68, 91-116 for some examples.

13. See Gleason L. Archer, Jr., *A Survey of Old Testament Introduction* (Chicago, Illinois: Moody Press, 1985), pp. 83-185, for a good, and quite readable, summary of this evidence.

14. One useful book is Gordon D. Fee and Douglas Stuart, *How to Read the Bible for All It Is Worth* (Grand Rapids, Michigan: Zondervan, 2003).

15. John R.W. Stott, *Understanding the Bible* (Grand Rapids, Michigan: Zondervan, 1982), p. 218.

16. See my paper, *Who Did Jesus Say He Is?* on my website (below). www.standingfirminthefaith.com

17. For a more detailed discussion of the evidence, see my paper, *Evidence That Jesus Was Resurrected,* on my website (below). Also see *Evidence*, pp. 203-284. www.standingfirminthefaith.com

18. I think it is in this sense that we should read 1 John 2:1-2, "If anyone sins we have an Advocate with the Father, Jesus Christ the righteous. And He Himself is the propitiation for our sins." This does not speak of Jesus as pleading for mercy, but rather as reminding the Father of what Jesus has already done.

19. J. Rodman Williams, *Renewal Theology*, Volume 3 (Grand Rapids, Michigan: Zondervan, 1992), p. 458.

20. James Strong, *Dictionary of the Greek Bible*. This is part of Strong's *Exhaustive Concordance* (Nashville, Tennessee: Abingdon Press, 1894). Spiros Zodhiates, Ed., *Hebrew-Greek Key Word Study Bible*, King James Version (Chattanooga, Tennessee: AMG Publishers, 1991), p. 1761.

21. See George Eldon Ladd, *The Gospel of the Kingdom* (Grand Rapids, Michigan: Wm. B. Eerdmans Publishing Co., 1986). (Especially see Chapter 3.)

22. James Strong.

23. W.E. Vine, Merrill F. Unger, and William White, Jr., *An Expository Dictionary of Biblical Words* (Nashville, Tennessee: Thomas Nelson, 1984). Also see James Strong, *Dictionary of the Greek Bible.*

24. For a fictional, but very perceptive, account of some of the devil's tactics, see C.S. Lewis, *The Screwtape Letters* (New York: MacMillan, 1982).

25. John R.W. Stott, *The Message of the Sermon on the Mount* (Downers Grove, Illinois: InterVarsity Press, 1978), p. 17.

26. Spiros Zodhiates, p. 1750.

27. Spiros Zodhiates, p. 1709.

28. James Strong.

29. Spiros Zodhiates, p. 1735.

30. J. Rodman Williams, *Renewal Theology*, Volume 2 (Grand Rapids, Michigan: Zondervan, 1990), p. 411.

31. J.I. Packer, *God's Words* (Intervarsity Press, 1981), p. 133.

32. Donald G. Bloesch, *Essentials of Evangelical Theology* (New York: Harper & Row, paperback edition, 1982), vol. 1, p. 224.

33. Two books I found helpful in dealing with this subject are: Philip Yancey, *Where Is God When It Hurts?* (Grand Rapids, Michigan: Zondervan, 1990); and James Dobson, *When God Doesn't Make Sense* (Carol Stream, Illinois: Tyndale House Publishers, 1993).

34. C.S. Lewis, *The Great Divorce* (New York: Collier Books, MacMillan Publishing Company, 1946), pp. 33-34.

35. Charles Colson and Nancy Pearcey, *How Then Shall We Live* (Carol Stream, Illinois: Tyndale House, 1999).

978-0-595-84194-3
0-595-84194-5

Lightning Source UK Ltd.
Milton Keynes UK
UKHW041841050421
381487UK00009B/294/J

9 780595 841943